The Communicant's Companion

THE
COMMUNICANT'S COMPANION;

OR,

INSTRUCTIONS FOR THE RIGHT RECEIVING

OF

THE LORD'S SUPPER.

BY THE
REV. MATTHEW HENRY.

WITH AN
INTRODUCTORY ESSAY
BY THE
REV. JOHN BROWN,
Of Edinburgh.

SOLID GROUND CHRISTIAN BOOKS
BIRMINGHAM, ALABAMA USA

Solid Ground Christian Books
2090 Columbiana Rd, Suite 2000
Birmingham, AL 35216
205-443-0311
sgcb@charter.net
http://solid-ground-books.com

The Communicant's Companion
INSTRUCTIONS FOR THE RIGHT RECEPTION OF THE LORD'S SUPPER

Matthew Henry (1662-1714)

Taken from 1843 edition by Presbyterian Board of Publications, Philadelphia

Solid Ground Classic Reprints

First printing of new edition June 2005

Cover work by Borgo Design, Tuscaloosa, AL
Contact them at nelbrown@comcast.net

ISBN: 1-932474-95-1

CONTENTS.

	Page
INTRODUCTORY ESSAY,	5
TO THE READER,	28
CHAPTER I.—The Names by which this Ordinance is usually called,	31
CHAPTER II.—The Nature of this Ordinance,	42
CHAPTER III.—An Invitation to this Ordinance,	57
CHAPTER IV.—Helps for Self-examination before we come to this Ordinance,	81
CHAPTER V.—Instructions for Renewing our Covenants with God in our Preparation for this Ordinance,	105
CHAPTER VI.—Helps for Meditation and Prayer in our preparation for this Ordinance,	125
CHAPTER VII.—Directions in what frame of spirit we should come to, and attend upon this Ordinance,	144
CHAPTER VIII.—Some account of the affecting sights that are to be seen by Faith in this Ordinance,	162
CHAPTER IX.—Some account of the precious Benefits which are to be received by Faith in this Ordinance,	179
CHAPTER X.—Helps for the exciting of those pious and devout affections which should be working in us while we attend this Ordinance,	199

CONTENTS.

	Page
CHAPTER XI.—Directions concerning the solemn Vows we are to make to God in this Ordinance,	219
CHAPTER XII.—Directions concerning the frame of our spirits when we come away from this Ordinance,	235
CHAPTER XIII.—An Exhortation to order the Conversation aright after this Ordinance,	259
CHAPTER XIV.—Some Words of Comfort which this Ordinance speaks to serious Christians,	276

INTRODUCTORY ESSAY.

THERE is an important, though often an overlooked difference between the results of human ingenuity, as embodied in the principles of science and the institutions of civil society, and the results of divine wisdom, as embodied in the doctrines of revelation and the ordinances of the Christian church. Human science is the offspring of the observations and experiments of beings limited in their faculties, and liable to error, and admits, from this very circumstance, of constant growth, frequent correction, and indefinite improvement. The principles of natural philosophy are much better understood at present, not only than they were, but than they could have been a hundred years ago; and it is highly probable, that, before the end of another century, they will be still better understood than they are at present: but, as the most finished work of the human mind is necessarily imperfect, there will always be room for the correction of mistakes, and the supply of deficiencies.

It is altogether otherwise with the doctrines of Revelation. They flow forth absolutely pure from the fountain of knowledge and of truth. They are an infallible statement of a portion of the mind of Him who alone hath wisdom. Human science is like the statue, which, under the successive strokes of the artist's chisel, from a rude unformed block, gradually assumes a striking resemblance to "the human form divine." Revealed truth is like our general parent, rising at once into perfect form, and beauty, and life, at the command of his Creator.

The improvement even of the most finished statue implies no absurdity; but the idea of mending the divine work were equally replete with impiety and folly. Human science, being the product of fallible reason, cannot be perfect. There must be deficiency, and there may be error; and it admits of improvement both by correction and addition. There is room for neither in the doctrines of revelation. Divine revelation is, from its very nature, free from error, proceeding from him who cannot be deceived, and who cannot deceive; and though imperfect, inasmuch as it does not extend to all possible objects of religious knowledge, it obviously admits of addition in no other way than by a new revelation. He who has made known to us a portion of his mind, may, if he pleases, make known to us another portion of it; but till he does so, the whole of our duty, in reference to the revelation given, is to endeavour distinctly to apprehend the meaning of its various parts, and the relations, connections, and dependencies of these various parts, and to yield up the whole of our intellectual and active nature to its influence. It is equally inconsistent with this duty to attempt to make corrections on the system of revealed truth, or to make additions to it.

It would have been a happy thing for the Christian world, if the obvious distinction which has now been pointed out, had been steadily kept in view by the teachers of religion. The "truth as it is in Jesus" would not then have been obscured by attempts to illustrate it; nor the dogmas of a vain philosophy mingled with the oracles of divine wisdom, or substituted in their room. The ingenuity, and learning, and labour, which have been often worse than wasted, in endeavouring, by working up into a complete system of religion and morals, such of the materials furnished by revelation, as seemed fit for their purpose, along with such materials as they could collect from other sources, while, without ceremony, such portions of revelation as appeared unsuitable to their object, were overlooked or rejected,—might have been devoted to a diligent inquiry into the meaning and connection of the sacred oracles; and thus have discovered there, made by his hand who made the world, what they must for ever in vain attempt to make for themselves; and we would not have had reason to doubt, in an age when human science has, in all its branches, attained to an unprecedented state of improvement, whether the principles of revealed truth are not worse understood, among those who profess to believe them, than they were seventeen hundred years ago.

A similar distinction ought to be made between the institutions of civil society and the ordinances of the Christian church. The principles of civil government are at present much better understood than they were, or could have been, in what are ordinarily called the dark ages; and it is certain, whatever a blind reverence for antiquity may urge to the contrary, that the social arrangements which prevail in our own country are incomparably superior to those which existed even in the most illustrious ages of Grecian and Roman history; and it is equally evident, whatever a partial fondness for the institutions of our own country and age may suggest, that a much more perfect form of social life is not only easily conceivable, but, at some future period, is likely to be realized, than any that has yet been established among mankind. These institutions are the result of human ingenuity, and therefore are imperfect. There is something wanting, and something wrong with the best of them.

But it is otherwise with the ordinances of the Christian church; for they are the appointments of infinite wisdom. They were originally given by one who had a perfect knowledge of the end of such institutions—the religious and moral improvement of his people; and a perfect knowledge, too, of that intellectual and moral constitution, for the improvement of which they are intended,—and, like all the divine works, they are perfect. They are all of them characterized by a beautiful simplicity, which ill accords with the ordinary, but depraved taste of mankind for what is complicated and difficult; but which is a leading feature in all the works and arrangements of infinite wisdom.

It might have been expected, that the institutions of Christianity, bearing on them the impress of supreme authority, would have been accounted too sacred things to be tampered with by those who admitted the divine origin of that religion. But what is there too presumptuous for man to attempt? The same principle which led professed Christians to modify the doctrines of Christ, led them to alter his institutions. In both cases, they flattered themselves that they were making improvements; but what was the truth? By their experiments on the doctrines of Christ, they, in many cases, converted the true elixir of immortal life into a deadly poison, and, at the very best, robbed it of its healing virtues, just in the proportion in which they have infused into it baser ingredients: and by their experiments on the institutions of Christ, they have rendered them utterly unfit for the purposes they were intended to answer; and, instead of important means of religious and moral improvement, they have made them mere vehicles of amusement to the senses or imagination, and, in many cases, the instruments of extensive demoralization and of fatal delusion.

No Christian ordinance has been more perverted by superstition than the Lord's Supper; and no portion of Christian truth has been more involved in obscurity and error than that which respects that ordinance. False opinions and superstitious usages mutually produce and support each other. By this malignant action and re-action, in reference to the Lord's Supper, where the emblematical nature of the institution, and the figurative language in which of course much of the truth respecting it was couched, afforded peculiar facilities for misapprehension, misrepresentation, and delusion, we find, within the course of a few centuries, the simple rite of an assembly of Christians eating bread and drinking wine, in grateful commemoration of the expiatory sufferings and death of Jesus Christ, converted into a splendid and complicated ceremony;* and the plain, intelligible doctrine, that in this ordinance we are presented with an emblematical representation and confirmation of the great principles of our religion, which, by strengthening our belief, contributes to our spiritual improvement, gives way to a portentous dogma, of which it is impossible to say whether it be more absurd or impious, that, in this ordinance, the bread and the wine are, by the mystic power of a priest's repeating the words of institution, converted into the body, and blood, and divinity of Jesus Christ; which, after having been offered to God by the priest, as an expiatory sacrifice for the sins of the living and the dead, are literally eaten and drunk by the recipients. So dangerous is it to deviate from the purity of scriptural truth, and the simplicity of primitive usage. It is impossible to say where we will stop. The probability is, that we will not stop till we land ourselves in the pravity of damnable error, and in the absurdity of senseless superstition.

At the Reformation, the doctrine of transubstantiation, and the practice of the sacrifice of the mass, were discarded by all the Protestant churches; but there was but a partial return to the purity and simplicity of primitive doctrine and observance. By the Lutheran church, a variety of unauthorized rites were retained, and the doctrine of consubstantiation, or the real, though impalpable and invisible, presence of the body and blood of Christ, along with, and under the substance of bread and wine in the consecrated elements, was substituted in the room of the not more absurd, and certainly not less intelligible dogma of transubstantiation; and, although most of the reformed churches rejected both these equally

* "That feast of free grace and adoption to which Christ invited his disciples to sit as brethren and co-heirs of the happy covenant which at that table was to be sealed to them, even that feast of love and heavenly-admitted fellowship, the seal of filial grace, became the subject of horror, and glouting admiration pageanted about like a dreadful idol."—MILTON.

unscriptural doctrines, and approximated much more closely to both the principles and practice of apostolical times, yet still it cannot be denied, that, in most of their symbolical books, there is much mystical statement, respecting the spiritual presence of Jesus Christ in the Lord's Supper, and the manner in which Christians participate of his body and blood when they observe it; as if Christ's presence in this ordinance, were not essentially the same as his presence in any other ordinance, when, by the operation of his Spirit, through the instrumentality of the truth, he communicates to the believing mind knowledge, and purification, and comfort;—as if "the eating Christ's flesh, and drinking Christ's blood," in this ordinance, were something else than that participation of those blessings procured by his sufferings and death, which all true Christians enjoy, whenever they believe the divine testimony respecting these sufferings and death;—and as if all the peculiarities of this ordinance did not originate in the emblematical form in which it brings Christian truth and its evidence before the mind.

It is obvious, that to be conducive to the spiritual improvement of those who engage in it, the Lord's Supper must be "a rational service,"—an exercise of the mind and of the heart: and it is equally obvious, that, for the purpose of rendering it a rational service, it is not our business to endeavour to invent a spiritual meaning to the emblems which are employed in it; but to endeavour to discover the spiritual meaning, which he who appointed the ordinances intended to be attached to these emblems. Some writers on the nature and design of this ordinance, seem to have overlooked this; and, of course, their works, though replete with pious fancies, are rather deficient in such distinct, scripturally supported views, as are calculated at once to satisfy the mind and guide the exercise of the devout Christian. It is often treated of as an oath of allegiance—a federal transaction between God and the communicant—an unbloody sacrifice, or a feast upon a sacrifice—and much fruitless controversy has taken place, which of these, or whether any of them, affords a just representation of its nature, design, and advantages. Figurative descriptions of an emblematical ordinance do not seem peculiarly well fitted for explaining it; and there is a considerable hazard lest, in our following out our tropical illustrations, we end in making the ordinance something altogether different from what Jesus Christ made it; and as the promise of his blessing is attached only to the observance of his institution, we shut ourselves out from the advantages we might have enjoyed from its observance, if we do not, in simple submission to his authority, and reliance on his Spirit, eat bread and drink wine, in believing remembrance and religious commemoration of his expiatory sufferings and death.

The simplest, and, to our own minds, the most satisfactory view of the Lord's Supper which we have been able to take, is that which considers it as, on the part of Him who instituted it, an emblematical representation and confirmation of the grand peculiarities of the Christian institution; and, on the part of him who observes it, an emblematical expression of a state of mind and heart in accordance with this statement of Christian truth and its evidence.

That there is something more in the Lord's Supper than meets the external senses—that its emblematical elements are meant to embody Christian doctrine, and its emblematical actions to express Christian thought and feeling,—there can be no doubt; and in order to discover what is the Christian truth which the instituted symbols represent, we are not left to conjecture how such emblems may be naturally interpreted. In the statements of our Lord, and of his inspired Apostles, we have abundant and satisfactory information. The following is a short account of the institution of the Lord's Supper, as narrated by Matthew, Mark, Luke, and Paul:—" The Lord Jesus, that night in which he was betrayed, while observing with his apostles the Jewish passover, took bread, and when he had given thanks, he brake it, and gave it to the disciples, and said, 'Take, eat; this is my body which is broken for you: this do in remembrance of me.' After the same manner he took the cup, when he had supped, and gave it to them, saying, 'This cup is my blood of the new covenant, which is shed for many, for the remission of sins: drink ye all of it. This do ye as oft as ye drink it, in remembrance of me.'"* The meaning of the highly figurative phrases, "eating Christ's flesh, and drinking Christ's blood," may be easily ascertained, from the following quotations from one of our Lord's discourses:—" He that believeth on me hath everlasting life. I am that bread of life. If any man eat of this bread, he shall live for ever: and the bread that I will give is my flesh, which I will give for the life of the world. Except ye eat the flesh of the Son of man, and drink his blood, ye have no life in you. Whoso eateth my flesh, and drinketh my blood, hath eternal life; and I will raise him up at the last day. For my flesh is meat indeed, and my blood is drink indeed."† The apostle Paul, in his first epistle to the Corinthians, makes the following observations in reference to the meaning of the emblems in the Lord's Supper:—" The cup of blessing, or thanksgiving, which we bless, or over which we give thanks, is it not the communion—the mutual participation, of the blood of Christ? the bread which we break, is it not the communion—the mutual participation, of the body of Christ? for we being many, are one bread and one body: for we are all partakers of that one bread."‡ These passages of Scripture are the legitimate materials from which we are to form our judgments as to the meaning of the emblems in the Lord's Supper; and they certainly warrant us to affirm, that this ordinance is an emblematical representation of all the grand peculiarities of the Christian system.

---

* Matt. xxvi. 26, &c. Mark xiv. 22, &c. Luke xxii. 19, &c. 1 Cor. xi. 23, &c.
† John vi. 47—55. ‡ 1 Cor. x. 16, 17.

Truth may be brought before the mind in two ways,—by verbal statement, or by emblematical representation. The first is best fitted for conveying new information; the second is admirably calculated for recalling, in a striking manner, to the mind, information formerly presented to it. The first method of presenting the leading truths of Christianity is adopted in the written and spoken gospel; the second, in the Lord's Supper: and it will be found, on examination, that that ordinance is, as it were, a miniature picture of the same series of divine dispensations, of which we have a detailed history in the word of the truth of the gospel.

It may be worth our while to expand this remark a little, and show how full of Christian truth is every part of this emblematical institution. Let us contemplate the symbolical elements and actions, and apply to our Lord and his Apostles for their spiritual signification. In this ordinance we have bread and wine: and of the bread, our Lord says, " This is my body;" and of the wine, " This is my blood." These words admit but of two modes of interpretation,—the literal, which conducts directly into all the absurdities and blasphemies of transubstantiation; and the figurative, which represents the bread and the wine, as emblems of the body and blood of the Redeemer; just in the same way as the rock which supplied the Israelites with water during their wanderings in the wilderness, is called Christ. The words plainly imply, that he who used them had a body and blood—was a possessor of human nature: and the elements, to a well-instructed Christian, naturally recall the grand fundamental doctrine of the incarnation. In silent, but expressive language, they proclaim, " The word was made flesh, and dwelt among men: inasmuch as the children were partakers of flesh and blood, he also took part of the same. Great is the mystery of godliness: God was manifest in the flesh."

But in the Lord's Supper we not only have bread and wine, but broken bread and poured-out wine. Our Lord has unfolded the meaning of these emblems also: "This is my body broken, my blood shed; my body broken, my blood shed for you; my body broken, my blood shed for remission of sin unto many." The broken bread and the poured-out wine are, when thus explained, calculated to suggest to Christian minds, that the incarnate Saviour, after a life of suffering, died a violent death; that these sufferings and this death were vicarious and expiatory, undergone in the room of sinners, to obtain their salvation. It concentrates, as it were, the principal statements both of the prophets and the evangelists; and, with one glance of the eye, we see the wondrous plan of human redemption through the mediation of the incarnate only-begotten. It tells us more touchingly than words could do, that "Christ died for our sins, according to the Scriptures; that he was wounded for our transgressions, and bruised for our iniquities; that in him we have redemption through his blood, even the forgiveness of sins; that he has given himself for us a sacrifice and an offering, and has thus brought us unto God."

But the doctrines of the incarnation and the atonement are not the only principles of Christian truth which are embodied in the Lord's Supper. Had their representation been its sole object, it might have been gained by the minister's exhibiting bread and wine; and, while he pointed to them, proclaiming, "This is Christ's body broken; this is Christ's blood shed for you." But this is not the Lord's Supper. In that ordinance, we have not only broken bread and poured-out wine; but the broken bread is eaten, and the poured-out wine is drunk. This also is replete with spiritual meaning. From the passage above quoted from one of our Lord's discourses, it is plain, that eating Christ's flesh and drinking Christ's blood, is significant of that interest in his sufferings and death, which, by the divine appointment, is connected with the belief of the truth respecting them: so that here we are furnished with an emblematical representation of that cardinal doctrine of Christianity, that "whosoever believeth in Christ Jesus shall not perish, but have everlasting life." As bread and wine, though in themselves most nutritious food, will not nourish us, unless we eat the one and drink the other; so the expiatory sufferings and death of the incarnate Son of God, though of themselves adequate to the salvation of the greatest sinner, will not save us unless we believe.

But we have not yet exhausted the spiritual meaning of the emblems in the Lord's Supper. Had it been our Lord's object merely to embody, in an emblematical institution, the principles, " that the only-begotten of God in human nature suffered and died in the room of sinners, to procure their salvation; and that faith in these truths is at once absolutely necessary, and completely sufficient to secure to the sinner an interest in this salvation;" it is probable that the sacred rite would have been of such a nature as admitted of performance by a single individual. But this is not the case with the Lord's Supper. It is a social institution, and Christians must "come together to eat the Lord's Supper." Without any explicit revelation on the subject, knowing, as we do, from other passages of Scripture, that a very intimate relation does subsist among all the true followers of Jesus Christ, we might perhaps have warrantably concluded, that this mystical feast was intended emblematically to represent their holy fellowship. But it is our wish to say nothing in reference to the meaning of this ordinance, but what we are distinctly taught in Scripture. Indeed, there is no necessity to have recourse to inference. The passage already quoted from the apostle Paul is most explicit. In partaking of the cup of blessing, there is a communion, or mutual participation of the blood of Christ; in partaking of the broken bread, there is a communion, or mutual participation of the body of Christ; and the consequence of this mutual participation is, that the partakers are all one body and one bread. The reality and the nature of that intimate relation which subsists among all Christ's genuine followers, is there strikingly exhibited. They are a holy society, bound together by their common faith in the grand leading truths of Christianity, embodied in this emblematical institution, and, by their common love to that Saviour who is in it, " evidently set forth crucified and slain."

It is deeply to be regretted, that this part of the meaning of the Lord's Supper has been so much overlooked and forgotten, and that " the symbol of our common Christianity" should have been almost universally converted into " the badge and criterion of a party, a mark of discrimination applied to distinguish the nicer shades of difference among Christians."* It was not so from the beginning. The church of Christ was originally one body: the ordinance of the Lord's Supper is suited to such an order of things; and however perverted from its original purpose, though, instead of the common place of friendly meeting for all who believe the truth and love the Saviour, it has in many cases become " the line of demarcation, the impassable boundary which separates and disjoins them," still, in its obvious emblematical meaning, it sounds a retreat from the unnatural divisions which prevail among the genuine followers of the Saviour, by proclaiming that they are indeed all " one in Christ Jesus."

There is just one other important principle of Christian truth which we consider as embodied in the Lord's Supper. The Lord's Supper is a positive institution. It is entirely founded on the authority of Jesus Christ, as Him to whom all power in heaven and earth belongs. It does not, like what may be termed the moral part of our religion, necessarily arise out of the relations in which we stand to God as the God of salvation, and to Jesus Christ as the Redeemer of mankind, such as faith, confidence, and obedience. The sole obligation of this ordinance arises out of its appointment by Christ. It would have been our duty to have gratefully and devoutly remembered our Saviour's dying love, though no express command had been given us to that effect;

* Hall.

but it would not have been our duty to have expressed this grateful and devout recollection by the eating bread, and drinking wine, had not Jesus Christ said, " Do this in remembrance of me." The ordinance, then, embodies in it Christ's claims on the implicit obedience of his followers, and holds him forth as their Lawgiver as well as their Saviour.

Thus have we seen how replete with Christian truth is this emblematical institution. It forcibly presents to the Christian's mind these great fundamental principles of his religion, " that Jesus Christ, the Son of God, assumed human nature, and suffered and died in the room of sinners, to obtain their salvation; that all who believe God's testimony concerning this method of salvation, shall be saved; that all who are thus interested in this Christian salvation form a holy fellowship, bound together by the faith of the same truth, and reliance on the same Saviour; and that all who belong to this Christian fellowship are bound to submit implicitly to the Saviour's authority, and to walk in all his ordinances and commandments blameless."

But the Lord's Supper contains in it an emblematical *confirmation*, as well as an emblematical *exhibition*, of Christian doctrine. It presents to us not only the truth, but its evidence. The Lord's Supper involves in it satisfactory evidence of the truth of Christianity in general. It has been remarked, by one of the most ingenious defenders of Christianity,[*] that there can be no reasonable doubt of the reality of any event which is of such a nature as that men's senses can clearly and fully judge of it, which took place publicly, and in commemoration of which public institutions were immediately appointed, and have continued to be observed, with uninterrupted succession, till the present time. The facts of our Lord's death and resurrection are facts to which these characters belong. They were events, of the reality of which, men, in the exercise of the senses common to the species, could clearly and fully judge—they

* Leslie.

took place publicly. In the institution of the Lord's Supper and the Lord's day, institutions more closely connected than seems generally to be apprehended by Christians in the present age, we have public observances instituted in commemoration of these events, and which we know, from the most indubitable evidence, have been uninterruptedly observed from the period of their institution down to our own times. It is impossible for the ingenuity of infidelity to account satisfactorily for these facts, on any principle which does not involve in it the truth of Christianity; and it does not seem possible to conceive of a more simple, yet more effectual method of transmitting unimpaired the principal evidences of the truth of Christianity, in the miraculous events accompanying the Saviour's death and resurrection, than by wrapping it up, if I may use the expression, in the two kindred positive institutions of the Lord's Supper and the Lord's day.

The use of the Lord's Supper, as confirming Christian truth, is however by no means confined to this general proof of the truth of Christianity, as a system which it involves. It not only proves that a certain system of principles, denominated Christianity, is true and divine, but it proves that the doctrines which it emblematically embodies, form the leading principles of that true and divine system. It does not, like some very clear and convincing statements of the evidences of Christianity, leave you in the dark as to what Christianity is. And here we have much reason to admire the "manifold wisdom" discovered in this emblematical institution. Even a slight variation in its details would have rendered it completely unfit for answering this most important purpose. Had our Lord merely enjoined that his followers should frequently assemble around the same board, and eat bread and drink wine together, the rite might have been plausibly represented as nothing more than an exhibition of the tendency and design of Christianity to put an end to all unfriendly divisions among mankind, and to bind them together in the bands of fraternal affection. Had he even gone somewhat farther, and, on appointing such an institution, proclaimed, " This is the bread of life; he who eateth of it shall never hunger—this is the wine of the kingdom; he that drinketh of it shall never thirst —eat, drink, and live for ever,"—still, without doing any violence to the meaning either of the symbols, or of the words explicatory of them, we might have been told, that all that was meant was an emblematical representation of the tendency and design of the doctrine of Jesus Christ, to make men good, and wise, and happy. But it is impossible thus to give meaning to the emblems in the Lord's Supper, as explained by our Lord, without admitting that the incarnation and the atonement are essential parts of Christianity: and the same evidence which proves Christianity to be divine, proves this to be Christianity. The doctrine of salvation, through the sufferings and death of Jesus Christ, as the substitute of sinners, is so wrought into the very substance of this ordinance, that no ingenuity can extract it. So long as the Lord's Supper continues in the church—so long as the words of the institution are repeated, and the instituted symbols displayed, there never shall be wanting in the church a clear demonstration, that the death of the Son of God, as a sacrifice for sin, was a doctrine of the primitive age of Christianity.

It is thus that the Lord's Supper confirms, as well as exhibits the leading principles of Christianity; and it is thus that it answers to the description which is often given of it as a *sealing* ordinance. To this denomination, which, by the way, is not a scriptural one, very confused, and, in some cases, dangerously mistaken ideas are attached. The covenant of mercy was ratified, or sealed, by the blood of the Son of God, shed on Calvary; and of this blood-shedding, the Lord's Supper is not the repetition, but the commemoration: and as to the Lord's Supper sealing to the recipient his individual interest in the blessings secured by that covenant, the only scriptural idea that can be attached to these words is, that this ordinance is fitted as an exhibition both of truth and its evidence, to confirm that faith in the gospel, which at once connects us with the Saviour, and produces the consciousness of enjoying some, and the well-grounded hope of enjoying all the blessings of his salvation.

The Lord's Supper, which is thus, on the part of him who instituted it, an emblematical exhibition and confirmation of the leading principles of Christianity, is, on the part of him who observes it, an emblematical expression of a state of mind and of heart, accordant with this statement of Christian truth and its evidence. And here lies one of the principal differences between the verbal exhibition of Christian truth and evidence, in the written or spoken gospel, and the emblematical exhibition of Christian truth and evidence in the Lord's Supper. In both cases, it is the duty of those to whom the exhibition is made, to meet it with a corresponding state of thought and affection; but it is in the latter case only that a solemn profession of such an accordance of mind and heart is made. The taking the bread into our hands and eating it, the taking the wine into our hands and drinking it, are the appointed emblematical method of professing our faith of the truths represented in this ordinance; our reliance on Jesus Christ as our own Saviour, our unreserved submission to his authority, and our cordial love to all who, through the faith of the truth, rely on this Saviour, and are interested in his salvation.

The intelligent and believing communicant responds, as it were, to the voice of the Saviour, "This is my body broken, my blood shed for many, for the remission of sins:" "It is thy body broken, it is thy blood shed for many, for the remission of sins. I know, and am sure, that this is a faithful saying, that Jesus Christ, God's Son in human nature, suffered and died in the room of sinners, to obtain their salvation, and that whosoever believeth in him shall not perish, but have everlasting life."

But, in observing the Lord's Supper, there is more

than an expression of the belief of the gospel testimony in its general form, as embodied in this emblematic institution; there is also a profession of personal reliance on the Saviour's sufferings and death, as the expiation of our guilt, and the price of our salvation. This is the necessary and immediate result of the belief of the testimony in its true extent, and is so closely connected with it, that it is not much to be wondered at, if it has sometimes been identified with it. The emblems, as explained by our Lord, not merely intimate in general that Christ died for men—for sinners; but that he died for those in particular for whom this ordinance is intended, that is, for believers:—" This is my body broken for *you*, this is my blood shed for *you*." The state of mind and heart corresponding to such a declaration, is a personal reliance on the Saviour, a cordial reception of his salvation; and the language of the conduct of the believing communicant is, MY Lord and MY God, MY Saviour and MY all.

In the observance of the Lord's Supper, there is also a profession of an accordance of mind and heart with the view which the ordinance emblematically exhibits of the unity of the body of Christ. The believing communicant embraces, in the arms of his affections, the whole brotherhood of believers, and the language of his conduct, in eating of the common loaf, and drinking out of the common cup of the Christian family, is, "I love them all in the truth, for the truth's sake which is in them, and will abide in them for ever." The observation of the Lord's Supper does not imply in it a profession of a complete accordance of sentiment with every individual, or even with the religious body, along with whom we observe it. It implies a profession of our union with them in the faith of the truth, which the ordinance emblematically represents. It necessarily implies this, but it implies no more.

Finally, in observing the Lord's Supper, there is plainly implied, a profession of unreserved and implicit submission to the authority of Jesus Christ.

The ordinance, as we have shown above, is a positive institution. It involves in it an assertion of the authority of Jesus Christ over the conscience; and the observance of the ordinance is an unequivocal acknowledgment of this authority. The only reason why we observe it is, that Jesus Christ has commanded us to observe it; and in observing it, we say, "We do this just because Christ has commanded us to do it, and we are ready to do whatever he commands us, and ask no better reason than that he hath commanded us." When Jesus Christ puts the cup into our hands, he as it were says, "The man in whose hand this cup is found shall be my servant for ever;" and on taking it, we as it were respond, "Truly, O Lord, we are thy servants—we are thy servants, thou hast loosed our bonds; thine we are, and thee we will serve: we will walk in all thy commandments and ordinances blameless."

This view of the Lord's Supper—as on the part of him who instituted it, an emblematical representation and confirmation of the grand peculiarities of the Christian institution; and on the part of him who observes it, an emblematical expression of a state of mind and of heart in accordance with this statement of Christian truth and its evidence—has at least this advantage, that it is completely free of mysticism; it enables us distinctly to see why the observance of this ordinance should be restricted to persons possessed of a peculiar character, to explain the manner in which this ordinance contributes to spiritual improvement, and furnishes us with a plain, palpable rule, to ascertain whether we may safely observe the Lord's Supper, and to guide our devotional exercises when at the communion table.

The exclusion of all but genuine Christians from a right to observe the Lord's Supper, is not an arbitrary arrangement: it rises out of the nature of the case, and, like all the appointments of the God of nature and of grace, is found characterized by wisdom, equity, and benignity. How can a grossly ignorant person derive any advantage from observing such an ordinance as the Lord's Supper? To a mind in some measure enlightened in the meaning and evidence of Christian truth, the ordinance is calculated to recall and impress the great realities of the Christian economy, and to subject the whole of the inner man to their purifying and blissful influence. But to the man who does not know well who Jesus Christ is, in what his mediation consists, what made it necessary, what blessings he has procured for mankind, and how we, as individuals, are to obtain these blessings, of what intellectual or moral benefit can it possibly be to observe the Lord's Supper? He eats a little bread and drinks a little wine, and profanes a divine institution, and sinks himself deeper in guilt and delusion than ever.

The unbeliever is obviously equally unfitted for deriving spiritual advantage from this ordinance, and indeed cannot observe it without making a false profession—without "lying, not to men, but to God." This remark is equally applicable to those who, instead of relying solely on Jesus Christ crucified for salvation, are going about to establish their own righteousness, not submitting themselves to the righteousness of God—to those who are strangers to the love of the Christian brotherhood—and to those who are living in the habitual neglect or violation of any of the laws of Jesus. From the very nature of the institution, it is impossible that such persons can engage in it without dishonouring God and injuring their own souls; and of course that law of Christ is a holy, and just, and good one, which forbids such persons to approach the communion table.

There is a beautiful unity of principle pervading all the various methods adopted in the scheme of grace, for promoting man's spiritual improvement. The truth as it is in Jesus, known, and believed, and meditated on, is the grand instrument by which the Holy Spirit performs all his wonders in the new creation. It is delightful to observe this principle exemplified even in the ritual part of Christianity. There are many who seem to ascribe a sort of magical power to the Lord's Supper. The *consecrated* elements, as they like to phrase it, (and with them consecration does not refer to the Saviour's appointment, but to the mysterious effects of certain words uttered by the officiating minister,) are considered as a species of talismans, of miraculous efficacy in guarding the soul from the attacks of the powers of darkness. The Lord's Supper does us good just in the same way as the gospel does us good. In both, the truth as it is in Jesus, in its meaning and evidence, is held forth to us; and just in the degree in which it is apprehended by us, will we be made good and happy. It is a great mercy that the communication of saving blessings by the Lord's Supper and other ordinances, is not confined to those who can satisfactorily explain to their own minds the manner in which these institutions work out their intended results. At the same time, there is no doubt that such knowledge is of high importance, and greatly and directly tends to promote both the holiness and comfort of the true Christian.

These observations will be strangely misconceived, if they are considered by any one, as intended to cast into the shade the cardinal doctrine of the necessity of the influence of the Holy Spirit, in order to our deriving saving advantage from the Lord's Supper. But the influence of the Holy Spirit operates not miraculously, but according to the established laws of the human mind; and in the Lord's Supper, it is by his fixing the mind, and keeping it fixed on the emblematical display of Christian truth and its evidence, that he renders the ordinance effectual to the strengthening of our faith, and through the strengthening of our faith, to the general improvement of our spiritual character.

The work of self-inquiry, which, from the nature of the case, ought to precede our observing the Lord's Supper, is often represented as a peculiarly difficult and operose business; but if the above views of that ordinance be correct, the point to be ascertained is brought within a narrow limit, and little, except an honest wish to know the truth, should be necessary, for the resolution of the question. If a man is ignorant of the way of salvation through Christ Jesus, if he does not really believe that the Son of God in human nature suffered and died, the just in the room of the unjust, that he might bring them to God, if he does not rely on Jesus Christ, and on him alone, for salvation, if he does not love genuine Christians, just because they are genuine Christians, and if he habitually neglects or violates any of the laws of Jesus Christ, in his present condition, he is utterly incapacitated from deriving any spiritual advantage from this ordinance. And on the other hand, if a man understands and believes the testimony of God concerning his Son, trusts in him as his only and all-sufficient Saviour, loves all who love him, and are like him, and while conscious of much wanting and much wrong, has the testimony of his conscience, that he delights in the law of the Lord after the inward man,—such a person ought to avail himself of every opportunity of obeying Christ's commandment, "Do this in remembrance of me," and may reasonably anticipate, from such obedience, both spiritual enjoyment and improvement.

If we wish to obtain either, however, it is of importance that we keep steadily in view the nature and design of the Lord's Supper. When engaged in eating bread and drinking wine, in obedience to our Redeemer's command, our great endeavour should be to yield up our minds to the native influence of the truth and its evidence, as represented to us in the ordinance. The business of the communicant is simple; and, were we in any good measure what we should be, easy. It is to look to Jesus, plainly set forth, crucified and slain—to behold the Lamb of God bearing, and bearing away the sin of the world, and to allow these truths, so strikingly exhibited, so powerfully confirmed, to produce that love to God and to his Son, that penitence, humility, and resignation, that love to the brotherhood, and benevolence to all men, that weanedness from the world, and that earnest longing for a better one, which are their natural results. The best preparation for comfortable, profitable communicating, is habitually to "let the word of Christ dwell in us richly." The more thoroughly we are acquainted with Christian truth, the more firmly we believe it, the more readily will the instituted symbols in the Lord's Supper recall that truth and its evidence, and, under the influence of the good Spirit, contribute the more to our sanctification and consolation.

It is to the Bible that we have endeavoured to send our readers for their views of the nature and design of the Lord's Supper; and it is to the Bible we would wish to send them, as furnishing them with the best of all "Sacramental Directories," the only infallible "Guide to the Lord's Table." At the same time, we are disposed to think, that, when kept in their own place, those Treatises, whether doctrinal or devotional, which pious men have given to the world, on the Lord's Supper, may be turned to good account by the intelligent Christian. From almost all of them, important and useful instruction may be derived; but, perhaps, none of these Treatises possess more excellencies, and fewer defects, than MATTHEW HENRY's COMMUNICANT's COMPANION. It is much more than a general account of the nature and design of the Lord's Supper, and a set of rules for the observance of that institution; it contains in it an admirable view of Christian doctrine, experience, and duty, and is peculiarly fitted to prevent persons from taking that insulated view of the ordinance, which, with too many, converts it into a mere rite, a piece of "bodily service, which profits little." It is distinguished, in a high degree, by the characteristic good qualities of the minor works of its Author, who, on a scale of literary merit, graduated on the principle which will regulate the judgment of the last day, would occupy a high place among English writers. It is very plain, very pious, and very practical. There is a simplicity, a naturalness, and a familiarity, which renders it peculiarly delightful reading, and makes us almost fancy ourselves enjoying the conversation of its venerable Author. With these views of the following Treatise, we cannot but apprehend that much good must be derived from its attentive, prayerful perusal; but the advice we would give, as to reading this or any other human composition, is that of the apostle—" PROVE ALL THINGS, HOLD FAST THAT WHICH IS GOOD."

J. B.

EDINBURGH, *April*, 1825.

TO THE READER.

I HERE humbly offer you, Christian reader, some assistance in that great and good work, which you have to do, and are concerned to do well, when you attend the table of your Lord; a work in which I have observed most serious people desirous of help, and willing to use the helps they have; which I confess was one thing that invited me to this undertaking.

I offer this service with all due deference and respect to the many excellent performances of this kind, with which we are already blessed, done by far better hands than mine; who yet have not so fully gathered in this harvest, but that those who come after may gather up plentiful gleanings, without robbing their sheaves:—" Lord, it is done as thou hast commanded, and yet there is room;" room enough to enlarge upon a subject so copious, and of so great a compass that it cannot be exhausted.

I do this also with a just sense of my own unworthiness, and unfitness to bear the vessels of the Lord, and to do any service in his sanctuary. Who am I, and what is my father's house, that I should have the honour to be " a door-keeper in the house of my God," to show his guests the way to his table? And that I should be employed thus to " hew wood, and draw water for the congregation of the Lord?" I reckon it true preferment, and " by the grace of God," his free grace, " I am what I am." It is service which is its own recompense;—work which is its own wages. In helping to feed others, we may feast ourselves; for our master hath provided that the mouth of the ox be not muzzled when he treads out the corn. For my part, I would not exchange the pleasure of converse with the Scriptures and divine things, for all "the delights of the sons and daughters of men, and the peculiar treasures of kings and provinces." It was a noble saying of the Marquis of Vico, "Let their money perish with them, who esteem all the wealth of this world worth one hour's communion with God in Jesus Christ."

In doing this, I hope I can truly say, my desire and design is to contribute something to the faith, holiness, and joy of those who in this ordinance have given up their names to the Lord Jesus. And if God, by his grace, will make this endeavour in some degree serviceable to that end, I have what I wish, I have what I aim at; and it will not be the first time that praise hath been perfected, and strength ordained out of the mouths of babes and sucklings.

In this essay I have an eye particularly to that little handful of people among whom I have been, in much weakness, ministering in these holy things seventeen years; during all which time, through the good hand of our God upon us, we have never once been disappointed of the stated solemnities, either of our new moons, or of our Sabbaths. As I designed my Scripture Catechism, and the other little one that followed it, to be a present, and perhaps ere long it may prove my legacy to the young ones, the lambs of the flock; so I recommend this to the adult, and leave it with them, being desirous that the sheep we are charged to feed, "may go in and out, and find pasture." And I earnestly wish, that both these may prove successful expedients to preserve some of those things they have been taught, from being quite forgotten; and that, after my decease, they and theirs will have those things always in remembrance.

And lastly, I send this abroad under the protection and blessing of heaven; with a hearty prayer to God to forgive whatever is mine, that is, what is amiss and defective in the performance; and graciously to accept what is his own, that is, whatever is good and profitable; hoping that, if God pardon my defects and infirmities, my friends also will overlook them; and that, if he favourably accept my endeavours through Christ, they also will accept them; for truly it is the height of my ambition to approve myself, a faithful servant to Christ and souls.

MATTHEW HENRY.

CHESTER, *June* 21, 1704.

THE COMMUNICANT'S COMPANION.

CHAPTER I.

THE NAMES BY WHICH THIS ORDINANCE IS USUALLY CALLED.

I. We call it the Sacrament; that is, a sign and an oath. II. The Lord's Supper; a supper, our Lord's Supper. III. The Communion; having in it communion with Christ, and with the universal church. IV. The Eucharist; Christ in the institution of it gave thanks, and we in the participation. V. The Feast; a royal feast, a marriage feast, a feast of memorial, a feast of dedication, a feast upon a sacrifice, and a feast upon a covenant.

In discoursing of this great and solemn ordinance, which every serious Christian looks upon with a peculiar regard and veneration, I purpose, as God shall enable me, to open the doctrine as well as the duty of it; it will, therefore, be proper enough, and I hope profitable, to take some notice of the several names by which it is known.

I. We call it *the* sacrament.—This is the name we commonly give it, but improperly, because it does not distinguish it from the ordinance of baptism, which is as much a sacrament as this; a sacrament which we have all received, by which we are all bound, and are concerned to improve, and live up to: but, when we call this ordinance, "the sacrament," we ought to remind ourselves that it is *a* sacrament; that is, it is a sign, and it is an oath.

1. It is a sign, an outward and visible sign of an inward and spiritual grace; for such sacraments are

designed to be.—It is a parable to the eye; and in it God uses similitudes, as he did of old by his servants the prophets. In it Christ tells us earthly things, that thereby we may come to be more familiarly acquainted, and more warmly affected, with spiritual and heavenly things. In it Christ speaks to us in our own language, and accommodates himself to the capacities of our present state. Man consists of body and soul, and the soul admits impressions, and exerts its power, by the body; here is an ordinance, therefore, which consists of body and soul too, wherein Christ, and the benefits of the new covenant, are, in the instituted elements of bread and wine, set before us, and offered to us. We live in a world of sense, not yet in the world of spirits; and, because we therefore find it hard to look above the things that are seen, we are directed, in a sacrament, to look through them, to those things not seen, which are represented by them. That things merely sensible, may not improve the advantage they have from our present state wholly to engross our thoughts and cares, in compassion to our infirmity, spiritual things are in this ordinance made in a manner sensible.

Let us, therefore, rest contented with this sign which Christ hath appointed, in which he is " evidently set forth crucified among us," and not think it can be any honour to him, or advantage to ourselves, but, on the contrary, a dishonour to him, and an injury to ourselves, to represent, by images and pictures, the same things of which this ordinance was designed to be the representation. If infinite wisdom thought this sign sufficient, and most proper to affect the heart, and excite devotion, and stamp it accordingly with an institution, let us acquiesce in it.

Yet let us not rest contented with the sign only, but converse by faith with the things signified, else we receive the grace of God in this appointment in vain; and sacraments will be to us, what parables were to them that were wilfully blind, blinding them the more. What will it avail us to have the shadow without the substance, the letter without the spirit?

"As the body without the soul is dead," so our seeing and receiving bread and wine, if therein we see and receive not Christ crucified, is dead also.

2. It is an oath.—That is the ancient signification of the word sacrament. The Romans called the oath which soldiers took to be true to their general, *Sacramentum militare;* and our law still uses it in this sense: *dicunt super sacramentum suum,* "they say upon their oath;" so that to take the sacrament, is to take an oath, a solemn oath, by which we bind our souls with a bond unto the Lord. It is an oath of allegiance to the Lord Jesus, by which we engage ourselves to be his dutiful and loyal subjects, acknowledging him to be our rightful Lord and Sovereign. It is as a freeman's oath, by which we enter ourselves members of Christ's mystical body, and oblige ourselves to observe the laws, and seek the good of that Jerusalem which is from above, that we may enjoy the privileges of that great charter by which it is incorporated. An oath is an appeal to God's knowledge of our sincerity and truth in what we assert or promise; and in this ordinance we make such an appeal as Peter did: "Lord, thou knowest all things, thou knowest that I love thee." An oath is an imprecation of God's wrath upon ourselves, if we deal falsely, and wilfully prevaricate; and something of that also there is in this sacrament; for if we continue in league with sin, while we pretend to covenant with God, "we eat and drink judgment to ourselves."

Let us, therefore, according to the character of a virtuous man, fear this oath; not fear to take it, for it is our duty, with all possible solemnity, to oblige ourselves to the Lord; but fear to break it, for oaths are not to be jested with. God hath said it, and hath sworn it by himself: "Unto me every tongue shall swear." But he hath also said, that we must swear to him "in truth, in judgment, and in righteousness;" and having sworn, we must perform it. If we come to this sacrament carelessly, and inconsiderately, we incur the guilt of rash swearing; if we go away from the sacrament, and walk contrary to the engagements of it, we incur the guilt of false swearing. Even natural religion teaches men to make conscience of an oath; much more does the Christian religion teach us to make conscience of this oath, to which God is not only a witness, but a party.

II. We call it the Lord's Supper, and very properly, for so the Scripture calls it, (1 Cor. xi. 20,) where the Apostle, reproving the irregularities that were among the Corinthians in the administration of this ordinance, tells them, "This is not to eat the Lord's Supper."

1. It is a supper.—A supper is a stated meal for the body; this is so for the soul, which stands in as much need of its daily bread as the body does. Supper was then accounted the principal meal; this ordinance is so among Christ's friends, and in his family it is the most solemn entertainment. It is called a supper, because it was first instituted in the evening, and at the close of the passover-supper; which, though it tie not us always to administer it about that time, because it would be inconvenient for religious assemblies; yet it signifies, 1st, That Christ now, in the end of the world, in the declining part of its day, as the great evening sacrifice, " hath appeared to put away sin." This glorious discovery was reserved for us, " upon whom the ends of the world are come." 2d. That comfort in Christ is intended for those only that dwell in God's house, and for those only that have done the work of the day in its day, according as the duty of every day required. They only that work with Christ, shall eat with him. 3d. That the chief blessings of the new covenant are reserved for the evening of the day of our life. The evening feast is a supper designed for us, when we have " accomplished as a hireling our day," and come home at night.

2. It is the Lord's Supper, the Lord Christ's Supper.—The apostle, in his discourse concerning this ordinance, (1 Cor. xi. 23, &c.) all along calls Christ

the Lord, and seems to lay an emphasis upon it; for as the ordaining of this sacrament was an act of his dominion, and as lord of his church, he appointed it; so, in receiving this sacrament we own his dominion, and acknowledge him to be our lord. This also puts an honour upon the ordinance, and makes it look truly great; however, to a carnal eye it hath no form nor comeliness, that it is the Supper of the Lord. The sanction of this ordinance, is the authority of Christ; the substance of this ordinance, is the grace of Christ. It is celebrated in obedience to him, in remembrance of him, and for his praise. Justly is it called the Lord's Supper; for it is the Lord Jesus that sends the invitation, makes the provision, gives the entertainment. In it we feed upon Christ, for he is the bread of life; we feed with Christ, for he is our beloved and our friend, and he it is that bids us welcome to his table. In it " Christ sups with us, and we with him;" he doth us the honour to sup with us, though he must bring his own entertainment along with him; he gives us the happiness of supping with him upon the dainties of heaven.

Let our eye, therefore, be to the Lord, to the Lord Christ, and to the remembrance of his name, in this ordinance. We see nothing here, if we see not the beauty of Christ; we taste nothing here, if we taste not the love of Christ. The Lord must be looked upon as the Alpha and the Omega, the beginning and the end, and all in all in this solemnity. If we receive not Christ Jesus the Lord here, we have the supper, but not the Lord's Supper.

III. We call it the Communion, the holy communion, and fitly do we call it so: for,

1. In this ordinance we have communion with Christ, our Head.—" Truly our fellowship is with him." He here manifests himself to us, and gives out to us his graces and comforts; we here set ourselves before him, and tender him the grateful returns of love and duty. A kind correspondence between Christ and our souls is kept up in this ordinance, such as our present state will admit. Christ, by his word

and spirit, abides in us: we by faith and love abide in him: here, therefore, where Christ seals his word, and offers his Spirit, and where we exercise our faith, and have our love inflamed, there is communion between us and Christ.

This communion supposes union; this fellowship supposes friendship; for, "can two walk together except they be agreed?" We must, therefore, in the bond of an everlasting covenant, join ourselves to the Lord, and combine our interest with his; and then, pursuant thereto, concern him in all the concerns of our happiness; and concern ourselves in all the concerns of his glory.

2. In this ordinance we have communion with the universal church, "even with all that in every place call on the name of Jesus Christ our Lord, both theirs and ours."—Hereby we profess, testify, and declare, that "we, being many, are one bread and one body," by virtue of our common relation to our Lord Jesus Christ; "for we are all partakers of that one bread, Christ, the bread of life," signified and communicated in this sacramental bread. All true Christians, though they are many, yet they are one; and we express our consent to, and complacency in that union, by partaking of the Lord's Supper. I say, though they are many, that is, though they are numerous, yet, as a vast number of creatures make one world, governed by one providence, so a vast number of Christians make one church, animated by one Spirit, the soul of that great body. Though they are various, far distant from each other in place, of distinct societies, different attainments, and divers apprehensions in lesser things; yet, all meeting in Christ, they are one. They are all incorporated in one and the same church, all interested in one and the same covenant, all stamped with one and the same image, partakers of the same new and divine nature, and all entitled to one and the same inheritance. In the Lord's Supper we are "made to drink into one Spirit." And therefore, in attending on that ordinance, we are concerned not only to preserve, but to culti-

vate and improve Christian love and charity; for what will this badge of union avail us without the unity of the Spirit?

IV. We call it the Eucharist; so the Greek church called it, and we from them. It signifies a *thanksgiving*, and it is so called,

1. Because Christ in the institution of it gave thanks.—It should seem that Christ frequently offered up his prayers in the form of thanksgivings, as, " Father, I thank thee that thou hast heard me;" and so he blessed the bread and the cup, by giving thanks over them; as the true Melchizedek, who, when he " brought forth bread and wine to Abraham, blessed the most high God." Though our Saviour, when he instituted the sacrament, had a full prospect of his approaching sufferings, with all their aggravations, yet he was not thereby indisposed for thanksgiving; for praising God is a work that is never out of season. Though the Captain of our salvation was now but girding on the harness, yet he gives thanks as though he had put it off, being confident of a glorious victory: in the prospect of which, even before he took the field, he did in this ordinance divide the spoil among his followers, and " gave gifts unto men."

2. Because we, in the participation of it, must give thanks likewise.—It is an ordinance of thanksgiving appointed for the joyful celebrating of the Redeemer's praises. This sacrifice of atonement Christ himself offered once for all, and it must not, it cannot be repeated; but sacrifices of acknowledgment Christians must offer daily, that is, " the fruit of our lips giving thanks to his name." The cup of salvation must be a cup of blessing, with which, and for which, we must bless God, as the Jews were wont to do very solemnly at the close of the passover supper; at which time Christ chose to institute this sacrament, because he intended it for a perpetual thanksgiving, till we come to the world of praise.

Come, therefore, and let us sing unto the Lord in this ordinance; let the high praises of our Redeemer be in our mouths and in our hearts; would we have the comfort, let him have the praise of the great things he has done for us; let us remember that thanksgiving is the business of the ordinance, and let that turn our complaints into praises; for, whatever matter of complaint we find in ourselves, in Christ we find abundant matter for praise, and that is the pleasant subject upon which, in this ordinance, we should dwell.

V. We call it the feast, the Christian feast.—Christ "our passover being sacrificed for us," in this ordinance we keep the feast, (1 Cor. v. 8.) They that communicate, are said to feast with us. This name, though not commonly used, yet is very significant; for it is such a supper as is a feast. Gospel preparations are frequently compared to a feast: "And in this mountain shall the Lord of hosts make unto all people a feast of fat things, a feast of wines on the lees; of fat things full of marrow, of wines on the lees well refined." The guests are many, the invitation solemn, and the provision rich and plentiful, and therefore fitly is called a feast of souls. "A feast is made for laughter," so is this for spiritual joy; the wine here designed to make glad the heart. A feast is made for free conversation, so is this for communion between heaven and earth; in this banquet of wine the golden sceptre is held out to us, and this fair proposal made, "What is thy petition, and it shall be granted thee?"

Let us see what kind of a feast it is.

1. It is a royal feast; "a feast like the feast of a king," that is, a magnificent feast. It is a feast like that of king Ahasuerus; "a feast for all his servants," and designed, as that was, not only to show his good will to those whom he had feasted, but to "show the riches of his glorious kingdom, and the honour of his excellent majesty." The treasures hid in Christ, even his unsearchable riches, are here set open, and the glories of the Redeemer illustriously displayed. He who is King of kings, and Lord of lords, here issues out the same order that we find him giving:

"Come gather yourselves together to the supper of the great God;" and that must needs be a great supper. The wisest of kings introduces Wisdom herself as a queen or princess making this feast: "Wisdom hath killed her beasts, and mingled her wine." At a royal feast, the provision, we may be sure, is rich and noble, such as becomes a king to give, though not such beggars as we are to expect; the welcome also we may be sure is free and generous; Christ gives like a king.

Let us remember, that in this ordinance we sit to eat with a Ruler, with a Ruler of rulers, and therefore "must consider diligently what is before us," and observe a decorum. He is a King that comes in to see the guests, and therefore we are concerned to behave ourselves well.

2. It is a marriage-feast; it is a feast made by a King, at the marriage of his Son: so our Saviour represents it, not only to speak exceeding rich and sumptuous, and celebrated with extraordinary expressions of joy and rejoicing, but because the covenant here sealed between Christ and his church is a marriage-covenant, such a covenant as makes two one; a covenant founded in the dearest love, founding the nearest relation, and designed to be perpetual. In this ordinance, 1st, We celebrate the memorial of the virtual espousals of the church of Christ when he died upon the cross, to "sanctify and cleanse it, that he might present it to himself." "That was the day of his espousals, the day of the gladness of his heart." 2d, The actual espousals of believing souls to Christ, are here solemnized, and that agreement ratified: "My beloved is mine, and I am his." The soul that renounces all other lovers that stand in competition with the Lord Jesus, and joins itself by faith and love to him only, is in this ordinance "presented as a chaste virgin to him." 3d, A pledge and earnest of the public and complete espousals of the church of Christ at his second coming, is here given; "then the marriage of the Lamb comes," and we, according to his promise, hereby declare that we look for it.

If we come to a marriage-feast, we must not come without a wedding garment, that is, a frame of heart, and a disposition of soul agreeable to the solemnity, conformable to the nature, and answering the intentions of the gospel, as it is exhibited to us in this ordinance. "Holy garments, and garments of praise," are the wedding garments: "Put on Christ, put on the new man," these are the wedding garments. In these we must, with our lamps in our hands, as the wise virgins, go forth, with all due observance, to attend the royal bridegroom.

3. It is a feast of memorial, like the feast of the passover, of which it is said, "This day shall be unto you for a memorial, and you shall keep it a feast to the Lord,—a feast by an ordinance for ever." The deliverance of Israel out of Egypt was a work of wonder never to be forgotten; the feast of unleavened bread was therefore instituted to be annually observed throughout all the ages of the Jewish church, as a solemn memorial of that deliverance, that the truth of it being confirmed by this traditional evidence, might never be questioned; and that the remembrance of it, being frequently revived by this service, might never be lost. Our redemption by Christ from sin and hell, is a greater work of wonder than that was, more worthy to be remembered, and yet (the benefits that flow from it being spiritual) more apt to be forgotten; this ordinance was therefore instituted, and instituted, in the close of the passover supper, (as coming in the room of it,) to be a standing memorial in the church, of the glorious achievements of the Redeemer's cross; the victories obtained by it over the powers of darkness, and the salvation wrought by it for the children of light. "Thus the Lord hath made his wonderful works to be remembered."

4. It is a feast of dedication.—Solomon made such a feast for all Israel, when he dedicated the temple, as his father David had done, when he brought the ark into the tabernacle. Even the children of the captivity "kept the dedication of the house of God

with joy." In the ordinance of the Lord's Supper, we dedicate ourselves to God as living temples; temples of the Holy Ghost, separated from every thing that is common and profane, and entirely devoted to the service and honour of God in Christ. To show that we do this with cheerfulness and satisfaction, and that it may be done with an agreeable solemnity, this feast is appointed for the doing of it, that we may, like the people of Israel, when Solomon dismissed them from his feast of dedication, " Go to your tents joyful, and glad of heart, for all the goodness that the Lord hath done for David his servant, and for Israel his people."

5. It is a feast upon a sacrifice.—This, methinks, is as proper a notion of it as any other. It was the law and custom of sacrifices, both among the Jews, and in other nations, that when the beast offered was slain, the blood sprinkled, the fat, and some select parts of it burnt upon the altar, and the priest had his share out of it, then the remainder was given back to the offerer; on which he and his family and friends feasted with joy. Hence we read of Israel after the flesh, eating the sacrifices, and so partaking of the altar: " Behold Israel after the flesh. Are not they which eat of the sacrifices partakers of the altar?" That is, in token of their partaking of the benefit of the sacrifice, and their joy therein. And this eating of the sacrifice was a religious rite, expressive of their communion with God in and by the sacrifice.

(1.) Jesus Christ is the great and only sacrifice, who, by being " once offered, perfected for ever them which are sanctified;" and this offering need never be repeated; that once was sufficient.

(2.) The Lord's Supper is a feast upon this sacrifice, in which we receive the atonement, as the expression is: " And not only so, but we also joy in God, through our Lord Jesus Christ, by whom we have now received the atonement." That is, we give consent to, and take complacency in the method which infinite wisdom has taken of justifying and saving us by the merit and mediation of the Son of God incarnate. In feasting upon the sacrifice, we apply the benefit of it to ourselves, and ascribe the praise of it to God with joy and thankfulness.

6. It is a feast upon a covenant.—The covenant between Isaac and Abimelech was made with a feast. So was that between Laban and Jacob, and their feasting upon the sacrifices was a federal rite, in token of peace and communion between God and his people. In the Lord's Supper we are admitted to feast with God, in token of reconciliation between us and him through Christ. Though we have provoked God, and been enemies to him in our minds by wicked works, yet he thus graciously provides for us, to show that now " he hath reconciled us to himself. His enemies hungering, he thus feeds them; thirsting, he thus gives them drink; which if, like coals of fire heaped upon their heads, it melts them into a compliance with the terms of his covenant, they shall henceforth, as his own familiar friends, eat bread at his table continually, till they come to sit down with him at his table in his kingdom.

CHAPTER II.

THE NATURE OF THIS ORDINANCE.

I. It is a commemorating Ordinance, in remembrance of the person of Christ, as an absent friend, and of the death of Christ as an ancient favour. Hereby we preserve the memory of it in the church, and revive the remembrance of it in our hearts. II. It is a Confessing Ordinance; we profess our value and esteem for Christ crucified, and our dependence upon, and confidence in Christ crucified. III. It is a Communicating Ordinance; Christ and all his benefits are here communicated to us, and are here to be received by us. IV. It is a Covenanting Ordinance; it is the New Testament, and the new covenant, opened distinctly; God seals to us to be to us a God, and we seal to him to be to him a people.

WHEN the Jews, according to God's appointment, observed the passover yearly throughout their generations, it was supposed that their children would ask them, "What mean you by this service?" and they were directed what answer to give to that inquiry. The question may very fitly be asked concerning our gospel passover. What mean we by this service? We come together in a public and select assembly of baptized Christians, under the conduct and presidency of a gospel minister; we take bread and wine, sanctified by the word and prayer, and we eat and drink together in a solemn religious manner, with an eye to a divine institution, as our warrant and rule in so doing. This we do often; this all the churches of Christ do, and have done in every age, from the death of Christ down to this day; and, we doubt not, but it will continue to be done till time shall be no more. Now, what is the true intent and meaning of this ordinance? What did Christ design it for in the institution? And what must we aim at in the observation of it?

It was appointed to be a commemorating ordinance, and a confessing ordinance, and a communicating ordinance, and a covenanting ordinance.

I. The ordinance of the Lord's Supper is a commemorating ordinance. This explanation our Lord himself gave of it, when he said, "Do this in remembrance of me." Do it for my memorial. Do it for a remembrance of me. In this ordinance he has recorded his name for ever, and this is his memorial throughout all generations.

We are to do this,

1. In remembrance of the person of Christ, as an absent friend of ours.—It is a common ceremony of friendship to lay up something in remembrance of a friend we have valued, which we say, we keep for his sake, when he is gone, or is at a distance; it is usual likewise to drink to one another, remembering such a friend that is absent. Jesus Christ is our beloved and our friend, the best friend that ever our souls had; he is now absent, he has left the world, and is gone to the Father, and the heavens must contain him till the time of the restitution of all things.

Now, this ordinance is appointed for a remembrance of him. We observe it in token of this, that though the blessed Jesus be out of sight, he is not out of mind. He that instituted this ordinance, did, as it were, engrave this on it for a motto:—

> When this you see,
> Remember me.

Remember him! Is there any danger of our forgetting him? If we were not wretchedly taken up with the world and the flesh, and strangely careless in the concerns of our souls, we could not forget him. But, in consideration of the treachery of our memories, this ordinance is appointed to remind us of Christ.

Ought we not to remember, and can we ever forget such a friend as Christ is:—a friend that is our near and dear relation; "bone of our bone, flesh of our flesh, and not ashamed to call us brethren?" A friend in covenant with us, who puts more honour upon us than we deserve, when he calls us his servants, and yet is pleased to call us friends. A friend that has so wonderfully signalized his friendship, and commended his love: he hath done that for us which no friend we have in the world did, or could do for us: he has laid down his life for us, when the redemption of our souls was grown so precious, as otherwise to have ceased for ever. Surely we must forget ourselves if ever we forget him, since our happiness is entirely owing to his kindness.

Ought we not to remember, and can we ever forget a friend, who, though he be absent from us, is negotiating our affairs, and is really absent for us? He is gone, but he is gone upon our business; as the forerunner he is for us entered; he is gone to appear in the presence of God for us, as our agent. Can we be unmindful of him who is always mindful of us, and who, as the great High Priest of our profession, bears the names of all his spiritual Israel on his breastplate, near his heart, within the veil!

Ought we not to remember, and can we ever forget a friend, who, though he be now absent, will be absent but a while? We see him not, but we expect to see him shortly, when he will "come in the clouds, and every eye shall see him;" will come to receive us to himself, to share in his joy and glory. Shall we not be glad of any thing that helps us to remember him, who not only remembered us once in our low estate, but, having once remembered us, will never forget us? Shall not his name be written in indelible characters upon the tables of our heart, who hath graven us upon the palms of his hands? Surely we must continually remember our Judge and Lord, when, behold, the Lord is at hand, and the Judge standeth before the door. Thus must we show him forth till he come; for he comes quickly.

2. We are to do this in the remembrance of the death of Christ, as an ancient favour done to us. This ordinance was instituted on the night wherein our Master was betrayed, that night of observations, as the first passover night is called, (Exod. xii. 42. margin,) which intimates the special reference this ordinance was to have to that which was done that night, and the day following. In it we are "to know Christ and him crucified," to remember his sufferings, and, in a special manner, to remember his bonds. All the saints and all the churches could not see Christ upon the cross; therefore, in this ordinance, that great transaction is set before us, upon which the judgment of this world turned: "Now is the judgment of this world." Here we remember the dying of the Lord Jesus: that is,

(1.) We endeavour to preserve the memory of it in the church, and to transmit it pure and entire through our age, to the children which shall be born, that the remembrance of it may be ever fresh, and may not die in our hand. That good thing which was committed to us as a trust, we must thus carefully keep, and faithfully deliver down, to the next generation; evidencing, that we firmly believe, and frequently think of Christ's dying for us, and desiring that those who should come after us may do so too.

(2.) We endeavour to revive and incite the remembrance of it in our own hearts.—This ordinance was intended "to stir up our pure minds," (our impure minds we have too much reason to call them,) by way of remembrance, that, giving such an earnest heed to the things that belong to the great salvation, as the solemnity of this ordinance calls for, we may not at any time let them slip; or if we do, we may, in the use thereof, speedily recover them. The instituted images of Christ crucified, are, in this ordinance, very strong and lively, and proper to make deep impressions of his grace and love, upon the minds that are prepared to receive them, and such as cannot be worn out.

We see, then, what we have to do in our attendance upon this ordinance; we must remember the sufferings of Christ there, else we do nothing.

1st. This supposes some acquaintance with Christ crucified; for we cannot be said to remember that which we never knew.—The ignorant, therefore, to whom the great things of the gospel are as a strange thing, with which they are not concerned to acquaint themselves, cannot answer the intention of this ordinance; but they offer the blind in sacrifice, not discerning the Lord's body, and the breaking of it. It concerns us, therefore, to cry after this knowledge, and to labour after a clearer insight into the mystery of our redemption by the death of Christ; for, if we be ignorant of this, and rest in false and confused notions of it, we are unworthy to wear the Christian name, and to live in a Christian nation.

2d. It implies a serious thought and contemplation of the sufferings of Christ, such as is fed and supplied with matter to work upon, not from a strong fancy, but from a strong faith. Natural passions may be raised by the power of imagination, representing the story of Christ's suffering as very doleful and tragical; but pious and devout affections are best kindled by the consideration of Christ's dying as a propitiation for our sins, and the Saviour of our souls; and this is the object of faith, not of fancy. We must here look unto Jesus as he is lifted up in the gospel, take him as the word makes him, and so behold him.

3d. The contemplation of the sufferings of Christ must make such an impression upon the soul, as to work it into a fellowship with, and conformity, to Christ in his sufferings. This was the knowledge and remembrance of Christ, of which blessed Paul was ambitious to "know Christ and the fellowship of his sufferings," and we all, by our baptism, are in profession "planted together in the likeness of his death." Then we do this in remembrance of Christ effectually, when we experience the death of Christ killing sin in us, mortifying the flesh, weaning us from this present life, weakening vicious habits and dispositions in us, and the power of Christ's cross, both as a moral argument, and as the spring of special grace, "crucifying us to the world, and the world to us," when, in "touching the hem of his garment," we find, like that good woman, virtue comes out of him to heal our souls, then we rightly remember Christ crucified.

II. It is a confessing ordinance.—If the heart believe unto righteousness, hereby confession is made unto salvation. The Lord's Supper is one of the peculiarities of our holy religion, by the observance of which, the professors of it are distinguished from all others. Circumcision, which was the initiating ordinance among the Jews, by leaving its mark in the flesh, was a lasting badge of distinction; baptism, which succeeds it, leaves no such indelible character on the body: but the Lord's Supper is a solemnity by which we constantly avow the Christian name, and declare ourselves not ashamed of the banner of the cross under which we were enlisted, but resolve to continue Christ's faithful servants and soldiers to the end of our lives, according to our baptismal vow.

In the ordinance of the Lord's Supper we are said to show forth the Lord's death, 1 Cor. xi. 26, that is,

1. We hereby profess our value and esteem for Christ crucified; ye show it forth with commendation and praise: so the word sometimes signifies. The cross of Christ was to the Jews a stumbling-block,

because they expected a Messiah in temporal pomp and power. It was to the Greeks foolishness, because the doctrine of man's justification and salvation by it, was not agreeable to their philosophy. The wisdom of this world, and the princes of it, judged it absurd to expect salvation by one that died a captive; and honour by one that died in disgrace; and turned it to the reproach of Christians, that they were the disciples and followers of one that was hanged on a tree at Jerusalem. They who put him to such an ignominious death, and loaded him with all the shame they could put upon him, hoped thereby to make every one shy of owning him, or expressing any respect for him; but the wisdom of God so ordered it, that the cross of Christ is that which above any thing else Christians have cause to glory in. Such are the fruits, the purchases, the victories, the triumphs of the cross, that we have reason to call it our crown of glory, and diadem of beauty. The politicians thought it had been the interest of Christ's followers to have concealed their Lord's death, and that they should have endeavoured to bury it in forgetfulness; but instead of that, they are appointed to show forth the Lord's death, and to keep it in everlasting remembrance before angels and men.

This, then, we mean, when we receive the Lord's Supper; we thereby solemnly declare that we do not reckon the cross of Christ any reproach to Christianity: and that we were so far from being ashamed of it, that, whatever constructions an unthinking, unbelieving world may put upon it, to us it is the wisdom of God and the power of God; it is all our salvation, and all our desire. We think never the worse of Christ's holy religion for the ignominious death of its great Author; for we see God glorified in it, man saved by it; then is the reproach of it rolled away for ever.

2. We hereby profess our dependence upon, and confidence in Christ crucified. As we are not ashamed to own him, so we are not afraid to venture our souls, and their eternal salvation with him,

believing him "able to save to the uttermost all that come to God by him;" and as willing as he is able, and making confession of that faith. By this solemn rite we deliberately, and of choice put ourselves under the protection of his righteousness, the influence of his grace, and the conduct and operation of his Holy Spirit. The concerns that lie between us and God, are of vast consequence, our eternal weal or woe depends upon the right management of them; now we hereby solemnly declare, that having laid them near our own hearts in a serious care about them, we choose to lodge them in the Redeemer's hands, by a judicious faith in him, for which we can give a good reason. God having declared himself well pleased in him, we hereby declare ourselves well pleased in him too; God having committed all judgment to the Son, we hereby commit all our judgment to him likewise, as the sole Referee of the great cause, and the sole Trustee of the great concern, "knowing whom we have believed, even one who is able and faithful to keep what we have committed to him against that day," that great day when it will be called for.

This then, we mean, when we receive the Lord's Supper; we confess that Jesus Christ is Lord, and we own ourselves to be his subjects, and put ourselves under his government; we confess that he is a skilful physician, and own ourselves to be his patients, resolving to observe his prescriptions; we confess that he is a faithful advocate, and own ourselves to be his clients, resolving to be advised by him in every thing. In a word, in this ordinance we profess that we are not ashamed of the gospel of Christ, nor of the cross of Christ, in which his gospel is all summed up, knowing it to be "the power of God unto salvation to all them that believe," and having found it so to ourselves.

III. It is a communicating ordinance: here are not only gospel truths represented to us, and confessed by us; but gospel benefits offered to us, and accepted by us; for it is not only a faithful saying, but well worthy of all acceptation, that Christ Jesus died to save sinners. This is the explication which the apostle gives of this ordinance: "The cup of blessing which we bless," that is, which we pray to God to bless, which we bless God with and for, and in which we hope and expect that God will bless us, it "is the communion (or the communication) of the blood of Christ; the bread which we break, is the communion (or communication) of the body of Christ," which was not only broken for us upon the cross, when it was made an offering for sin, but is broken to us, as the children's bread is broken to the children in the everlasting gospel, wherein it is made the food of souls.

By the body and blood of Christ, of which this ordinance is the communion, we are to understand all those precious benefits and privileges, which were purchased for us by the death of Christ, and are assured to us upon gospel terms, in the everlasting covenant.

When the sun is said to be with us, and we say we have the sun, as in the day, or as in the summer, it is not the body and bulk of the sun that we have, but his rays and beams are darted down upon us, and by them we receive the light, warmth, and influence of the sun, and thus the sun is communicated to us, according to the laws of creation: so in this ordinance we are partakers of Christ, not of his real body and blood, (it is senseless and absurd, unchristian and inhuman to imagine so,) but of his merits and righteousness for our justification, his Spirit and grace for our sanctification. We must not dream of ascending up into heaven, or of going down to the depth, to fetch Christ into this ordinance, that we may partake of him; no, the word is nigh thee, and Christ in the word.

Unworthy receivers, that is, those who resolve to continue in sin, because grace has abounded, partake of the guilt of Christ's body and blood, and have communion with those that crucified him; for, as much as in them lies, they crucify him afresh. What they do, speaks such ill thoughts of Christ, that we may conclude, that if they had been at Jerusalem when he was put to death, they would have joined with those that cried, "Crucify him, crucify him."

But humble and penitent believers partake of the blessed fruits of Christ's death; "his body and blood" are their food, their medicine, their cordial, their life, their all. All the riches of the gospel are virtually in them.

1. Christ and all his benefits are here communicated to us; here is not only bread and wine set before us, to be looked at, but given to us to be eaten and drunk; not only Christ made known to us, that we may contemplate the mysteries of redemption, but Christ made over to us, that we may participate of the benefits of redemption. God, in this ordinance, not only assures us of the truth of the promise, but, according to our present case and capacity, conveys to us, by his Spirit, the good things promised. Receive Christ Jesus the Lord, Christ and pardon, Christ and peace, Christ and grace, Christ and heaven; it is all your own, if you come up to the terms on which it is offered in the gospel.

Fountains of life are here broken up, wells of salvation are here opened, the stone rolled away from the well's mouth, and you are called upon to come and draw water with joy. The well is deep, but this ordinance is a bucket by which it is easy to draw: let us not forsake these living streams for stagnant water. These are wisdom's gates, where we are appointed to wait for wisdom's gifts; and we shall not wait in vain.

2. Christ and all his benefits are here to be received by us. If we do indeed answer the intention of the ordinance, in receiving the bread and wine, we accept the offer that is made us: "Lord, I take thee at thy word; be it unto thy servant according to it." We hereby interest ourselves in Christ's mediation between God and man, and take the benefit of it according to the tenor of the everlasting gospel. Christ, in this ordinance, is graciously condescending to show

us the print of the nails, and the mark of the spear, to show us his pierced hands, his pierced side, those tokens of his love and power as a Redeemer; we, by partaking of it, comply with his intentions, we consent to him, and close with him, saying, as Thomas did, " My Lord, and my God!" None but Christ, none but Christ.

We do here likewise set ourselves to participate of that spiritual strength and comfort, which, through grace, flows into the hearts of believers, from their interest in Christ crucified. The gospel of Christ here solemnly exhibited, is meat and drink to our souls: it is bread that strengthens man's heart, and is the staff of life; it is wine that makes glad the heart, and revives the spirits. Our spiritual life is supported and maintained, and the new man enabled for its work and conflicts, by the spiritual benefits of which we here communicate; as the natural life, and the natural body, are by our necessary food. From the fulness that is in Christ crucified, we here derive grace for grace, grace for gracious exercises, as the branches derive sap from the root, and as the lamps derive oil from the olive trees; and so, like healthful grown children, are nourished " up in the words of faith and of good doctrine," till we all come to the perfect man, to the measure of the stature of the fulness of Christ. Thus it is our communion with, and communicating of, Christ's body and blood.

IV. It is a covenanting ordinance.—This cup, our Saviour tells us, (that is, this ordinance,) is the New Testament; not only pertaining to the New Testament, but containing it; it has the whole New Testament in it, and has the sum and substance of it. It is, in general, an instrument by which a right passes, and is conveyed; and a title to some good thing given. The gospel revelation of God's grace and will, is both a testament and a covenant, and the Lord's Supper has a reference to it as both.

1. It is the New Testament.—The everlasting gospel is Christ's last will, by which he has given and bequeathed a great estate to his family on earth,

with certain precepts and injunctions, and under certain provisions and limitations. This will is become of force, by the death of the Testator, and is now unalterable; it is proved in the court of heaven, and administration given to the blessed Spirit, who is as the executor of the will; for of him the Testator said, "He shall receive of mine, and show it unto you." Christ, having purchased a great estate by the merit of his death, by his testament left it to all his poor relations, that had need enough of it, and for whom he bought it: so that all those who can prove themselves akin to Christ, by their being born from above, their partaking of a divine nature, and their doing the will of God, may claim the estate by virtue of the will, and shall be sure of a present maintenance, and a future inheritance out of it.

The Lord's Supper is the New Testament; it is not only a memorial of the Testator's death, but it is the seal of the Testament. A true copy of it attested by this seal and pleadable, is hereby given into the hands of every believer, that he may have strong consolation. The general record of the New Testament, which is common to all, is hereby made particular.

The charge given by the will is hereby applied and enforced to us. The Testator has charged us to remember him, has charged us to follow him whithersoever he goes; he has charged us to love one another, and the estate he has left us is so devised, as not to give any occasion to quarrel, but rather to be a bond of union. He has charged us to espouse his cause, serve his interest, and concern ourselves in his concerns in the world, to seek the welfare of the great body, and all the members of it. He has likewise charged us to expect and prepare for his second coming: his word of command is, "Watch." Now, in the Lord's Supper, we are reminded of this charge, and bound afresh faithfully to observe whatsoever Christ has commanded, as the Rechabites kept the command of their father.

The legacies left by the will, are hereby particularly consigned to us; paid in part, and the rest secured to be paid when we come to age, even at the time appointed by the Testator. What is left for us is not only sufficient to answer the full intention of the will, enough for all, enough for each; but is left in good hands, in the hands of the Spirit of truth, who will not deal unfaithfully with us; for, as Christ tells us, "we know him." Nay, Christ himself is risen from the dead, to be the overseer of his own will, and to see it duly executed: so that we are in no danger of losing our legacies, unless by our own fault. These are good securities, and upon which we may with abundant satisfaction rely; and yet our Lord Jesus, "more abundantly to show the heirs of promise the immutability of his counsel, has confirmed it by an oath, (by a sacrament, which is his oath to us, as well as ours to him,) that by all those immutable things, in which it is impossible for God to lie, we might have strong consolation," that have ventured our all in the New Testament.

2. It is the new covenant.—Though God is our sovereign Lord, and owner, and we are in his hand, as the clay in the hand of the potter; yet he condescends to deal with us about our reconciliation and happiness in the way of a covenant, that they which are saved may be the more comforted, and they which perish may be rendered the more inexcusable. The tenor of this covenant is, "Believe on the Lord Jesus Christ, and thou shalt be saved." Salvation is the great promise of the covenant, believing in Christ the great condition of the covenant; now, this cup is the covenant, that is, it is the seal of the covenant. There seems to be an allusion to that solemnity, which we read of where Moses read the book of the covenant in the audience of the people, and the people declared their consent to it, saying, "All that the Lord hath said we will do, and will be obedient. And then Moses took the blood, and sprinkled it upon the people, (part of it having before been sprinkled upon the altar,) and said, Behold the blood of the covenant, which the Lord hath made with you

concerning all these words." Thus the covenant being made by sacrifice, and the blood of the sacrifice being sprinkled both upon the altar of God and upon the representatives of the people, both parties did, as it were, interchangeably put their hands and seals to the articles of agreement. So the blood of Christ having satisfied for the breach of the covenant of innocency, and purchased a new treaty, and being the sacrifice by which the covenant is made, is fitly called the blood of the covenant. Having sprinkled this blood upon the altar in his intercession, when by his own blood he entered in once into the holy place, he does in this sacrament sprinkle it upon the people; as the apostle explains this mystery, Heb. ix. A bargain is a bargain, though it be not sealed, but the sealing is the ratification and perfection of it. The internal seal of the covenant, as administerd to true believers, is the spirit of promise " whereby we are sealed to the day of redemption." But the external seals of the covenant, as administered in the visible church, are the sacraments, particularly this of the Lord's Supper. Sealing ordinances are appointed to make our covenanting with God the more solemn, and consequently the more affecting, and the impressions of it the more abiding. The covenant of grace is a " covenant never to be forgotten." This ordinance, therefore, was instituted to assure us, that God will never forget it, and to assist us, that we may never forget it. It is the seal of the new covenant; that is,

1. God does in, and by this ordinance, seal to us, to be to us a God. This article of the covenant is inclusive of all the rest; in giving himself to us to be ours, he gives us all things, for he is God all sufficient. This is the grant, the royal grant which the eternal God here seals, and delivers to true believers, as his act and deed. He gives himself to them, and empowers them to call him theirs. What God is in himself, he will be to them for their good. His wisdom theirs, to counsel and direct them; his power theirs, to protect and support them; his justice theirs,

to justify them; his holiness theirs, to sanctify them; his goodness theirs, to love and supply them; his truth is the inviolable security of the promise, and his eternity the perpetuity of their happiness. He will be to them a Father, and they shall be his sons and daughters, dignified by the privileges of adoption, and distinguished by the spirit of adoption. Their Maker is their husband, and he hath said, that "he is married to them, and rejoiceth in them as the bridegroom in his bride." The Lord is their shepherd, and the sheep of his pasture shall not want. He is the portion of their inheritance in the other world, as well as of their cup in this; he has prepared for them a city, and thereby " is not ashamed to be called their God."

2. We do in and by this ordinance, seal to him to be to him a people. We accept the relation by our voluntary choice and consent, and bind our souls with a bond, that we will approve ourselves to him in the relation. We hereby resign, surrender, and give up our whole selves, body, soul, and spirit, to God, the Father, Son, and Holy Ghost, covenanting and promising, that we will, by his strength, serve him faithfully, and walk closely with him in all manner of gospel obedience all our days. Claiming the blessings of the covenant, we put ourselves under the bonds of the covenant. O Lord, truly I am thy servant, I am thy servant: wholly, and only, and for ever thine. And this is the meaning of this service.

CHAPTER III.

AN INVITATION TO THIS ORDINANCE.

All things are ready, (opened in many particulars,) therefore come. I. Those that are unmeet for this ordinance, must qualify themselves and come; a serious address to such in three things. II. Those that are in some measure meet for it, must enter themselves. Young people reasoned with in four questions; those who are cold and indifferent, put upon considering two things; those that are timorous counselled and encouraged in two things. III. Those that have given up themselves to God in this ordinance must be constant; this largely urged.

PLENTIFUL and suitable provision is made in this ordinance out of the treasures of the Redeemer's grace; and ministers, as servants, are sent to bid to the feast, to invite those that the master of the feast has designed for his guests, and to hasten those that are invited to this banquet of wine. Wisdom hath sent forth her maidens on this errand, and they have words put in their mouths—" Come, for all things are now ready." This is our message.

I. We are to tell you that all things are ready, now ready; he that hath an ear, let him hear this: All things are now ready in the gospel-feast, that are proper for, or will contribute to, the full satisfaction of an immortal soul, that knows its own nature and interest, and desires to be truly and eternally happy in the love and favour of its Creator.

All things are ready; all things requisite to a noble feast. Let us a little improve the metaphor.

1. There is a house ready for the entertainment of the guests, the gospel church, wisdom's house, which she hath built upon seven pillars. God hath set up his tabernacle among men, and the place of his tent is enlarged, and made capacious enough; so that though the table has been replenished with guests, yet still there is room.

2. There is a table ready spread in the word and ordinances, like the table in the temple on which the

show-bread was placed, a loaf for every tribe. The Scripture is written, the canon of it completed, and in it a full declaration made of God's good-will towards men.

3. There is a laver ready for us to wash in. As at the marriage-feast at Cana, there were six water-pots set for purification. Lest sense of pollutions contracted should deter us from the participation of these comforts, behold there is "a fountain opened," come and wash in it, that, being purged from an evil conscience by the blood of Jesus, you may, with humble confidence, compass God's altar.

4. There are servants ready to attend you, and those are the ministers, whose work it is to direct you to the table, and "to give every one their portion of meat in due season, rightly dividing the word of truth." They are not masters of the feast, but only stewards, and "your servants for Christ's sake."

5. There is much company already come; many have accepted the invitation, and have found a hearty welcome: why then should your place be empty? Let the communion of saints invite you into communion with Christ.

6. A blessing is ready to be craved. He is ready to bless the sacrifice. The great High Priest of our profession, ever living to intercede for us, and attending continually to this very thing, is ready to command a blessing upon our spiritual food.

7. The Master of the feast is ready to bid you welcome; as ready as the father of the prodigal was to receive his repenting, returning son, whom he saw when "he was yet a great way off." God's ear is open to hear, and his hand open to give.

8. The provision is ready for your entertainment.

1. All things are ready: (1.) For our justification.—divine justice is satisfied, an everlasting righteousness is brought in, an act of indemnity has passed the royal assent, and a throne of grace is erected, at which all that can make it appear that they are interested in the general act, may sue out their particular charter of pardon. There is a plea ready, an advocate

ready: "Behold, he is near that justifieth us." (2.) For our sanctification—there is a fulness of grace in Christ, from which we may all receive; the word of grace is ready as the means, the Spirit of grace is ready as the author; every thing ready for the mortification of sin, the confirming of faith, and our furtherance in holiness. (3.) For our consolation—a well of living water is ready, if we can but see it; peace is left us for a legacy, which we may claim if we will; promises are given us for our support, of which, if we have not the benefit, it is our own fault. There is something in the new covenant to obviate every grief, every challenge, every fear, if we will use it. (4.) For our salvation ready to be revealed—angels upon the wing are ready to convey us; Jesus, standing at the Father's right hand, is ready to receive us; the many mansions are ready prepared for us: "All things are ready."

2. All things are now ready, just now, for "Behold, now is the accepted time."

1. All things are now readier than they were under the law. Grace then lay more hid than it does now, when life and immortality are brought to so clear a light by the gospel. Christ in a sacrament is much readier than Christ in a sacrifice.

2. All things are now readier than they will be shortly, if we trifle away the present season. Now the door of mercy stands open, and we are invited to come and enter; but it will shortly be shut. Now the golden sceptre is held out, and we are called to come and touch the top of it; but it will be otherwise when the days of our probation are numbered and finished, and he that now saith, "Come for a blessing," will say, "Depart with a curse."

II. We must call you to come: this is now the call, Come, come; "the Spirit saith, Come, and the bride saith, Come." Come to Christ in the first place, and then come to this ordinance. All things are ready, be not you unready.

This exhortation must be directed to three sorts of persons: 1. Those who are utterly unmeet for this ordinance, must be exhorted to qualify themselves, and then come. 2. Those who, through grace, are in some measure meet for this ordinance, must be exhorted speedily to enter themselves. 3. Those who have entered themselves, must be exhorted to be constant in their attendance upon it.

1. I must apply myself to those that, by their ignorance, profaneness, irreligion, or reigning worldliness, put a bar in their own way, and may not be admitted to this ordinance. If these lines should fall under the eye of any such, let them know I have a message to them from God, and I must deliver it, whether they will hear, or whether they will forbear.

Dost thou live a carnal wicked life, in the service of sin and Satan, without fear, and without God in the world? Light is come into the world, and dost thou love darkness rather, not knowing nor desiring to know the way of the Lord, and the judgment of thy God? Art thou a drunkard, a swearer, a Sabbath-breaker? Art thou an adulterer, fornicator, or unclean person? Art thou a liar, a deceiver, a railer, or a contentious person? Art thou a mere drudge to the world, or a slave to any base lust? Doth thy own conscience tell thee thou art the man, or would it not tell thee so, if thou wouldst suffer it to deal faithfully with thee?

(1.) Know then, that thou hast no part nor lot in this matter; whilst thou continuest thus, thou art not an invited guest to this feast; the servants dare not bid thee welcome, for they know the Master will not, but will ask thee, "Friend, how camest thou in hither? What hast thou to do to take God's covenant and the seal of it into thy mouth, seeing thou hatest instruction?" Read that scripture, and hear God speaking to thee in it: "It is not meet to take the children's bread, and cast it to dogs." Thou art forbidden to touch these sacred things with thine unhallowed hands: for "what communion hath Christ with Belial?" If thou thrust thyself upon this ordinance, whilst thou continuest under such a character, instead of doing honour to the Lord Jesus, thou puttest a daring affront upon him, as if he were altogether such a one as thyself; instead of deriving any true comfort to thy own soul, thou dost but aggravate thy guilt and condemnation; thy heart will be more hardened, thy conscience more seared, Satan's strong holds more fortified, and thou eatest and drinkest judgment to thyself, not discerning the Lord's body; nor puttest a difference between this bread and other bread; but trampling under foot the blood of the covenant, as a profane and common thing.

(2.) Know also, that thy condition is very miserable whilst thou debarrest thyself from this ordinance, and art, as polluted, put from this priesthood. How light soever thou mayest make of it, this is not a small portion of thy miseries, that thou shuttest thyself out of covenant and communion with the God that made thee; and, in effect, disclaimest any interest in the Christ that bought thee, as if thou hadst taken the devils' words out of their mouths, " What have we to do with thee, Jesus, thou Son of God?" And if thou persist in it, so shall thy doom be; thou thyself hast decided it. If now it be as nothing to thee, to be separated from the sheep of Christ, and excluded from their green pastures, yet it will be something shortly, when thou shalt accordingly have thy place among the goats, and thy lot with them for ever. Thou thinkest it no loss now to want the cup of blessing, because thou preferrest the cup of drunkenness before it; but what dost thou think of the cup of trembling, that will ere long be put into thy hand if thou repent not? Thou hast no desire to the wine of the love of God, but rather choosest the puddle water of sensual pleasures; but canst thou "drink of the wine of the wrath of God," which shall be poured out without mixture in the presence of the Lamb? Thou thinkest thyself easy and happy, that thou art not under the bonds and checks of this ordinance; but dost thou not see thyself extremely miserable, whilst thou hast no right to the blessings and comforts of this ordinance? If there were not another life after this, thou mightest have some colour for blessing thyself thus in thine own wicked way; (and yet, if so, I should see no cause to envy thee;) but, wretched soul, "what wilt thou do in the day of visitation?" Thou that joinest thyself with the sinners in Zion, and choosest them for thy people, "Canst thou dwell with devouring fire? Canst thou inhabit everlasting burnings?" May God by his grace open thine eyes, and give thee to see thy misery and danger before it be too late!

(3.) Yet know, that though thy condition is very sad, it is not desperate. Thou hast space yet given thee to repent, and grace offered thee. O refuse not that grace, slip not that opportunity! Leave thy sins, and turn unto God in Christ; cast away from thee all thy transgressions, make thee a new heart, begin a new life, forsake the foolish, and live to some purpose, and go in the way of understanding: and then in wisdom's name, I am to tell thee, that notwithstanding all thy former follies, thou art welcome to her house, welcome to her table, freely welcome to "eat of her bread, and to drink of the wine which she hath mingled." "Now at least, now at last, in this thy day, know the things that belong to thy peace;" be wise for thyself, be wise for thine own soul, and cheat not thyself into thine own ruin.

Poor sinner! I pity thee, I would gladly help thee; the Lord pity thee and help thee! He will, if thou wilt pity thyself, and help thyself. Wilt thou be persuaded by one that wishes thee well, to exchange the service of sin, which is perfect slavery, for the service of God, which is perfect liberty? to exchange the base and sordid pleasures of a sensual life, which level thee with the beasts, for the pure and refined pleasures of a spiritual and divine life, which will raise thee to a communion with the holy angels? I am confident thou wilt quickly find it a blessed change. "Awake, shake thyself from the dust, loose thyself from the bands of thy neck." Give up thyself in sincerity to Jesus Christ, and then come and feast with him: thou shalt then have in this ordinance the pledges of his favour, assurances of thy reconciliation to him, and acceptance with him, and all shall be well, for it shall end everlastingly well.

2. I must next apply myself to those, who, having a competent knowledge in the things of God, and making a justifiable profession of Christ's holy religion, cannot be denied admission to this ordinance, and yet deny themselves the benefit and comfort of it. Such are hereby exhorted, without further delay, solemnly to give up their names to the Lord Jesus, in and by this sacrament. Hear Hezekiah's summons to the passover: "Yield yourselves unto the Lord, give the hand unto the Lord;"—so the Hebrew phrase is: join yourselves to him in the bond of the covenant, and then exchange the ratifications; enter into the sanctuary. First give your own selves unto the Lord, and then confirm the surrender by the solemnity of this ordinance.

Let me direct this exhortation to young people that were in their infancy baptized into the Christian faith, and have been well educated in the knowledge of God and of his holy ways, and are now grown up to years of discretion, are capable of understanding what they do, of discerning between their right hand and their left in spiritual things, and of choosing and refusing for themselves accordingly; and that have had some good impressions made upon their souls by divine things, and some good inclinations towards God, and Christ, and heaven: such are invited to the table of the Lord, and called upon to come, for all things are now ready, and it is not good to delay.

You that are young, will you now be prevailed with to be serious, and resolved for God? You now begin to act with reason, and to put away childish things; you are come to be capable of considering, and you are thinking how you must live in this world. O that I could prevail with you to think first how you may live for another world! I am not persuading you to come rashly and carelessly to the Lord's table, as when you were little children you went to church for fashion's sake, and because your parents took you with them; but I am persuading you now, in the days of your youth, from a deep conviction of your duty and interest, and a serious concern about your souls and eternity, intelligently, deliberately, and with a fixed resolution, to join yourselves unto the Lord in an everlasting covenant, and then to come and seal that covenant at his table. You are now come to the turning time of life, to those years when ordinary people fix for their whole lives; I beg of you for Christ's sake, and for your own precious souls' sake, that now you will turn to God, and fix for him, and set your faces heavenwards.

Come, and let us reason together a little, and I beseech you to reason with yourselves:

1. Are you not by baptism given up unto the Lord? Are not the vows of God already upon you? Is not your baptism your honour? Is it not your comfort? It is so; but you are unworthy of that honour, unworthy of that comfort, if, when you arrive at a capacity for it, you decline doing that for yourselves, which was done for you when you were baptized. How can you expect that your parents' dedication of you to God then, should avail you any thing, if you do not now make it your own act and deed? Might not your backwardness to confirm the covenant, by this solemn taking of it upon yourselves, be construed as an implicit renunciation of it, and be adjudged a forfeiture of the benefit of it? I believe you would not for a world disclaim your baptism, nor disown the obligation of it: you will not, I am confident you will not, throw off your Christianity, nor join with those that say, We have no part in David, or inheritance in the Son of David. Come then and ratify your baptism; either let these articles be cancelled, or now, that you are of age, come and seal them yourselves; either be Christians complete, Christians by your own consent, or not Christians at all. The matter is plain; the bonds of both the sacraments are the same: you are under the bonds of the one, which I know you dare not renounce; therefore,

come under the bonds of the other. Consider, take advice, and speak your minds.

2. How can you dispose of yourselves better now in the days of your youth, than to give up yourselves to the Lord? These are your choosing days; you are now choosing other settlements, in callings, relations, and places of abode; why should you not now close this settlement in the service of God, which will make all your other settlements comfortable? Choose you, therefore, this day whom you will serve —God, or the world; Christ, or the flesh; and be persuaded to bring the matter to a good issue; determine the debate in that happy resolution to which the people of Israel came, when they said, " Nay, but we will serve the Lord." Why should not he, who is the first and the best, have the first and best of your days? Which I am sure you cannot bestow better, and which it is both your duty and interest to bestow thus.

3. What will you get by delaying it? You intend some time or other solemnly to give up yourselves unto the Lord in this ordinance, and you hope then to receive the benefit and comfort of it: but the tempter tells you, 'Tis all good in time; and you dismiss your convictions, as Felix did Paul, with a promise, that "at a more convenient season you will send for them." You are ready to say, as the people did, " The time is not come, the time that the Lord's house should be built:" you think you must build your own first; and what comes of those delays? Satan, ere you are aware, gets advantage by them, and cheats you of all your time, by cheating you of the present time; your hearts are in danger of being hardened, the Spirit of grace may hereby be provoked to withdraw, and strive no more; and what will become of you, if death surprise you before your great work be done?

4. What better provision can you make for a comfortable life in this world, than by doing this great work betimes? You are setting out in a world of temptations more than you think of; and how can

you better arm yourselves against them, than by coming up to that fixed resolution which will silence the tempter, "Get thee behind me, Satan?" When Naomi saw that Ruth was "steadfastly resolved, she left off speaking to her." The counsel of the ungodly will not be so apt to court you to the way of sinners, and the seat of the scornful, when you have avowed yourselves set out in the way of God, and seated already at the table of the Lord. You are launching forth into a stormy sea, and this will furnish you with ballast; your way lies through a vale of tears, and therefore you have need to be well stocked with comforts: and where can you stock yourselves better than in this ordinance, which seals all the promises of the new covenant, and conveys all the happiness included in them?

And now, shall I gain this point with young people? Will they be persuaded betimes to resolve for God and heaven? "Remember thy Creator, remember thy Redeemer in the days of thy youth;" and then it is to be hoped thou wilt not forget them, nor will they forget thee when thou art old.

Let me address this exhortation to those whose inclinations are good, and their conversation blameless, but their desires are weak, and their affections cool and indifferent, and therefore they keep off from this ordinance. This is the character of very many who are honest, but they want zeal and resolution enough to bring them under this engagement. They can give no tolerable reason why they do not come to the sacrament: it may be they have bought a piece of ground, or a yoke of oxen; their hands are full of the world, and they are too busy, they are unsettled, or not settled to their minds, and this makes them uneasy, and they hope that therefore they may be excused; but the true reason is, they are slothful and dilatory, and the things that remain are ready to die; they cannot find in their hearts to take pains, the pains they know they must take in a work of this nature; they are not willing to be bound to that strict care and watchfulness to which this sacrament will oblige them; they will be as they are, and make no advances; they "have hid their hand in their bosom, and it grieves them to bring it to their mouth again;" that is, they will not be at the pains to feed themselves.

What shall we say to rouse these sluggards; to persuade them to press forward in their profession, forgetting the things that are behind, and not resting in them? Hear, ye virgins, that slumber and sleep, and let your lamps lie by neglected—hear the cry, " Behold the bridegroom cometh, (cometh in this ordinance to espouse you to himself; stir up yourselves, and) go ye forth to meet him." Hear, ye servants, ye slothful servants, your Master's voice, " How long wilt thou sleep, O sluggard?" Is it not high time to awake out of sleep, and apply thyself more closely and vigorously to the business of a Christian? Is it not far in the day with thee, perhaps the sixth hour, or further on; and yet hast thou no appetite to this spiritual feast to which thou art invited? Thou hast lost a great deal of time already, shouldst not thou now think of redeeming time for thy soul and eternity? And how can that be better done, than by improving such advantageous opportunities as sacraments are? Hear that call to careless and trifling professors, as if thou thyself wert called by name in it: " Awake, thou that sleepest, and arise from the dead, and Christ shall give thee light."

1. Consider what an affront you put upon the Lord Jesus, while you live in the neglect of this ordinance; you contemn his authority, who hath given this command to all his disciples, (and among them you reckon yourselves,) " Do this in remembrance of me." And is it nothing to live in the omission of a known duty, and in disobedience to an express precept? Is the law of Christ nothing with you? If you know to do good, and do it not, is it not sin? Is not this as much an ordinance of Christ, as the word and prayer? You would not live without them; nor would you be yourselves, or suffer your children to be, without baptism; why then is this neglected? You

arraign Christ's wisdom: he instituted this ordinance for your spiritual good, your strength, and nourishment; and you think you need it not, you can do as well without it: this appointment, you think, might have been spared; that is, you think yourselves wiser than Christ. You likewise hereby put a great slight upon the grace and love of Christ, which has made such rich provision for you, and given you so kind an invitation to it.

This is excellently well urged in the public form of invitation to the holy communion, which warns those that are scandalous to keep off, in these words: "If any of you be a blasphemer of God, a hinderer or slanderer of his word, an adulterer, or be in malice or envy, or in any other grievous crime; repent you of your sins, or else come not to that holy table; lest, after the taking of that holy sacrament, the devil enter into you, as he entered into Judas, and fill you full of all iniquities, and bring you to destruction of both body and soul."

But the other exhortation stirs up those that are negligent, in these words: "Ye know how grievous and unkind a thing it is, when a man hath prepared a rich feast, decked his table with all kind of provision, so that there lacketh nothing but the guests to sit down, and yet they who are called (without any cause) most unthankfully refuse to come. Which of you in such a case would not be moved? Who would not think it a great injury and wrong done unto him? Wherefore, most dearly beloved in Christ, take ye good heed, lest ye, withdrawing yourselves from this holy supper, provoke God's indignation against you. It is an easy matter for a man to say, I will not communicate, because I am otherwise hindered with worldly business; but such excuses are not so easily accepted and allowed before God. If any man say, I am a grievous sinner, and therefore am afraid to come; wherefore then do you not repent and amend? When God calls you, are ye not ashamed to say, ye will not come? When ye should return to God, will you excuse yourselves, and say, you are not ready? Consider earnestly with yourselves, how little such feigned excuses will avail before God. They that refused the feast in the gospel, because they had bought a farm, or would try their yokes of oxen, or because they were married, were not so excused, but counted unworthy of the heavenly feast."

2. Consider what an injury you hereby do to your own souls. You know not what you lose while you live in the neglect of this ordinance. If you be deprived of opportunities for it, that is an affliction, but not a sin; and, in such a case, while you lament the want of it, and keep up desires after it, and improve the other helps you have, you may expect that God will make up the want some other way; though we are tied to ordinances, God is not: but if you have opportunities for it, and yet neglect it, and when it is to be administered, turn your back upon it, you serve your souls as you would not serve your bodies; for you deny them their necessary food, and the soul that is starved is as certainly murdered as the body that is stabbed, and his blood shall be required at thy hands. "No man ever yet hated his own flesh, but nourisheth and cherisheth it;" yet thou deniest thine own soul that which would nourish and cherish it, and thereby showest how little thou lovest it. If thou didst duly attend on this ordinance, and improve it aright, thou wouldst find it of unspeakable use to thee for the strengthening of thy faith, the exciting of holy affections in thee, and thy furtherance in every good word and work. So that to thy neglect of it, thou hast reason to impute all thy weakness, and all the strength and prevalency of thy temptations; all the unsteadiness of thy resolutions, and all the unevenness of thy conversation. How can we expect the desired end, while we persist in the neglect of the appointed means?

Think not to say within yourselves, We are not clean, surely we are not clean, therefore we come not to the feast. If you are not, why are you not? Is there not a fountain opened? Have you not been many a time called to wash you, and make you clean? You are not ready, and therefore you excuse yourselves from coming: but is not your unreadiness your sin, and will one sin justify you in another? Can a man's offence be his defence? You think you are not serious enough, nor devout enough, nor regular enough, in your conversations, to come to the sacrament; and perhaps you are not: but why are you not? What hinders you? Is any more required to fit you for the sacrament, than is necessary to fit you for heaven? And dare you live a day in that condition, in which, if you die, you will be rejected and excluded as unmeet for heaven? Be persuaded, therefore, to put on the wedding-garment, and then come to the wedding-feast. Instead of making your unreadiness an argument against coming to this ordinance, make the necessity of your coming to this ordinance an argument against your unreadiness. Say not, I am too light, airy, too much addicted to sports and pleasures; I am linked too close in vain and carnal company, or plunged too deep in worldly care and business, and therefore I must be excused from attending this ordinance; for this is to make ill worse: but rather say, It is necessary I come to the Lord's Supper, and come in a right manner; my soul withers and languishes, dies and perishes, if I do not; and therefore I must break off this vain and sensual course of life, which unfits me for and indisposes me to that ordinance; I must disentangle myself from that society, and disengage myself from that encumbrance, whatever it is, which cools pious affections, and quenches the coal. Shake off that, whatever it is, which comes between you and the comfort and benefit of this ordinance; trifle no longer in a matter of such vast moment, but speedily come to that resolution: "Depart from me, ye evil-doers, and evil doings; for I will keep the commandment of my God."

Let me address this exhortation to those whose desires are strong towards the Lord, and towards the remembrance of his name in this ordinance; but they are timorous, and are kept from it by prevailing fears. This is the case of many, who, we hope, "fear the Lord, and obey the voice of his servant, but they walk in darkness, and have no light;" who follow Christ, but they follow him trembling. Ask them why they do not come to this sacrament, and they will tell you they dare not come; they are unworthy, they have no faith, no comfort in God, no hope of heaven; and therefore, if they should come, they should "eat and drink judgment to themselves." They find not in themselves that fixedness of thought, the flame of pious and devout affections, which they think should be; and, because they cannot come as they should, they think it better to stay away. What is said for the conviction and terror of hypocrites and presumptuous sinners, notwithstanding our care to distinguish between the precious and the vile, they misapply to themselves: and so the heart of the righteous is made sad, which should not be made sad. We are commanded to "strengthen the weak hands, and confirm the feeble knees; to say to them that are of a fearful heart, Be strong; fear not." But wherewith shall we comfort such, whose souls many times refuse to be comforted? If we tell them of the infinite mercy and goodness of God, the merit and righteousness of Christ, the precious promises of the covenant, their jealous hearts reply, All this is nothing to them; the Lord, they think, has forgotten them, their God has forsaken them, and utterly separated them from his people: "As vinegar upon nitre, so is he that singeth songs to a heavy heart."

But O ye of little faith, who thus doubt, would you not be made whole? Would you not be strengthened? Is it not a desirable thing to attain to such a peace and serenity of mind, as that you may come with an humble, holy boldness to this precious ordinance?

For your help, then, take these two cautions:—

1. Judge not amiss concerning yourselves. As it is a damning mistake, common among the children of men, to think their spiritual state and condition

to be good, when it is very bad; for "there is that maketh himself rich, and yet hath nothing,"—so it is a disquieting mistake, common among the children of God, to think their spiritual state and condition to be bad, when it is very good; for "there is that maketh himself poor, and yet hath great riches." But it is a mistake which, I hope, by the grace of God, may be rectified: and though a full assurance is rarely attained to, and we ought always to keep up a godly jealousy over ourselves, and a holy fear, lest we seem to come short; yet such good hope through grace, as will enable us to rejoice in God, and go on cheerfully in our work and duty, is what we should aim at, and labour after, and of which we ought not to deny ourselves the comfort, when God by his grace has given us cause for it: wherever there is such a serious concern about the soul and another world, as produces a holy fear, even that gives ground for a lively hope.

You think you have no grace, because you are not yet perfect; but why should you look for that on earth, which is to be had in heaven only? A child will at length be a man, though as yet he "think as a child, and speak as a child." Blessed Paul himself had not yet attained, nor was already perfect. Gold in the ore is truly valuable, though it be not yet refined from its dross. "Despise not the day of small things," for God does not. Deny not that power and grace which has brought you out of the land of Egypt, though you be not yet come to Canaan.

You think you have no grace, because you have not that sensible joy and comfort which you would have; but those are spiritually enlightened who see their own deformity, as well as those that see Christ's beauty. "The child that cries, is as sure alive as the child that laughs." Complaints of spiritual burdens are the language of the new nature, as well as praises for spiritual blessings.

Drooping soul, thou art under grace, and not under the law; and therefore judge of thyself by the measures of grace, and not by those of the law. Thou hast to do with one that is willing to make the best of thee, and will accept the willingness of the spirit, and pardon the weakness of our flesh. Take thy work before thee, therefore, and let not the penitent, humble sense of thy own follies and corruptions eclipse the evidence of God's graces in thee, nor let the diffidence of thyself shake thy confidence in Christ. Thank God for what he has done for thee: let him have the praise of it, and then thou shalt have the joy of it. And this is certain, either thou hast an interest in Christ, or thou mayest have. If thou doubt, therefore, whether Christ be thine, put the matter out of doubt, by a present consent to him: I take Christ to be mine, wholly, only, and for ever mine: Christ upon his own terms, Christ upon any terms.

2. Judge not amiss concerning this ordinance. It was instituted for your comfort, let it not be a terror to you; it was instituted for your satisfaction, let it not be your amazement. Most of the messages from heaven which we meet with in Scripture, delivered by angels, began with "Fear not;" and particularly that to the women who attended Christ's sepulchre: "Fear not ye; for I know that ye seek Jesus." And do not you seek him? Be not afraid then. Chide yourselves out of these disquieting fears, which steal away your spear and your cruse of water, rob you both of your strength and of your comfort.

You say you are unworthy to come; so were all that ever came, not worthy to be called children, nor to eat of the children's bread: in yourselves there is no worthiness; but is there none in Christ? Is not he worthy, and is not he yours? Have you not chosen him? Appear therefore before God in him. Let faith in his mediation silence all your fears; and dismiss their clamours with that—"But thou shalt answer, Lord, for me."

You say you dare not come, lest you should eat and drink judgment to yourselves; but ordinarily those that most fear that, are least in danger of it.

That dreadful word was not intended to drive men from the sacrament, but to drive them from their sins. Can you not say, through grace you hate sin, you strive against it, you earnestly desire to be delivered from it? Then certainly your league with it is broken; though the Canaanites be in the land, you do not make marriages with them. Come then and seal the covenant with God, and you shall be so far from eating and drinking judgment to yourselves, that you shall eat and drink life and comfort to yourselves.

You dare not come to this sacrament; yet you dare pray, you dare hear the word. I know you dare not neglect either the one or the other; and what is the sacrament but the doing the same thing by a visible sign, which is and ought to be done in effect by the word and prayer? Nor ought we to put such an amazing distance between this and other ordinances. If we pray in hypocrisy, our prayers are an abomination; if we hear the word and reject it, it is a savour of death unto death: shall we therefore not pray, not hear? God forbid. Commanded duty must be done: appointed means must be used: and that which unfits and hinders us must be removed, and we must in sincerity give up ourselves to serve God; do as well as we can, and be sorry we can do no better: and then, having a High Priest, who is touched with the feeling of our infirmities, we may come boldly to the throne of grace, and to this table of grace.

You say your faith is weak, pious affections are cool and low, your resolutions unsteady, and therefore you keep away from this ordinance. That is as if a man should say, he is sick, and therefore he will take no physic; he is empty, and therefore will take no food; he is faint, and therefore he will take no cordials. This ordinance was appointed chiefly for the relief of such as you are; for the strengthening of faith, the inflaming of holy love, and the confirming of good resolutions: in God's name, therefore, use it for these purposes; pine not away in thy weakness, while God has ordained thee strength; perish not for hunger, while there is bread enough in thy father's house, and to spare; die not for thirst, while there is a well of water by thee.

III. This chapter must conclude with an exhortation to those who have given up their name to the Lord in this ordinance, and have sometimes sealed their covenant with God in it, but they come very seldom to it, and allow themselves in the neglect and omission of it. Frequent opportunities they have for it, stated meals provided for them, the table spread and furnished. Others come, and they are invited; but time after time they let it slip, and turn their backs upon it, framing to themselves some sorry excuse or other to shift it off.

I desire such to consider seriously,

1. How powerful the engagements are which we lie under, to be frequent and constant in our attendance on the Lord in this ordinance. It is plainly intimated in the institution, that the solemnity is oft to be repeated; for it is said, "Do this, as oft as ye drink it, in remembrance of me." Baptism is to be administered but once, because it is the door of admission, and we are but once to enter in by that door: but the Lord's Supper is the table in Christ's family, at which we are to eat bread continually. The law of Moses prescribed how oft the passover must be celebrated, under very severe penalties; but the gospel being a dispensation of a greater love and liberty, only appoints us to observe its passover oft, and then leaves it to our own ingenuity and pious affections to fix the time, and determine how oft. If a deliverance out of Egypt merited an annual commemoration, surely our redemption by Christ merits a more frequent one, especially since we need not go up to Jerusalem to do it. If this tree of life, which bears more than twelve manner of fruits, yieldeth her fruit to us every month, I know not why we should neglect it any month. Where there is the truth of grace, this ordinance ought to be improved, which, by virtue of divine appointment, has a moral influence upon our growth in grace. The great Master

of the family would have none of his family missing at meal-time.

While we are often sinning, we have need to be often receiving the seal of our pardon; because, though the sacrifice be perfect, and "able to perfect for ever them which are sanctified," so that that needs never to be repeated; yet the application of it being imperfect, has need to be often made afresh. The worshippers, though once purged, having still consciences of sin in this defective state, must oft have recourse to the fountain opened for the purging of their consciences, from the pollutions contracted daily by dead works, to serve the living God. Even he that is washed thus, needs to wash his feet, or he cannot be easy.

While we are often in temptation, we have need to be often renewing our covenants with God, and fetching strength from heaven for our spiritual conflicts. Frequent fresh recruits and fresh supplies, are necessary for those that are so closely besieged, and are so vigorously attacked, by a potent adversary. He improves all advantages against us, therefore it is our wisdom not to neglect any advantage against him, and particularly this ordinance.

While we are often labouring under great coldness and deadness of affection towards divine things, we need oft to use those means which are proper to kindle that holy fire, and keep it burning. We find, by sad experience, that our coal from the altar is soon quenched, our thoughts grow flat and low, and unconcerned about the other world, by being so much conversant with this; we have therefore need to be often celebrating the memorial of Christ's death and sufferings, than which nothing can be more affecting to a Christian, nor more proper to raise and refine the thoughts; it is a subject that more than once has made the disciples' hearts to burn within them.

Much of our communion with God is kept up by the renewing of our covenant with him, and the frequent interchanging of solemn assurances. It is not superfluous, but highly serviceable, both to our holiness and our comfort, oft to present ourselves to God as living sacrifices, alive from the dead. It is a token of Christ's favour to us, and must not be slighted, that he not only admits, but invites us oft to repeat this solemnity, and is ready again to seal to us, if we be but ready to seal to him. Jonathan, therefore "caused David to swear again, because he loved him." And an honest mind will not startle at assurances.

2. Consider how poor the excuses are with which men commonly justify themselves in this neglect. They let slip many an opportunity of attending upon the Lord in this ordinance, and why do they?

Perhaps they are so full of worldly business, that they have neither time nor heart for that close application to the work of a sacrament which they know is requisite: the shop must be attended, accounts must be kept, debts owing them must be got in, and debts they owe must be paid; it may be, some affair of more than ordinary difficulty and importance is upon their hands, of which they are in care about the issue, and till that be over, they think it not amiss to withdraw from the Lord's Supper. And is this thy excuse? Weigh it in the balances of the sanctuary then, and consider, is any business more necessary than the doing of thy duty to God, and the working out of thine own salvation? Thou art careful and troubled about many things; but is not this the one thing needful, to which every thing else should be obliged to give way? Dost thou not think thy worldly business would prosper and succeed the better for thy care about the main matter? If it were left whilst thou comest hither to worship, mightest thou not return to it with greater hope to speed in it? And dost thou not spare time from thy business for things of much less moment than this? Thou wilt find time, as busy as thou art, to eat and drink, and sleep, and converse with thy friends; and is not the nourishment of thy soul, its repose in God, and communion with him, much more necessary? I dare say, thou wilt own it is.

If indeed thou canst not allow so much time for solemn secret worship in preparation for this ordinance, and reflection upon it, as others do, and as thou thyself sometime hast done, and wouldst do, yet let not that keep thee from the ordinance; thy heart may be in heaven, when thy hands are about the world; and a serious Christian may, through God's assistance, do a great deal of work in a little time. If the hours that should be thus employed, be trifled away in that which is idle and impertinent, it is our sin; but if they be forced out of our hands by necessary and unavoidable avocations, it is but our affliction, and ought not to hinder us from the ordinance. The less time we have for preparation, the more close and intent we should be in the ordinance itself, and so make up the loss. A welcome guest never comes unseasonably to one that always keeps a good house.

But if, indeed, thy heart is so set upon the world, so filled with the cares of it, and so eager in the pursuits of it, that thou hast no mind to the comforts of this ordinance, no spirit nor life for the business of it,—surely thou hast left thy first love, and thou hast most need of all to come to this ordinance for the recovery of the ground thou hast lost. Dost thou think that the inordinacy of thine affections to the world, will be a passable excuse for the coldness of thine affections to the Lord Jesus? Make haste, and get this matter mended, and conclude, that thy worldly business then becomes a snare to thee, and thy concern about it is excessive and inordinate, and an ill symptom, when it prevails to keep thee back from this ordinance.

Perhaps some unhappy quarrels, with some relations or with neighbours, some vexatious law-suit they are engaged in, or some hot words that have passed, are pleaded as an excuse for withdrawing from the communion. They are not in charity with others, or others are not in charity with them; and they have been told, and it is undoubtedly true, that it is better to stay away than come in malice; but then the malice is so far from being an excuse for the staying away, that really the staying away is an aggravation of the malice. The law in this case is very express: If thy brother has ought against thee, that is, if thy conscience tell thee that thou art the party offending, do not therefore leave the altar, but leave thy gift before the altar, as a pawn for thy return, and go first and be reconciled to thy brother, by confessing thy fault, begging his pardon, and making satisfaction for the wrong done, and then be sure to come and offer thy gift. But, on the other hand, if thou have ought against any, if thou be the party offended, then forgive. Lay aside all uncharitable thoughts, angry resentments, and desire of revenge, and be in readiness to confirm and evidence your love to those that have injured you; and then, if they will not be reconciled to you, yet your being reconciled to them, is sufficient to remove that bar in your way to this ordinance. In short, strife and contention, as far as it is our fault, must be truly repented of, and the sincerity of our repentance evidenced by amendment of life, and then it needs not hinder us; as far as it is our cross, it must be patiently borne, and we must not be disturbed in our minds by it, and then it need not hinder us. And that law-suit which cannot be carried on without malice and hatred of our brother, had better be let fall, whatever we lose. Law is costly indeed, when it is followed at the expense of love and charity.

3. If the true reason of your absenting yourselves so often from the Lord's Supper be, that you are not willing to take that pains with your own hearts, and to lay that restraint upon yourselves both before and after, which you know you must if you come; if, indeed, you are not willing to have your thoughts so closely fixed, your consciences so strictly examined, and your engagements against sin so strongly confirmed, as they will be by this ordinance; if this be your case, you have reason to fear that " the things which remain are ready to die, and your works are not found filled up before God." It is a sad sign

of spiritual decay, and it is time for thee to "remember whence thou art fallen, and to repent, and do thy first works." Time was, when thou hadst a dear love to this ordinance, when thou longedst for the returns of it, and it was to thee "more than thy necessary food: such was the kindness of thy youth, such the love of thine espousals;" but it is otherwise now. Do you now sit loose to it? Are you indifferent whether you enjoy the benefit of it or not? Can you live contentedly without it? You have reason to fear lest you are of those that are drawing back to perdition. Having "begun in the spirit, will you now end in the flesh?" What iniquity have you found in this ordinance, that you have thus forsaken it? Has it been "as a barren wilderness to you, or as waters that fail?" If ever it were so, was it not your own fault? Return, therefore, ye backsliding children, be persuaded to return; return to God, return to your duty, to this duty; be close and constant to it, as you were formerly; for I dare say, "then it was better with you than now."

Those that, by the grace of God, do still keep up a love for this ordinance, should contrive their affairs so, as if possible not to miss any of their stated opportunities for it. Thomas, by being once absent from a meeting of the disciples, lost that joyful sight of Christ which the rest then had. It is good to have a nail in God's holy place. Blessed are they that dwell in his house; not those that turn aside to tarry but for a night, but those that take it for their home, their rest for ever.

Yet, if God prevent our enjoyment of an expected opportunity of this kind; though we must lament it as an afflictive disappointment, yet we may comfort ourselves with this, that though God has tied us to ordinances, he has not tied himself to them, but by his grace can make providences work for the good of our souls. It is better to be, like David, under a forced absence from God's altar, and have our hearts there, than to be, like Doeg, present under a force, "detained before the Lord," and the heart going after covetousness. It is better to be lamenting and longing in the want of ordinances, than loathing in the fulness of them.

CHAPTER IV.

HELPS FOR SELF-EXAMINATION BEFORE WE COME TO THIS ORDINANCE.

What it is to examine ourselves, illustrated in six similitudes, particularly six questions to be put to ourselves. I. What am I? Four inquiries by which to find out what our spiritual state is; two directions what to do thereupon. II. What have I done? Twelve questions to be put to ourselves, to bring to remembrance, and directions thereupon. III. What am I doing? In two things. IV. What ground do I get? Four questions by which to try our growth in grace. V. What do I want? What grace? What comfort? VI. What shall I resolve to do? In two things.

How earnest soever we are in pressing people to join themselves to the Lord in this ordinance, we would not have them to be "rash with their mouth, nor hasty to utter any thing before God." It must be done, but it must be done with great caution and consideration. Bounds must be set about the mount on which God will descend, and we must address ourselves to solemn services with a solemn pause. It is not enough that we seek God in a due ordinance, but we must "seek him in a due order," that is, we must "stir up ourselves to take hold on him." "Prepare to meet thy God, O Israel." Those that labour under such an habitual indisposition to communion with God, and are liable to so many actual discomposures, as we are conscious of to ourselves, have need to take pains with their heart, and should, with a very serious thought and steady resolution, engage them to approach unto God.

Now, the duty most expressly required in our preparation for the ordinance of the Lord's Supper, is that of self-examination. The apostle, when he would rectify the abuses which had sullied the beauty of this sacrament in the church of Corinth, prescribes this great duty as necessary to the due management of it, and a preservative against sharing in the guilt of such corruptions. "But let a man examine himself, and so let him eat of that bread, and drink of that cup." He that desires the Lord's Supper, desires a good work; but let these also first be proved, let them prove their own selves, and *so* let them come; *so*, upon that condition, and with that preparation; as, "I will wash my hands in innocency, *so* will I compass thine altar." In this method we must proceed.

"Let a man examine himself." The word signifies either to prove, or to approve, and appoints such an approbation of ourselves, as is the result of a strict and close probation; and such a probation of ourselves as issues in a comfortable approbation according to the tenor of the new covenant. It is so to prove ourselves, as to approve ourselves to God in our integrity. "Lord, thou knowest all things, thou knowest that I love thee;" so as to appeal to God's inquiry, "Examine me, O Lord, and prove me."

To examine ourselves is to discourse with our own hearts; it is to converse with ourselves; a very rational, needful, and improving piece of conversation. When we go about this work we must retire from the world, "sit alone, and keep silence;" we must retire into our own bosoms, and consider ourselves, reflect upon ourselves, inquire concerning ourselves, enter into a solemn conference with our own souls, and be anxious concerning their state. Those who are ignorant and cannot do this, or careless and secure, and will not do it, are unmeet for this ordinance.

I shall illustrate this by some similitudes.

1. We must examine ourselves, as metal is examined by the touchstone whether it be right or counterfeit. We have a show of religion; but are we what we seem to be? Are we current coin, or only washed over, as "a potsherd covered with silver dross?" Hypocrites are reprobate silver. True

Christians, when they are tried, come forth as gold. The word of God is the touchstone by which we must try ourselves. Can I through grace answer the characters which the Scriptures give of those whom Christ will own and save? It is true, the best coin has an alloy which will be allowed for in this state of imperfection; but the question is, Is it sterling,—is it standard? Though I am conscious to myself there are remainders of a baser metal, yet is love to God the predominant principle? Are the interests of Christ the prevailing interests in my soul, above those of the world and the flesh? I bear God's image and superscription: Is it of God's own stamping? Is it upon an honest and good heart? It is a matter of great consequence, and in which it is very common but very dangerous to be imposed upon, and therefore we have need to be jealous over ourselves. When we are bid to try the spirits, it is supposed we must begin with our own, and try them first.

2. We must examine ourselves, "as a malefactor is examined by the magistrate," that we may find out what we have done amiss. We are all criminals; that is readily acknowledged by each of us, because it is owned to be the common character: "All have sinned, and come short of the glory of God." We are all prisoners to the divine justice, from the arrests of which we cannot escape, and to the processes of which we lie obnoxious: being thus in custody, that we may not be judged by the Lord, we are commanded to judge ourselves. We must inquire into the particular crimes we have been guilty of, and their circumstances, that we may discover more sins, and more of the evil of them, than at first we were aware of. Dig into the wall as Ezekiel did, and see the secret abominations of your own hearts; look further, as he did, and you will see more and greater. The heart is deceitful, and has many devices, many evasions to shift convictions; we have therefore need to be very particular and strict in examining them, and to give them that charge which Joshua gave to

Achan, when he had him under examination: "Give glory unto the God of Israel, and make a confession unto him; tell me now what thou hast done, hide it not from me."

3. We must examine ourselves, as a copy is examined by the original to find out the errata, that they may be corrected. As Christians, we profess to be "the epistles of Christ," to have his law and love transcribed into our hearts and lives; but we are concerned to inquire, whether it be a true copy, by comparing ourselves with the gospel of Christ, whether our affections and conversation be conformable to it, and such as become it. How far do I agree with it, and where are the disagreements? What mistakes are there? What blots and what omissions? That what has been amiss may be pardoned, and what is amiss may be rectified. In this examination faith must read the original, and then let conscience read the copy, and be sure that it read true, because there will shortly be a review.

4. We must examine ourselves, as a candidate is examined that stands for preferment. Inquiry is made into his fitness for the preferment he stands for; we are candidates for heaven, the highest preferment, to be to our God kings and priests. We stand for a place at the wedding-feast: Have we on the wedding-garment? Are we made meet for the inheritance? What knowledge have we? What grace? Are we skilled in the mystery we make profession of? What improvement have we made in the school of Christ? What proficiency in divine learning? What testimonials have we to produce? Can we show the seal of the Spirit of promise? If not, we shall not be welcome.

5. We must examine ourselves, as a wife is examined of her consent to the levying of a fine for the confirming of a covenant. It is a common usage of the law. A covenant is to be ratified between God and our souls in the Lord's Supper: Do we freely and cheerfully consent to that covenant, not merely through the constraint of natural conscience, but be-

cause it is a covenant highly reasonable in itself, and unspeakably advantageous to us? Am I willing to make this surrender of myself unto the Lord? Am I freely willing, not because I cannot help it, but because I cannot better dispose of myself? We must examine ourselves as Joshua examined the people, whether they would choose to serve the Lord or not; and the product of the inquiry must be a fixed resolution, like theirs, " Nay, but we will serve the Lord."

6. We must examine ourselves, as a way-faring man is examined concerning his business. Our trifling hearts have need to be examined as vagrants, whence they come, whither they go, and what they would have. We are coming to a great ordinance, and are concerned to inquire what is our end in coming? What brings us thither? Is it only custom or company that draws us to this duty? or is it a spiritual appetite to the dainties of heaven? Our hearts must be catechized, as Elijah was: " What dost thou here, Elijah?" That we may give a good account to God of the sincerity of our intentions in our approaches to him, we ought, before we come, to call ourselves to an account concerning them.

More particularly, to examine ourselves, is to put serious questions to ourselves, and to our own hearts; and to prosecute them till a full and true answer be given to them. These six questions (among others,) are good for each of us to put to ourselves in our preparation to the Lord's Supper, both at our admission, and in our after approaches to it: " What am I? What have I done? What am I doing? What progress do I make? What do I want? and, What shall I resolve to do?"

I. Inquire, What am I?—It needs no inquiry, but it calls for serious consideration, that I am a reasonable creature, lower than the angels, higher than the brutes, capable of knowing, serving, and glorifying God in this world, and of seeing and enjoying him in a better. I am made for my Creator, and am accountable to him. God grant I have not such a noble and excellent being in vain! But here this question has another meaning. All the children of men, by the fall of the first Adam, are become sinners; some of the children of men, by the grace of the second Adam, are become saints: some remain in a state of nature, others are brought into a state of grace: some are sanctified, others unsanctified. This is a distinction which divides all mankind, and which will last when all other divisions and subdivisions shall be no more: for according to this will the everlasting state be determined. Now, when I ask, What am I? the meaning is, To which of these two do I belong? Am I in the favour of God, or under his wrath and curse? Am I a servant of God, or a slave to the world and the flesh? Look forward and ask, Whither am I going? To heaven or hell? If I should die this night, (and I am not sure to live till to-morrow,) whither would death bring me? Where would death lodge me? In endless light, or in utter darkness? Am I in the narrow way that leads to life, or in the broad way that leads to destruction? I am called a Christian, but am I a Christian, indeed? Have I a nature answerable to the name?

It highly concerns us all to be strict and impartial in this inquiry. What will it avail us to deceive ourselves? God cannot be imposed upon, though men may. It is undoubtedly true, if we be not saints on earth, we shall never be saints in heaven. It is not a small thing about which I am now persuading thee to inquire: no, it is thy life, thy precious life, the life of thy soul, thine eternal life, which depends upon it. Multitudes have been deceived in this matter, whose way seemed right, but the end of it proved the ways of death; and after they had long flattered themselves in their own eyes, they perished at last, with a lie in their right hand. We also are in danger of being deceived, and therefore have need to be jealous over ourselves with a godly jealousy; and being told that many who eat and drink in Christ's presence, will be disowned and rejected by him in the great day, we have each of us more reason to suspect ourselves than the disciples had, and to ask, "Lord, is it I?"

But it especially concerns us to insist upon this inquiry, when we draw near to God in the Lord's Supper. It is children's bread that is there prepared: Am I a child? If not, I have no part nor lot in the matter. I am there to seal a covenant with God; but, if I never made the covenant, never in sincerity consented to it, I shall put the seal to a blank, nay, to a curse.

Therefore, that I may discover, in some measure, what my spiritual state is, let me seriously inquire,

1. What choice have I made?—Have I chosen God's favour for my felicity and satisfaction, or the pleasures of sense, and the wealth of this world? Since I came to be capable of acting for myself, and discerning between my right hand and my left, have I made religion my deliberate choice? Have I chosen God for my portion, Christ for my master, the Scripture for my rule, holiness for my way, and heaven for my home and everlasting rest? If not, how can I expect to have what I never chose? If my covenant with the world and the flesh (which certainly amounts to a covenant with death, and an agreement with hell,) be still in force, and never yet broken, never yet disannulled, what have I to do to take God's covenant, and the seal of it into my mouth? But if I have refused Satan's offers of the kingdoms of this world, and the glory of them, and given the preference to the gospel offer of a kingdom in the other world, and the glory of that, I have reason to bless the Lord who gave me that counsel, and to hope that he, who hath directed me to choose the way of truth, will enable me to "stick to his testimonies."

2. What change have I experienced?—When I ask, Am I a child of wrath, or a child of love? I must remember that I was by nature a child of wrath. Now, can I witness to a change? Though I cannot exactly tell the time and manner, and the steps of that change, yet "one thing I know, that whereas I was blind, now I see." Though, in many respects,

it is still bad with me, yet thanks be to God, it is better with me than it has been. Time was, when I minded nothing but sport and pleasure, or nothing but the business of this world; when I never seriously thought of God and Christ, and my soul and another world: but now it is otherwise; now I see a reality in invisible things. I find an alteration in my care and concern; and now I ask more solicitously, "What shall I do to be saved?" than ever I asked, "What shall I eat, or what shall I drink, or wherewithal shall I be clothed?" Time was, when this vain and carnal heart of mine had no relish at all of holy ordinances, took no delight in them, called them a task and a weariness. But now it is otherwise; I love to be alone with God, and though I bring little to pass, yet I love to be doing in his service. If I have, indeed, experienced such a change as this; if this blessed turn be given to the bent of my soul, grace, free grace, must have the glory of it, and I may take the comfort of it. But if I have not found any such work wrought in my heart; if I am still what I was by nature, vain, and carnal, and careless: if Jordan runs still in the old channel, and was never yet driven back before the ark of the covenant; I have reason to suspect the worst by myself. If all go one way without struggle or opposition, it is to be feared it is not the right way.

3. What is the bent of my affections?—The affections are the pulse of the soul. If we would know its state, we must observe how that pulse beats. How do I stand affected to sin? Do I dread it as most dangerous, loathe it as most odious, and complain of it as most grievous? Or do I make a light matter of it, "as the madman that casteth firebrands, arrows, and death, and saith, Am not I in sport?" Which lies heavier, the burden of sin, or the burden of affliction; and of which am I most desirous to be eased? What think I of Christ? How do I stand affected to him? Do I love him, and prize him as the fairest among ten thousand? Or hath he in mine eyes no form nor comeliness, and is he no more than

another beloved? How do I stand affected to the word and ordinances? Are God's tabernacles amiable with me, or are they despicable? Am I in God's service, as in my element, as one that calls it a delight? Or am I in it as under confinement, and as one that calls it a drudgery? How do I stand affected to good people? Do I love the image of Christ wherever I see it, though it be in rags, or though not in my own colour? Do I honour them that fear the Lord, and choose his people for my people, in all conditions? Or do I prefer the gaieties of the world before the beauties of holiness? How do I stand affected to this world? Is it under my feet, where it should be; or in my heart, where Christ should be? Do I value it, and love it, and seek it with a prevailing concern? Or do I look upon it with a holy contempt and indifference? Which have the greater command over me, and which, in my account, have the most powerful and attractive charms; those riches, honours, and pleasures that are worldly, or those that are spiritual and divine? How do I stand affected to the other world? Do I dread eternal misery in a world of spirits, more than the greatest temporal calamities here in this world of sense? Do I desire eternal happiness in a future state, more than the highest contentments and satisfactions to which this present state can pretend? Or are the things of the other world, though sure and near, looked upon as doubtful and distant, and consequently little? By a close prosecution of such inquiries as these, with a charge to conscience, in God's name, to make a true answer to them, we may come to know our own selves.

4. What is the course and tenor of our conversations?—The tree is known by its fruits. Do I work the works of the flesh, or bring forth the fruits of the Spirit? The apostle gives us instances of both. Be not deceived yourselves, neither let any man deceive you: "He that doth righteousness, is righteous." And the surest mark of uprightness is, " keeping ourselves from our own iniquity." Do I allow myself

in any known sin, under the cloak of a visible profession? Dare I, upon any provocation, swear or curse, or profane God's holy name, and therein speak the language of his enemies? Dare I, upon any allurement to please my appetite, or please my company, drink to excess, and sacrifice my reason, honour, and conscience, to that base and brutish lust? Dare I defile a living temple of the Holy Ghost by adultery, fornication, uncleanness, or any act of lasciviousness? Dare I tell a lie for my gain or reputation? Dare I go beyond or defraud my brother in any matter, cheat those I deal with, or oppress those I have advantage against? Dare I deny relief to the poor that really need it, when it is in the power of my hand to give it? Dare I bear malice to any, and study revenge? If so, I must know that these are not the spots of God's children. If this be the life I live, I am certainly a stranger to the life of God. But if, upon search, my own heart tells me that I keep myself pure from these pollutions, and "herein exercise myself, to have always a conscience void of offence, both towards God and towards man;" if I have respect to all God's commandments, and make it my daily care in every thing to frame my life according to them, and to keep in the fear of God every day, and all the day long; and wherein I find I am defective, and come short of my duty, I repent of it, and am more watchful and diligent for the future: I have reason to hope, that though I have not yet attained, neither am already perfect, yet there is a good work begun in me, which shall be performed unto the day of Christ.

Thus we must examine our spiritual state; and, that the trial may come to an issue, we must earnestly pray to God to discover us to ourselves, and must be willing to know the truth of our case: and the result must be this:—

1. If we find cause to fear that our spiritual state is bad, and that we are yet unsanctified and unregenerate, we must give all diligence to get the matter mended. If our state be not good, yet, thanks be to

God, it may be made good: "There is hope in Israel concerning this thing." Rest not, therefore, in thy former faint purposes and feeble efforts; but consider more seriously than ever the concerns of thy soul. Pray more seriously than ever for the sanctifying grace of God; put forth thyself more vigorously than ever to improve that grace; resolve more firmly than ever to live a holy life, and depend more closely than ever upon the merit and strength of Jesus Christ, and I hope thou wilt soon experience a blessed change.

2. If we find cause to hope that our spiritual state is good, we must take the comfort of it, and give God the praise, and not hearken to the tempter when he would disturb our peace, and hinder our progress, by calling it in question. Though we must always abase ourselves, and be jealous over ourselves, yet we must not derogate from the honour of God's grace, nor deny its work in us. God keep us all, both from deceiving ourselves with groundless hopes, and from disquieting ourselves with groundless fears.

II. Inquire, What have I done?—We come to the ordinance of the Lord's Supper, to receive the remission of our sins, according to the tenor of the new covenant. Now, one thing required of us, in order to peace and pardon, is, that we confess our sins. If we do that, "God is faithful and just to forgive them." But if we cover them, we cannot prosper. Not that we can, by our confessions, inform God of any thing he did not know before, as earthly princes are informed by the confessions of criminals; but thus we must give glory to God, and take shame to ourselves, and strengthen our own guard against sin for the future. In the confession of sin, it is requisite that we be particular; the high priest, on the day of atonement, must confess, over the scape-goat, "all the iniquities of the children of Israel, and all their transgressions in all their sins." It is not enough to say, as Saul, "I have sinned;" but we must say, as David, "I have sinned, and done this evil;" as Achan, "I have sinned, and thus and thus have I done." A broken heart will thereby be more broken, and better prepared to be bound up; a burdened conscience will thereby be eased, as David's was when he said, "I will confess." Commonly, the more particular and free we are in confessing our sins to God, the more comfort we have in the sense of the pardon: deceit lies in generals.

It is therefore necessary, in order to a particular confession of sin, that we "search and try our ways;" that we examine our consciences, look over their records, examine the actions of our past life, and seriously call to mind wherein we have offended God in any thing. The putting of this question is spoken of as the first step towards repentance: " No man repented him of his wickedness, saying, What have I done?" For want of this inquiry duly made, when men are called to return, they baffle the call with that careless question, "Wherein shall we return?" Let us therefore set ourselves to look back, and remember our faults this day: it is better to be minded of them now, when the remembrance of them will open to us a door of hope, than be minded of them in hell, where sin remembered will aggravate an endless despair.

We ought to be often calling ourselves to an account: in the close of every day, of every week, the day's work, the week's work should be reviewed. It is one of the richest of Pythagoras' golden verses, wherein, though a heathen, he advises his pupil, every night before he sleeps, to go over the actions of the day, and revolve them three times in his mind, asking himself seriously these questions:—" Wherein have I transgressed? What have I done? What duty hath been omitted?" The oftener it is done, the easier it is done: even reckonings make long friends. But it is especially necessary that it be done before a sacrament: former reflections made, ought then to be repeated; and with a particular exactness we must consider what our ways have been since we were last renewing our covenants with God at his table, that we may be humbled for the follies to which we have returned since God spoke peace to us, and may be more particular and steady in our resolutions for the future.

To give some assistance in this inquiry, I shall instance some heads of it. Let the interrogatories be such as these:—

1. How have I employed my thoughts? Has God been in all my thoughts?—It is well if he has been in any. When I awake, am I still with him? Or am I not still with the world and the flesh? When I should have been contemplating the glory of God, the love of Christ, and the great things of the other world, has not my heart been with the fool's eyes in the ends of the earth, " following after lying vanities, and forsaking mine own mercies?" How seldom have I thought seriously, and with any fixedness, on spiritual and divine things? I set myself sometimes to meditate, but I soon break off abruptly, and this treacherous heart starts aside like a broken bow, and nothing that is good is brought to any head; but how have vain and vile thoughts lodged within me, gone out and come in with me, lain down and risen up with me, and crowded out good thoughts? Has not the " imagination of the thoughts of my heart" been evil, only evil, and that continually?

2. How have I governed my passions?—Have they been kept under the dominion of religion and right reason? Or have they not grown intemperate and headstrong, and transgressed due bounds? Have not provocations been too much resented, and made too deep an impression? Has not my heart many times been hot within me, too hot, so that its heat has consumed the peace of my own mind, and the love I owe my brother? Has not anger rested in my bosom? Have not malice and uncharitableness, secret enmities and antipathies, been harboured there, where love and peace should have reigned and given law?

3. How have I preserved my purity?—Have I possessed my vessel in sanctification and honour, or am I not conscious to myself of indulging the lust of uncleanness? If, by the grace of God, I have kept

my body pure, yet has not my spirit been defiled by impure thoughts and affections? I have made a covenant with mine eyes not to look and lust, but have I made good that covenant? Have I in no instance transgressed the laws of chastity in my heart, and modesty in my behaviour? Let this inquiry be made with a strict guard upon the soul, lest that which should not be named among Christians, be thought of without that just abhorrence and detestation which becomes saints.

4. How have I used my tongue?—It was designed to be my glory, but has it not been my shame? Has not much corrupt communication proceeded out of my mouth, and little of that which is good, which might either manifest grace, or minister grace? Have not I sometimes spoken unadvisedly, and said that in haste which at leisure I could have wished unsaid? Have not I said that, by which God's great name has been dishonoured, or my brother's good name reproached, or my own exposed? If, for every idle word that I speak, I must give account to God, I had best call myself to an account for them, and I shall find innumerable evils compassing me about.

5. How have I spent my time?—So long as I have lived in the world, to what purpose have I lived? What improvement have I made of my days for doing or getting good? It is certain I have lost time; have I yet begun to redeem it, and to repair those losses? How many hours have I spent that might have been spent much better? There is a duty which every day requires, but how little of it has been done in its day!

6. How have I managed my worldly calling?— Have I therein abode with God, or have I not in many instances of it wandered from him? Have I been just and fair in all my dealings, and spoken the truth from my heart? Or have I not sometimes dealt deceitfully in bargaining, and said that which bordered upon a lie? Has not fleshly wisdom governed me more than that simplicity and godly sincerity which becomes an Israelite indeed? Have I no wealth got

by vanity, no unjust gain, no blot of that kind cleaving to my hand?

7. How have I received my daily food?—Have I never transgressed the law of temperance in meat and drink, and so made my table my snare? Have not God's good gifts been abused to luxury and sensuality, and the body, which, by the sober use of them, should have been fitted, by the excessive use of them, unfitted to serve the soul in the service of God? Have I not eaten to myself, and drunk to myself, when I should have eaten and drunk to the glory of God?

8. How have I done the duty of my particular relations?—The word of God has expressly taught me my duty as a husband, a wife, a parent, a child, a master, a servant; but have I not in many things failed of my duty? Have not I carried myself disrespectfully to my superiors, disdainfully to my inferiors, and disingenuously to my equals? Have I given to each that which is just and right, and rendered to all their dues? Have I been a comfort to my relations, or have I not caused grief?

9. How have I performed my secret worship?—Have I been constant to it, morning and evening; or have I not sometimes omitted it, and put it by with some frivolous excuse? Have I been conscientious in it, and done it with an eye to God; or have I not kept it up merely as a custom, and suffered it to degenerate into a formality? Have I been lively and serious in secret prayer and reading; or have I not rested in the outside of the performance, without any close application and intention of mind in it?

10. How have I laid out what God has given me in the world?—I am but a steward; have I been faithful? Have I honoured the Lord with my substance, and done good with it; or have I wasted and misapplied my Lord's goods? Hath God had his dues, my family and the poor their dues, out of my estate? What should have been consecrated to piety and charity, has it not been either sinfully spared, or sinfully spent?

11. How have I improved the Lord's day, and the other helps I have had for my soul?—I enjoy great plenty of the means of grace; have I grown in grace in the use of those means, or have I not received the grace of God therein in vain? Have I "called the Sabbath a delight, the holy of the Lord, and honourable;" or have I not snuffed at it, and said, "When will the Sabbath be gone?" How have I profited by sermons and sacraments, and the other advantages of solemn assemblies? Have I received and retained the good impressions of holy ordinances; or have I not lost them, and let them slip?

12. How have I borne my afflictions?—When Providence has crossed me, and frowned upon me, what frame have I been in, repining or repenting? Have I submitted to the will of God in my afflictions, and patiently accepted the punishment of my iniquity; or have I not striven with my Maker, and quarreled with his disposals? When mine own foolishness has perverted my way, has not my heart fretted against the Lord? What good have I gotten to my soul by my afflictions? What inward gain by outward losses? Has my heart been more humbled and weaned from the world; or have I not been hardened under the rod, and trespassed yet more against the Lord?

Many more such queries might be adduced, but these may suffice for a specimen. Yet it will not suffice to put these questions to ourselves, but we must diligently observe what reply conscience, upon an impartial search, makes to them. We must not do as Pilate did, when he asked our Saviour, What is truth? but would not stay for an answer. No, we must take pains to find out what has been amiss, and herein must accomplish a diligent search.

And, as far as we find ourselves not guilty, we must own our obligations to the grace of God, and return thanks for that grace, and let the testimony of conscience for us be our rejoicing. "If our hearts condemn us not, then we have confidence towards God."

As far as we find ourselves guilty, we must be humbled before God for it, mourn and be in bitterness at the remembrance of it, cry earnestly to God for pardon of it, and be particular in our resolutions, by God's grace, to sin no more. Pray as Job is taught—" That which I see not teach thou me;" and promise as it follows there—" Wherein I have done iniquity, I will do no more."

III. Inquire, What am I doing?—When we have considered what our way has been, it is time to consider what it is. " Ponder the path of thy feet."

1. What am I doing in the general course of my conversation? Am I doing any thing for God, for my soul, for eternity; any thing for the service of my generation; or am I not standing all the day idle? It is the law of God's house, as well as of ours, " He that will not labour, let him not eat."

If I find that, according as my capacity and opportunity is, through the grace of Christ, I am going on in the way of God's commandments, this ordinance will be comforting and quickening to me; but if I give way to spiritual sloth and slumber, and do not mind my business, let this shame me out of it, and humble me for it: How unworthy am I to eat my master's bread, while I take no care to do my master's work!

2. What am I doing in this approach to the ordinance of the Lord's Supper?—I know what is to be done, but am I doing it? Do I apply myself to it in sincerity, and with a single eye; in a right manner, and for right ends? Am I by repentance undoing that which I have done amiss? And am I, by renewing my covenant with God, doing that better, which I have formerly done well? Am I joining myself unto the Lord, with purpose of heart to cleave unto him to the end? It is the preparation of the passover; am I doing the work of that day in its day? Am I purging out the old leaven, buying such things as I have need of against the feast, without

money and without price? Am I engaging my heart to approach unto God, or am I thinking of something else? Am I slothful in this business, or do I make a business of it?

Here it is good to examine, whether, beside the common and general intentions of this ordinance, there be not something particular, which I should more especially have in my eye, in my preparation for it. Do I find my heart at this time more than usually broken for sin, and humbled at the remembrance of it? Let me then set in vigorously with those impressions, and drive that nail. Or is my heart in a special manner affected with the love of Christ, and enlarged in holy wonder, joy, and praise? Let its outgoings that way be quickened, and those thoughts imprinted deep, and improved.

IV. Inquire, What progress do I make?—If, upon examination, there appear some evidences of the truth of grace, I must then examine my growth in grace; for grace, if it be true, will be growing: "That well of water will be springing up, and he that hath clean hands will be stronger and stronger." There is a spiritual death, or at least some prevailing spiritual disease, where there is not some improvement and progress towards perfection.

By what measures, then, may I try my growth in grace?

1. Do I find my practical judgment more settled and confirmed in its choice of holiness and heaven? If so, it is a sign I am getting forward. We cannot judge of ourselves by the pangs of affection; those may be more sensible and vehement at first; and their being less so afterwards, ought not to discourage us. The fire may not blaze so high as it did, and yet may burn better and stronger. But do I see more and more reason for my religion? Am I more strongly convinced of its certainty and excellency, so as to be able, better than at first, to "give a reason of the hope that is in me?" My first love was able to call religion a comfortable service; was my after light better able to call it a reasonable service? I

was extremely surprised, when, at first, "I saw men as trees walking;" but, am I now better satisfied, when I begin to see all things more clearly? Am I, through God's grace, better rooted? Or am I, through my own folly, still as a "reed shaken with the wind?"

2. Do I find my corrupt appetites and passions more manageable; or are they still as violent and headstrong as ever? Does the house of Saul grow weaker and weaker, and its struggles for the dominion less frequent, and more feeble? If so, it is a good sign: the house of David grows stronger and stronger. Though these Canaanites are in the land, yet if they do not make head as they have done, but are under tribute, then the interests of Israel are gaining ground. Do I find that my desires towards those things that are pleasing to sense are not so eager as they have been, but the body is kept more under, and brought into subjection to grace and wisdom; and is it not so hard a thing to me, as it has been sometimes to deny myself? Do I find that my resentments of those things which are displeasing to the flesh, are not so deep and keen as they have been? Can I bear afflictions from a righteous God, and provocations from unrighteous men, with more patience, and better composure and command of myself, than I could have done? Am I not so peevish and fretful, and unable to bear an affront or disappointment, as sometimes I have been? If so, surely He that has "begun the good work, is carrying it on." But if nothing be done towards the suppressing of these rebels, towards the weeding out of these "roots of bitterness which spring up and trouble us," though we lament them, yet we do not prevail against them; it is to be feared we stand still, or go back.

3. Do I find the duties of religion more easy and pleasant to me; or am I still as unskilful and unready in them as ever? Do I go dexterously about a duty, as one that understands it, and is used to it, and as a man that is master of his trade goes on with the business of it; or do I go awkwardly about it, as one not versed in it? When God calls, Seek ye my

face; do I, like the child Samuel, run to Eli, and terminate my regards in the outside of the service; or do I, like the man David, cheerfully answer, "Thy face, Lord, will I seek;" and so enter into that within the veil? Though, on the one hand, there is not a greater support to hypocrisy, than a formal, customary road of external performances; yet, on the other hand, there is not a surer evidence of sincerity and growth, than an even, constant, steady course of lively devotion, which, by daily use, becomes familiar and easy, and, by the new nature, natural to us. A growing Christian takes his work before him, and sings at it.

4. Do I find my heart more weaned from this present life, and more willing to exchange it for a better; or am I still loath to leave it? Are thoughts of death more pleasing to me than they have been, or are they still as terrible as ever? If, through grace, we are got above the fear of death, by reason of which many weak and trembling Christians are all their life-time subject to bondage, and can truly say, "We desire to depart and to be with Christ, which is far better," it is certain we are gaining ground, though we have not yet attained.

5. If, upon search, we find that we make no progress in grace and holiness, let the ordinance of the Lord's Supper be improved for the furtherance of our growth, and the removal of that, whatever it is, which hinders it; if we find we thrive, though but slowly, and though it is not so well with us as it should be, yet, through grace, it is better with us than it has been, and that we are not always babes, let us be encouraged to abound so much the more. "Go and prosper; the Lord is with thee, whilst thou art with him."

V. Inquire, What do I want?—A true sense of our spiritual necessities is required to qualify us for spiritual supplies. The hungry only are filled with good things. It concerns us, therefore, when we come to an ordinance, which is as a spiritual market, to consider what we have occasion for, that we may know what to lay hold on, and may have an answer ready to that question which will be put to us at that banquet of wine—" What is thy petition, and what is thy request?" Or that which Christ put to the blind men—" What will ye that I shall do unto you?"

" Grace and peace from God the Father, and from our Lord Jesus Christ," are inclusive of all the blessings we can desire, and have in them enough to supply all our needs. Since, therefore, we must ask and receive, that our joy may be full, it concerns us to inquire what particular grace and comfort we need, that we may, by faith and desire, reach forth towards that in a special manner.

1. What grace do I most want?—Wherein do I find myself most defective, weakest, and most exposed? What corruption do I find working most in me? The grace that is opposite to that, I most need. Am I apt to be proud or passionate? Humility and meekness, then, are the graces I most want. Am I apt to be timorous and distrustful? Faith and hope, then, are the graces I most want. With what temptations am I most frequently assaulted? Which way does Satan get most advantage against me,—by my constitution, calling, or company? There I most want help from heaven, and strength to double my guard. Am I in danger of being drawn by my outward circumstances to intemperance or deceit, or oppression or dissimulation? Then sobriety, justice, and sincerity are the graces I most want. What is the nature of the duties I am mostly called out to, and employed in? Are they such as oblige me to stoop to that which is mean? Then self-denial is the grace I most want. Are they such as oblige me to struggle with that which is difficult and discouraging? Then courage and wisdom are the graces I most want. Whatever our wants are, there are promises in the new covenant adapted to them, which, in this ordinance, we must, in a particular manner, apply to ourselves, and claim the benefit of, and receive as sealed to us. If we cannot bethink ourselves of

particular promises suited to our case, yet there is enough in the general ones: "I will put my Spirit within you, and cause you to walk in my statutes." "I will put my law in your hearts," "and my fear," and many such like. And we know who has said, "My grace is sufficient for thee."

2. *What comfort do I most want?*—What is the burden that lies most heavy? I must seek for support under that burden. What is the grief that is most grieving? I must seek for a balance to that grief. The guilt of sin is often disquieting to me: O for the comfort of a sealed pardon! The power of corruption is very discouraging: O for the comfort of victorious grace! I am often tossed with doubts and fears about my spiritual state, as if the Lord had "utterly separated me from his people, and I were a dry tree:" O for the comfort of clear and unclouded evidences! I am sometimes tempted to say, "The Lord hath forsaken me, my God hath forgotten me:" O that he would seal to my soul that precious promise, "I will never leave thee nor forsake thee!" But my greatest trouble arises from the sense of my own weakness, and tendency to backslide; and I am sometimes ready to make that desperate conclusion, "I shall one day perish by the hand of Saul:" O that I may have the comfort of that promise, "I will put my fear in their hearts, that they shall not depart from me." There is, in the covenant of grace, a salve for every sore, a remedy for every malady, comforts suited to every distress and sorrow; but that we may have the benefit of them, it is requisite that we "know every one his own sore, and his own grief," that we may spread it before the Lord, and may apply to ourselves that relief which is proper for it, and "from the fulness which is in Jesus Christ, may receive, and grace for grace," grace for all occasions.

Here it may be of use to take cognizance even of our outward condition, and inquire into the cares and burdens, the crosses and necessities of it; for even against those there is comfort provided in the new covenant, and administered in this ordinance,

"Godliness hath the promise of the life that now is." When Christ was inviting his disciples to come and dine with him, he asked them first, "Children, have ye any meat?" Christ's inquiry into our affairs, directs us to make known before him in particular, the trouble of them. Let every care be cast upon the Lord in this ordinance, lodged in his hands, and left with him; and let our own spirits be eased of it, by the application of that general word of comfort to this particular case, whatever it is, "He careth for you." What is the concern I am most thoughtful about, relating to myself, my family, or friends? Let that way be committed to the Lord, and to his wise and gracious conduct and disposal; and then let my thoughts concerning it be established. What is the complaint I make most feelingly? Is it of a sickly body, disagreeable relations, a declining estate, the removal of those by death that were very dear? Whatever it is, spread it before the Lord, as Hezekiah did Rabshakeh's letter, and allow no complaint that is not fit to be spread before him. When God came to renew his covenant with Abraham, and to tell him that he was his shield, and his exceeding great reward, Abraham presently puts in a remonstrance of his grievance: "Behold, to me thou hast given no seed." Hannah did so, when she came up to worship. And we also must bring with us such a particular sense of our afflictions, as will enable us to receive and apply the comforts here offered to us, and no more. Holy David observed how his house was with God, and that it was not made to grow, when he was taking the comfort of this, that, however it were, "God had made with him an everlasting covenant."

VI. Inquire, What shall I resolve to do?—This question is equivalent to that of Paul, "Lord, what wilt thou have me to do?" We come to this ordinance solemnly to engage ourselves against all sin, and to all duty; and therefore it is good to consider what that sin is which we should particularly covenant against, and what that duty to which we should most expressly oblige ourselves. Though the general covenant suffice to bind conscience, yet a particular article will be of use to remind conscience, and to make the general engagement the more effectual. It is good to be particular in our pious resolutions, as well as in our penitent reflections.

For our assistance herein let us inquire,

1. Wherein have we hitherto missed it most?—Where we have found ourselves most assaulted by the subtlety of the tempter, and most exposed by our own weakness, there we should strengthen our defence and double our guard. What is the sin that has most easily beset me—the well-circumstanced sin? That is it which I must more particularly resolve against in the strength of the grace of God. What is the duty I have most neglected, have been most backward to, and most careless in? To that I must most solemnly bind my soul with this bond.

2. Wherein may we have the best opportunity of glorifying God?—What can I do in my place for the service of God's honour, and the interests of his kingdom among men? "The liberal deviseth liberal things," and so the pious devises pious things, that he may both engage and excite himself to those liberal pious things, in and by this ordinance. What is the talent I am entrusted with the improvement of? My Lord's goods I am made steward of. What is it that is expected from one in my capacity? What fruit is looked for from me? That is it that I must especially have an eye to in my covenants with God; to that I must bind my soul; for that I must fetch in help from heaven, that, having sworn, I may perform it.

CHAPTER V.

INSTRUCTIONS FOR RENEWING OUR COVENANT WITH GOD IN OUR PREPARATION FOR THIS ORDINANCE.

I. In what method we must renew our covenant with God. (I.) We must repent of our sins, by which we have rendered ourselves unworthy to be taken into covenant: three things to be lamented. (II.) We must renounce the devil, the world, and the flesh: opened in three things. (III.) We must receive Christ as offered to us, consenting to his grace, and to his government. (IV.) We must resign, and give up ourselves to God in Christ; devote ourselves to his praise, and submit ourselves to his power: in three things. (V.) We must resolve to abide in it: opened in two things. (VI.) We must rely on the righteousness and strength of Christ herein: opened in two things. II. After what manner we must renew our covenant; intelligently, considerately, humbly, cheerfully, and in sincerity.

It is the wonderful condescension of the God of heaven, that he has been pleased to deal with man in the way of a covenant, that, on the one hand, we might receive strong consolations from the promises of the covenant, which are very sweet and precious; and, on the other hand, might lie under strong obligations from the conditions of the covenant, which, on this account, have greater cogency in them than mere precept, that we ourselves have consented to them, and that we have therein consulted our own interest and advantage.

The ordinance of the Lord's Supper, being a seal of the covenant, and the solemn exchanging of the ratifications of it, it is necessary we make the covenant before we pretend to seal it. In this order, therefore, we must proceed,—first give the hand to the Lord, and then enter into the sanctuary; first in secret consent to the covenant, and then solemnly testify that consent: this is like a contract before marriage. They that "ask the way to Zion, with their faces thitherward, must join themselves to the Lord in a perpetual covenant." The covenant is mutual, and in vain do we expect the blessings of the covenant, if we be not truly willing to come under the bonds of the covenant. We must "enter into covenant with the Lord our God, and into his oath;" else he doth not "establish us this day for a people unto himself." We are not owned and accepted as God's people, though we "come before him as his people come," and sit before him as his people sit, if we do not in sincerity "avouch the Lord for our God." In our baptism this was done for us, in the Lord's Supper we must do it for ourselves, else we do nothing.

Let us consider then, in what method, and after what manner, we must manage this great transaction.

I. In what method we must renew our covenant with God in Christ, and by what steps we must proceed.

(1.) We must repent of our sins, by which we have rendered ourselves unworthy to be taken into covenant with God. Those that would be exalted to this honour, must first humble themselves. "God layeth his beams in the waters." The foundations of spiritual joy are laid in the waters of penitential tears, therefore this sealing ordinance sets that before us which is proper to move our godly sorrow: in it we look on him whom we have pierced, and if we do not mourn and be not in bitterness for him, surely "our hearts are as hard as a stone, yea, harder than a piece of the nether millstone." Those that join themselves to the Lord, must go weeping to do it: so they did— "In those days, and in that time, saith the Lord, the children of Israel shall come, they and the children of Judah together, going and weeping: they shall go, and seek the Lord their God. They shall ask the way to Zion, with their faces thitherward, saying, Come, and let us join ourselves to the Lord in a perpetual covenant that shall not be forgotten." That comfort is likely to last, which takes rise from deep humiliation and contrition of soul for sin. Those only that go forth weeping, bearing this precious seed, shall come again rejoicing in God as theirs, and bringing the sheaves of covenant blessings and comforts with them. Let us therefore begin with this:

1. We have reason to bewail our natural estrangement from this covenant. When we come to be for God, we have reason to be affected with sorrow and shame, that ever we were for any other; that ever there should have been occasion for our reconciliation to God, which supposes that there has been a quarrel. Wretch that I am, ever to have been a stranger, an enemy to the God that made me, at war with my Creator, and in league with the rebels against his crown and dignity! O the folly, and wickedness, and misery, of my natural estate! My first father an Amorite, and my mother a Hittite, and myself a transgressor from the womb, alienated from the life of God, and cast out in my pollution. Nothing in me lovely, nothing amiable, but a great deal loathsome and abominable. Such as this was my nativity, my original.

2. We have reason to bewail our backwardness to come into this covenant. Well may we be ashamed to think how long God called, and we refused; how oft he stretched forth his hand before we regarded; how many offers of mercy we slighted, and against how many kind invitations we stood out; how long Christ stood at the door and knocked before we opened to him; and how many frivolous excuses we made to put off this necessary work. What a fool was I to stand in my own light so long! How ungrateful to the God of love, who waited to be gracious! How justly might I have been for ever excluded from this covenant, who so long neglected that great salvation! Wherefore I abhor myself.

3. We have reason to bewail the inconsistency of our hearts and lives with the terms of this covenant, since first we professed our consent to it. In many instances we have dealt foolishly, it is well if we have not dealt falsely, in the covenant. In our baptism we were given up to Christ to be his, but we have lived as if we were our own; we then put on the Christian livery, but we have done little of the Christian's

work; we were called by Christ's name to take away our reproach, but how little have we been under the conduct and government of the Spirit of Christ! Since we became capable of acting for ourselves, perhaps we have oft renewed our covenant with God, at his table, and upon other occasions; but we have despised the oath, "in breaking the covenant, when, lo, we had given the hand!" Our performances have not answered the engagements we have solemnly laid ourselves under. Did we not say, and say it with the blood of Christ in our hands, that we would be the faithful servants of the God of heaven? We did; and yet instead of serving God, we have served divers lusts and pleasures, we have made ourselves slaves to the flesh, and drudges to the world; and this "hath been our manner from our youth up." Did we not say, "we would not transgress, we would not offend any more?" We did; and yet "our transgressions are multiplied, and in many things we offend daily. Did we not say, we would walk more closely with God, more circumspectly in our conversation, we would be better in our closets, better in our families, better in our callings, every way better? We did; and yet we are still vain and careless, and unprofitable; all those good purposes have been to little purpose; this is a lamentation, and should be for a lamentation. Let our hearts be truly broken for our former breach of covenant with God, and then the renewing of our covenant will be the recovery of our peace, and that which was broken shall be bound up, and made to rejoice.

(II.) We must renounce the devil, the world, and the flesh, and every thing that stands in opposition to, or competition with, the God to whom we join ourselves by covenant. If we will indeed deal sincerely in our covenanting with God, and would be accepted of him therein, our "covenant with death must be disannulled, and our agreement with hell must not stand." All these foolish, sinful agreements, which were indeed null and void from the beginning, by which we had alienated ourselves from our rightful owner, and put ourselves in possession of the usurper, must be revoked and cancelled, and our consent to them drawn back with disdain and abhorrence. When we take an oath of allegiance to God in Christ as our rightful king and sovereign, we must herein abjure the tyranny of the rebellious and rival powers. "O Lord our God, other lords besides thee have had dominion over us," while sin has reigned in our mortal bodies, in our immortal souls, and every lust has been a lord; but now we are weary of that heavy yoke, and through God's grace it shall be so no longer; for, from henceforth, "by thee only will we make mention of thy name."

The covenant into which we are to enter is a marriage covenant, "thy Maker is to be thy husband," and thou art to be betrothed to him; and it is the ancient and fundamental law of that covenant, that all other lovers be renounced, all other beloved ones forsaken; and the same is the law of this covenant: "Thou shalt not be for another man, so will I also be for thee." Quitting all others, we must cleave to the Lord only; lovers and crowned heads will not endure rivals; on these terms, and no other, we may covenant with God: "If ye do return unto the Lord with all your hearts, then put away the strange gods and Ashtaroth," else it is not a return to God.

1. We must renounce all subjection to Satan's rule and government. Satan's seat must be overturned in our hearts, and the Redeemer's throne set up there upon the ruins of it. We must disclaim the devil's power over us, cast off that iron yoke, and resolve to be deceived by him no more, and led captive by him at his will no more. We must quit the service of the citizen of that country, and feed his swine no longer, feed upon his husks no more, that we may return to our father's house, where there is bread enough and to spare. We must renounce the treacherous conduct of the evil spirit, that we may put ourselves under the guidance of the holy and good Spirit. All that turn to God, must turn from the power of Satan: for what communion has Christ

with Belial? Our covenant with God engages us in a war with Satan; for the controversy between them is such as will by no means allow us to stand neutral.

2. We must renounce all compliance with the wills and interests of the flesh. The body, though near and dear to the soul, yet must not be allowed to have dominion over it. The liberty, sovereignty, and honour of the immortal spirit, by which we are allied to the upper world, that world of spirits, must be asserted, vindicated, and maintained against the usurpation and encroachments of the body, which is of the earth earthly, and by which we are allied to the beasts that perish. The elder too long has served the younger, the nobler has served the baser; it is time that the yoke should be broken from off its neck, and that that part of the man should rule under Christ, whose right it is. The servants on horseback must be dismounted, the lusts of the flesh denied, and its will no longer admitted to give law to the man: and the princes, who have walked like servants upon the earth, must be raised from the dunghill, and made to inherit the throne of glory; the dictates, I mean, of right reason, guided by revelation, and consulting the true interests of the better part, must have the commanding sway and empire in us. We must never more make it our chief good to have the flesh pleased, and the desires of it gratified, nor ever make it our chief business to make provision for the flesh, that we may fulfil the lusts of it. Away with them, away with them; crucify them, crucify them; for, like Barabbas, they are robbers, they are murderers, they are enemies to our peace. We will not have them to reign over us; no, no, we know them too well; we have no king but Jesus.

3. We must renounce all dependence upon this present world, and conformity to it. If we enter into a covenant which ensures us a happiness in the other world, on which we look with a holy concern, we must disclaim the expectations of happiness in

this world, and therefore look upon this with a holy contempt. God and mammon, God and gain, these are contrary the one to the other. So that if we will be found loving God, and cleaving to him, we must despise the world, and sit loose to it. We must so far renounce the way of the world, as not to govern ourselves by it, and take our principles and measures from it; for we must not be "conformed to this world," nor "walk according to the course of it." We must so far renounce the men of the world, as not to incorporate ourselves with them, nor choose them for our people; because, though we are in the world, we are not of the world, nor have we received the spirit of the world, but Christ has chosen and called us out of it. We must so far renounce the wealth of the world, as not to portion ourselves out of it, nor lay up our treasure in it; nor to take up with the things of this world, as our good things, as our consolation, as our reward, as the penny we agree for. For in God's favour is our life, and not in the smiles of this world. The Lord make us cordial in thus renouncing these competitors, that we may be found sincere in covenanting with God in Christ!

(III.) We must receive the Lord Jesus Christ, as he is offered to us in the gospel. In renewing our covenants with God, it is not enough to enter our dissent from the world and the flesh, and to shake off Satan's yoke, but we must enter our consent to Christ, and take upon us his yoke. In the everlasting gospel, both as it is written in the Scripture, and as it is sealed in this sacrament, salvation by Christ, that great salvation, is fairly tendered to us who need it, and are undone for ever without it. We then come into covenant with God, when we accept of this salvation, with an entire complacency and confidence in those methods which infinite wisdom has taken, of reconciling a guilty and obnoxious world to himself by the mediation of his own Son, and a cheerful compliance with those methods for ourselves and our own salvation.—Lord, I take thee at thy word: be it unto thy servant according to that word, which is so well ordered in all things, and so sure!

We must accept the salvation in Christ's way, and upon his terms, else our acceptance is not accepted.

By a hearty consent to the grace of Christ, we must accept the salvation in his own way, in such a way as for ever excludes boasting, humbles man to the dust, and will admit no flesh to glory in his presence; such a way as, though it leaves the blood of them that perish upon their own heads, yet lays all the crowns of them that are saved at the feet of free grace. This method we must approve of, and love this salvation; not going about to establish our own righteousness, as if, by pleading not guilty, we could answer the demands of the covenant of innocency, and so be justified and saved by it,—but submitting "to the righteousness of God by faith." All the concerns that lie between us and God, we must put into the hands of the Lord Jesus, as the great Mediator, the great manager; we must be content to be nothing, that the Lord alone may be exalted, and Christ may be all in all. God hath declared more than once by a voice from heaven, "This is my beloved Son, in whom I am well pleased." To consent to Christ's grace, and accept of salvation in his way, is to echo back that solemn declaration,— This is my beloved Saviour in whom I am well pleased: the Lord be well pleased with me in him; for out of him I can expect no favour.

By a hearty consent to the government of Christ, we must accept the salvation on his own terms. When we receive Christ, we must receive an entire Christ; for, "is Christ divided?"—a Christ to sanctify and rule us, as well as a Christ to justify and save us; for he is a priest upon his throne, and the council of peace is between them both. What God has joined together, let us not think to put asunder. He saves his people from their sins, not in their sins; and is the author of eternal redemption to those only that obey him. That very "grace of God which bringeth salvation, teacheth us to deny ungodliness, and worldly and fleshly lusts, and to live soberly, righteously, and godly in this world." Life and peace are to be had on these terms, and on no other; and are we willing to come up to these terms? Will we receive Christ and his law, as well as Christ and his love? Christ and his cross, as well as Christ and his crown? Lord, I will, saith the believing soul; Lord, I do. "My beloved is mine, and I am his," to all the intents and purposes of the covenant.

(IV.) We must resign and give up ourselves to God in Christ.—God in the covenant makes over not only his gifts and favours, but himself to us: "I will be to them a God." What he is in himself, he will be to us, a God all-sufficient: so we in the covenant must offer up, not only our services, but ourselves; our own selves, body, soul, and spirit, to God the Father, Son, and Holy Ghost, according to the obligations of our baptism, as those that are bound to be to him a people. This surrender is to be solemnly made at the Lord's table, and sealed there; it must therefore be prepared and made ready before. Let us see to it, that it be carefully drawn up without exception or limitation, and the heart examined, whether a free and full consent be given to it. We must first give our own selves unto the Lord, and I know not how we can dispose of ourselves better. By the mercies of God, which are inviting, and very encouraging, we must be wrought upon to present our bodies and souls to God a living sacrifice of acknowledgment, not a dying sacrifice of atonement; which, if it be holy, shall be acceptable, and it is our reasonable service. Thus he that covenants with God, is directed to say, "I am the Lord's," and for the greater solemnity of the transaction, to subscribe with his hand unto the Lord. Not that we do, or can hereby transfer or convey to God any right to us which He had not before. He is our absolute Lord and owner, and has an incontestable sovereignty over us and propriety in us, as he is our Creator, Preserver, Benefactor, and Redeemer; but hereby we recognize and acknowledge his right to us. We are his already by obligation, more his than our own; but, that we may have the benefit and comfort of being so, we must be his by our own consent. More particularly,

1. To resign ourselves to God, is to "dedicate and devote ourselves to his praise." It is not enough to call ourselves by his name, and associate ourselves with those that do so, to take away our reproach; but we must consecrate ourselves to his name, as living temples. It is a gift, a gift to God; all I am, all I have, all I can do is so; it is a dedicated thing, which it is sacrilege to alienate. All the powers and faculties of our souls, all the parts and members of our bodies, we must, as those that are alive from the dead, freely yield unto God as instruments of righteousness, to be used and employed in his service for his glory. All our endowments, all our attainments, all those things we call accomplishments, must be accounted as talents, which we must trade with for his honour. All being of him and from him, all must be to him and for him. Our tongues must not be our own, but his, in nothing to offend him, but to speak his praise, and plead his cause, as there is occasion. Our time not our own, but as a servant's time, to be spent according to our Master's directions, and some way or other to our Master's glory, every day being in this sense our Lord's day. Our estates not our own, to be spent or spared by the direction of our lusts, but to be used as God directs: "God must be honoured with our substance,"—"and our merchandise and our hire must be holiness to the Lord." Our interest not our own, with it to seek our own glory, but to be improved in seeking and serving God's glory; that is, God's glory must be fixed and aimed at, as our highest and ultimate end, in all the care we take about our employments, and all the comforts we take in our enjoyments. "As good stewards of the manifold grace of God," we must have this still in our eye, "that God in all things may be glorified through Jesus Christ." By this pious intention common actions must be sanctified, and done "after a godly sort." Our giving up ourselves to be to God a

people, is thus explained: it is "to be to him for a name, and for a praise, and for a glory."

2. To resign ourselves to God, "is to subject and submit ourselves to his power;" to the sanctifying power of his Spirit, the commanding power of his law, and the disposing power of his providence. Such as this is the subjection to which we must consent, and it has in it so much of privilege and advantage, as well as duty and service, that we have no reason to stumble at it.

(1.) We must submit ourselves to the sanctifying power of God's Spirit.—We must lay our souls as soft wax under this seal, to receive the impressions of it; as white paper under this pen, that it may write the law there. Whereas we have resisted the Holy Ghost, quenched his motions, and striven against him when he has been striving with us, we must now yield ourselves to be led and influenced by him, with full purpose of heart in every thing to follow his conduct, and comply with him. When Christ in his gospel breathes on us, saying, "Receive ye the Holy Ghost," my heart must answer, "Lord, I receive him," I bid him welcome into my heart; though he comes as a spirit of judgment, and a spirit of burning, as a refiner's fire, and fuller's soap, yet, "blessed is he that cometh in the name of the Lord." Let him come and mortify my lusts and corruptions, I do not desire that any of them should be spared; let them die, let them die by the sword of the Spirit, Agag himself not excepted, though he comes delicately. Let every thought within me, even the inward thought, "be brought into captivity to the obedience of Christ." Let the blessed Spirit do his whole work in me, and fulfil it with an almighty power.

(2.) We must submit ourselves to the commanding power of God's law. The law, as it is in the hand of the Mediator, is God's instrument of government; if I yield myself to him as a subject, I must in every thing be observant of, and obedient to, that law: and now I covenant to be so, in all my ways to walk according to that rule; all my thoughts and affections, all my words and actions, shall be under the direction of the divine law, and subject to its check and restraint. God's judgments will I lay before me, and have respect to all his commandments; by them I will always be ruled, overruled. "Let the word of the Lord come," as a good man once said, "and if I had six hundred necks, I would bow them all to the authority of it." Whatever appears to me to be my duty, by the grace of God, I will do it, how much soever it interfere with my secular interest; whatever appears to me to be a sin, by the grace of God I will avoid it, and refrain from it, how strong soever my corrupt inclination may be to it: "All that the Lord shall say to me, I will do, and will be obedient."

(3.) We must submit ourselves to the disposing power of God's providence. This must be the rule of our patience and passive obedience, as the former of our practice and active obedience. All my affairs relating to this life, I cheerfully submit to the divine disposal; let them be directed and determined as infinite wisdom sees fit, and I will acquiesce. Let the Lord save my soul, and then as to every thing else, "let him do with me and mine as seemeth good unto him." I will never find fault with any thing that God does. "Not as I will, but as thou wilt." I know I have no wisdom of my own; I am a fool, if I lean to my own understanding; and therefore I will have no will of my own: "Father, thy will be done." The health of my body, the success of my calling, the prosperity of my estate, the agreeableness of my family, the continuance of my comforts, and the issue of any particular concern my heart is upon, I leave in the hands of my heavenly Father, who knows what is good for me, better than I do for myself. If in any of these I be crossed, by the grace of God I will submit without murmuring or disputing. All is well that God does, and therefore welcome the will of God in every event; while he is mine and I am his, nothing shall come amiss to me.

(v.) We must resolve to abide by it as long as we live, and to live up to it. In our covenanting with God, there must be, not only a present consent—Lord, I do take thee for mine, I do give up myself to thee, to be thine,—but this must be ripened into a resolution for the future, " with purpose of heart to cleave unto the Lord." We must lay hold on wisdom, so as to retain it; and choose the way of truth, so as to stick to it. " The nail in the holy place must be well clenched, that it may be a nail in a sure place." Many a pang of good affections, and many a hopeful turn of good inclinations, comes to nothing for want of resolution. It is said of Rehoboam, that he " did evil, because he prepared not, or he fixed not, his heart;" so the word is in the margin, " to seek the Lord." The heart that is unfixed, is unprepared. Joshua took pains with the people, to bring them up to that noble resolution, " Nay, but we will serve the Lord." And we should not be content till we are also in like manner resolved, and firmly fixed, for God and duty, for Christ and heaven. This is the preparation of the gospel of peace, wherewith our feet must be shod.

Let us inquire what that resolution is, to which, in an entire dependence upon the grace of Christ, we should come up, in our covenanting with God.

1. We must come up to such a settled resolution as does not reserve a power of revocation for ourselves. The covenant is in itself a perpetual covenant, and as such we must consent to it; not as servants hire themselves, for a year, or to be free at a quarter's warning; not as apprentices bind themselves, for seven years, to be discharged at the expiring of that term; but it must be a covenant for life, a covenant for eternity, a covenant never to be forgotten; and in this even beyond the marriage-covenant, for that is made with this proviso, " Till death us do part:" but death itself must not part us and Christ. Our covenant must be made like that servant's, who loved his master, and would not go out free; our ears must be nailed to God's door-post, and

we must resolve to serve him for ever. A power of revocation reserved, is a disannulling of the covenant. It is no bargain, if it be not for a perpetuity, and if we consent not to put it past recal.

Let not those that are young, and under tutors and governors, think to discharge themselves of those obligations, when they come to be of age, and to put them off with their childish things; no, you must resolve to adhere to it, as Moses did, when you come to years. As children are not too little, so grown people are not too big, to be religious. You must resolve to live under the bonds of this covenant, when you come to live of yourselves, to be at your own disposal, and to launch out never so far into this world. Your greatest engagements in care and business, cannot disengage you from these. Whatever state of life you are called to, you must resolve to take your religion with you into it.

Let not those who are in the midst of their days think it possible or desirable to outlive the binding force of this covenant. If now we set out in the way we should go, it must be with a resolution, if we live to be old, how wise and honourable soever old age be, yet then we " will not depart from it;" as knowing that the hoary hairs are then only "a crown of glory, when they are found," as having been long before fixed, " in the way of righteousness."

2. We must come up to such a strong resolution as will not yield to the power of temptation from the enemy. When we engage ourselves for God, we engage ourselves against Satan, and must expect his utmost efforts to oppose us in our way, and to draw us out of it. Against these designs we must therefore arm ourselves, resolving to stand in the evil day, and having done all in God's name, to stand our ground, saying to all that which would either divert or deter us from prosecuting the choice we have made, as Ruth did to Naomi, when she was steadfastly resolved:—Entreat me not to leave Christ, or turn from following after him: for whither he goes, I

will follow him, though it be to banishment; where he lodges, I will lodge with him, though it be in a prison; for death itself shall never part us.

We must resolve, by God's grace, never to be so elevated or enamoured with the smiles of the world, as by them to be allured from the paths of serious godliness; for our religion will be both the safety and honour of a prosperous condition, and will sanctify and sweeten all the comforts of it to us.

And we must in like manner resolve never to be so discouraged and disheartened by the frowns of the world, as by the force of them to be robbed of our joy in God, or by the fear of them to be driven from our duty to God. We must come to Christ with a steady resolution to abide by him in all conditions: "Lord, I will follow thee whithersoever thou goest. Though I should die with thee, yet will I not deny thee. None of these things move me."

(VI.) We must rely upon the righteousness and strength of our Lord Jesus Christ in all this.—Christ is the Mediator of this peace, and the guarantee of it, the surety of this better covenant, that blessed days-man, who has laid his hand upon us both, who has so undertaken for God, that "in him all God's promises to us, are yea and amen;" and unless he undertakes for us too, how can our promises to God have any strength or stability in them? When, therefore, we enter into covenant with God, our eye must be to Christ, the Alpha and Omega of that covenant. When God had "sworn by himself, that unto him every knee should bow, and every tongue should swear," immediately it follows: "Surely shall one say," every one that vows and swears to God, "in the Lord have I righteousness and strength;" in the Lord Jesus is all my sufficiency for the doing of this well. In making and renewing our covenant with God, we must take instructions from that of David: "I will go in the strength of the Lord God; I will make mention of thy righteousness, even of thine only."

1. We must depend upon the strength of the Lord

for assistance, and for the working of all our works in us and for us. In that strength we must go, go forth, and go on, as those that know we can do nothing that is good of ourselves; our own hands are not sufficient for us, but we can "do all things through Christ strengthening us." Our work then goes on, and then only, when we are "strengthened with all might by his Spirit." This way we must look for spiritual strength, as Nehemiah did: "Now, therefore, O God, strengthen my hands." On this strength we must stay ourselves, in this strength we must engage ourselves, and put forth ourselves, and with it we must encourage ourselves.

We cannot keep this covenant when it is made, nor make it at all, but in the strength of Christ. Nature, corrupt nature, inclines to the world and the flesh, and cleaves to them; without the influences of special grace, we should never move towards God, much less resolve for him; we cannot do it well, but in Christ's strength, and in a dependence upon that. If, like Peter, we venture on our own sufficiency, and use those forms of speech which import a reliance on the divine grace, only as words of course, and do not by faith trust to that grace, and derive from it, we forfeit the aids of it, our covenant is rejected as presumptuous, and shall not avail us. Promises made in our own strength betray us, and do not help us, like the house built on the sand. We cannot keep this covenant, when it is made, but in the strength of Christ: for we stand no longer than he by his grace upholds us; we go no further than he by his grace, not only leads us, but carries us. His promises to us are our security, not ours to him; from his fulness, therefore, we must expect to receive grace for grace: for it is not in ourselves, nor is it to be had any where but in him.

We then that are principals in the bond, knowing ourselves insolvent, must put him in as surety for us. He is willing to stand, and without him our bond will not be taken. We are too well known to be trusted; for all men are liars, and the heart is deceitful above all things. Go to Christ, therefore, with that address—" Be surety for thy servant for good." " I am oppressed, undertake for me."

2. We must depend on the righteousness of Christ, making mention of that, even of that only, for acceptance with God in our covenanting with him: we have nothing in us to recommend us to God's favour, no righteousness of our own wherein to appear before him; we have by sin not only forfeited all the blessings of the covenant, but incapacitated ourselves for admission into it. By sacrifice therefore, by a sacrifice of atonement, sufficient to expiate our guilt, and satisfy the demands of injured justice, we must make a covenant with God; and there is none such but that one offering by which Christ has "perfected forever them which are sanctified;" that is, the blood of the covenant, which must be sprinkled upon our consciences, when we join ourselves to the Lord. That everlasting righteousness, which Messiah the prince hath brought in, must be the cover of our spiritual nakedness, our wedding-garment to adorn our nuptials, and the foundation on which we must build all our hopes, to find favour in the sight of God.

I shall not here draw up a form of covenanting with God, both because such may be found drawn up by far better hands than mine, as Mr. Baxter, Mr. Alleine, and others, and because a judicious Christian may, out of the foregoing heads, easily draw up one for himself.

II. After what manner we must renew our covenant with God, that we may therein please God, and experience the good effect of it on our souls.

1. We must do it intelligently.—Blind promises will produce lame performances, and can never be acceptable to the seeing God: ignorance is not the mother of this devotion. Satan indeed puts out men's eyes, and so brings them into bondage to him, and leads them blindfold; for he is a thief and a robber, that comes not in by the door, but climbeth up some other way: and therefore to him we must not open. But the grace of God takes the regular way of dealing

with reasonable creatures,—opening the understanding first, and then bowing the will: this is entering in by the door, as the shepherd of the sheep does. In this method, therefore, we must see that the work be done. We must first acquaint ourselves with the tenor of the covenant, and then consent to the terms of it. Moses read the book of the covenant in the audience of the people, and then sprinkled upon them the blood of the covenant. And we must take the same method: first peruse the articles, and then sign them. That faith which is without knowledge, is not the faith of God's elect.

2. We must do it considerately. We need not take time to consider whether we should do it or not; the matter is too plain to bear that debate; but we must seriously consider what we do, when we go about it. Let it be done with a solemn pause, such as Moses put Israel upon, when he said, " Ye stand this day all of you before the Lord your God, that thou shouldest enter into covenant with the Lord thy God, and into his oath." Consider how weighty the transaction is; that it may be managed with due seriousness: and of what consequence it is that it be done well; for it is to be hoped, if it be once well done, it is done for ever. We must sit down and count the cost, consider the restraints this covenant will put upon the flesh, the loss and expense we may sustain by our adherence to it, the hazards we run, and the difficulties we must reckon upon, if we will be faithful unto death—and in the view of these, consent to the covenant, that hereafter, when tribulation and persecution arise because of the word, we may not say, This was what we did not think of. Do it deliberately therefore, and then it will not be easily undone. The rule in vowing is, " Be not rash with thy mouth, neither let thy heart be hasty to utter any thing before God." It is the character of the virtuous woman, that " she considers a field and buys it." And it hath been thought a dictate of prudence, though it seem a paradox,—" Take time, and you will have done the sooner." Many that, without

consideration, have put on a profession, when the wind hath turned, have in like manner, without consideration, thrown it off again. Light come, light go. Those, therefore, that herein would prove themselves honest, must prove themselves wise.

3. We must do it humbly.—When we come to covenant with God, we must remember what we are, and who he is with whom we have to do, that the familiarity to which we are graciously admitted, may not beget a contempt of God, or a conceit of ourselves; but rather, the more God is pleased to exalt us, and condescend to us, the more we must honour him, and abase ourselves. "Abraham fell on his face," in a deep sense of his own unworthiness, when God said, "I will make my covenant between me and thee," and began to talk with him concerning it. And afterwards, when he was admitted into an intimate communion with God, pursuant to that covenant, he drew near as one that knew his distance, expressing himself with wonder at the favour done him: "Behold, now I have taken upon me to speak unto the Lord, who am but dust and ashes." When the covenant of royalty was confirmed to David, and " God regarded him according to the estate of a man of high degree," he sits down as one astonished at the honour conferred upon him, and humbly expresses himself thus—"Who am I, O Lord God, and what is mine house, that thou hast brought me hitherto?" Thus must we cast ourselves down at the footstool of God's throne, if we would be taken up into the embraces of his love. He that humbles himself, shall be exalted.

4. We must do it cheerfully: for here, in a special manner God loves a cheerful giver, and is pleased with that which is done, not of constraint, but willingly. In our covenanting with God, we must not be actuated by a spirit of fear, but by a spirit of adoption, a spirit of power and love, and a sound mind. We must join ourselves to the Lord, not only because it is our duty, and that which we are bound to, but because it is our interest, and that by which

we shall be unspeakably gainers,—not with reluctance and regret, and with a half consent extorted from us; but with an entire satisfaction, and the full consent of a free spirit. Let it be a pleasure to us to think of our interest in God as ours, and our engagement to him as his; a pleasure to us to think of the bonds of the covenant, as well as of the blessings of the covenant. Much of our communion with God (which is so much the delight of all that are sanctified) is kept up by the frequent recognition of our covenant with him, which we should make as those that like their choice too well to change; and as the men of Judah did, when "they sware unto the Lord with a loud voice, and with shouting and with trumpets, and all Judah rejoiced at the oath; for they had sworn with all their heart, and sought him with their whole desire." Christ's soldiers must be volunteers, not pressed men; and we must repeat our consent to him with such joy and triumph as appears in that of the spouse, "This is my beloved, and this is my friend."

5. *We must do it in sincerity.*—This is the chief thing required in every thing wherein we have to do with God: "Behold, he desires truth in the inward parts." When God took Abraham into covenant with himself, this was the charge he gave him, "Walk before me and be thou perfect," that is, upright; for uprightness is our gospel perfection. Writing the covenant, and subscribing it, signing and sealing it, may be proper expressions of seriousness and resolution in the transaction, and of use to us in the review; but, if herein we "lie unto God with our mouth, and flatter him with our tongue," as Israel did, though we may put a cheat upon ourselves and others, yet we cannot impose upon him: "Be not deceived, God is not mocked." If we only give the hand unto the Lord, and do not give our hearts to him, whatever our pretensions, professions, and present pangs of devotion may be, we are but as sounding brass, and a tinkling cymbal. What will it avail us to say, we covenant with God, if we still keep our league with

the world and the flesh, and have a secret antipathy to serious godliness? Dissembled piety is no disguise before God, but is hated as double iniquity. It is certain thou hast no part or lot in the matter, whatever thou mayest claim, if thy heart be not right in the sight of God. I know no religion but sincerity; our vows to God are nothing, if they be not bonds upon the soul.

CHAPTER VI.

HELPS FOR MEDITATION AND PRAYER IN OUR PREPARATION FOR THIS ORDINANCE.

I. Of meditation, opened in general. It is thought engaged, and thought inflamed. Particularly meditate, (I.) On the sinfulness and misery of man's fallen state. (II.) The glory of God's attributes in man's redemption. (III.) The person of the Redeemer and his undertakings. (IV.) His sufferings. (V.) His present glories. (VI.) The riches of the new covenant. (VII.) The communion of saints, and, (VIII.) The happiness of heaven. All these enlarged upon. II. Of prayer; why we must pray before the sacrament, and what we must pray for; four things to be prayed for.

MEDITATION and prayer are the daily exercise and delight of a devout and pious soul. In meditation we converse with ourselves; in prayer we converse with God. And what converse can we desire more agreeable and more advantageous? They who are frequent and serious in these holy duties at other times, will find them the easier and the sweeter on this occasion; the friends we are much with, we are most free with. But if at other times, we be not so close and constant to them as we should be, we have the more need to take pains with our own hearts, that we may effectually engage them in these services, when we approach the ordinance of the Lord's Supper.

Enter into thy closet, therefore, and shut the door of that against diversions from without: be not shy of being alone. The power of godliness withers and declines, if secret devotion be either neglected, or negligently performed. Enter into thy heart also, and do what thou canst to shut the door of that against distraction from within. Compose thyself for the business, and summon all that is within thee to attend on it: separate thyself from the world, and thoughts of it; leave all its cares at the bottom of the hill, as Abraham did his servants, when he was going up into the mount to worship God, and then set thyself about thy work: gird up thy loins, and trim thy lamp. Up and be doing, and the Lord be with thee.

I. We must set ourselves to meditate on that which is most proper for the confirming of our faith, and the kindling of pious and devout affections in us. Good thoughts should be often in our minds, and welcome there; so should our souls often breathe towards God in pious ejaculations that are short and sudden. But as good prayers, so good thoughts must sometimes be set and solemn: morning and evening they must be so, on the Lord's day also, and before the Lord's Supper.

Meditation is thought engaged, and thought inflamed.

It is thought engaged.—In it the heart fastens upon, and fixes to a select and certain subject with an endeavour to dwell and enlarge upon it; not matters of doubtful disputation, or small concern, but those things that are of greatest certainty and moment. And since few of the ordinary sort of Christians can be supposed to have such a treasury of knowledge, such a fruitfulness of invention, and so great a compass and readiness of thought, as to be able to discourse with themselves, for any time, upon any one subject so closely, methodically, and pertinently as one would wish, it may be advisable, either to fasten upon some portion of Scripture, and to read that over and over, with a closeness of observation and application, or to recollect some profitable sermon lately heard, and think that over; or to make use of some books of pious meditations or practical discourses, (of which, blessed be God, we have great plenty and variety,) and not only read them, but descant and enlarge upon them in our minds, still giving liberty to our own thoughts to expatiate, as they are able; but, borrowing help from what we read, to reduce them when they wander, refresh them when they tire, and to furnish them with matter when they are barren. In the choice of helps for this work, wisdom and experience are profitable to direct, and no rule can be given to fit all capacities and all cases; the end may be attained by different methods.

It is thought inflamed.—To meditate, is not only to think seriously of divine things, but to think of them with concern and suitable affection. "While we are thus musing, the fire must burn." When the heart meditates terror, the terrors of the Lord, it must be with a holy fear; when we contemplate the beauty of the Lord, his bounty, and his benignity, which is better than life, we must do it with a holy complacency, solacing ourselves in the Lord our God. The design of meditation is to improve our knowledge, and to affect ourselves with those things with which we have acquainted ourselves, that those impressions of them upon our souls may be deep and durable, and that, by "beholding the glory of the Lord, we may be changed into the same image."

Serious meditation before a sacrament will be of great use to us, to make those things familiar to us, with which in that ordinance we are to be conversant: that good thoughts may not be to seek when we are there, it is our wisdom to prepare them, and lay them ready before hand. Frequent acts confirm a habit, and pious dispositions are greatly helped by pious meditations. Christian graces will be the better exercised in the ordinance when they are thus trained and disciplined, and drawn out in our preparation for it.

For our assistance herein, I shall mention some few of those things which may most properly be pitched upon for the subject of our meditations before a sacrament: I say, before a sacrament; because though this be calculated here for the sacrament of the Lord's Supper, yet it may equally serve us in our preparations for the other sacrament, both that we may profit by the public administration of it, and especially that we may, in an acceptable manner, present our children to it; for which service we have as much need carefully to prepare ourselves as for this. As we must in faith join ourselves to the Lord, so we must in faith dedicate our children to him.

That our hearts, then, may be raised and quickened, and prepared for communion with Christ at his table,

(1.) Let us set ourselves to think of the sinfulness and misery of man's fallen state. That we may be taught to value our recovery and restoration by the grace of the second Adam, let us take a full and distinct view of our ruin by the sin of the first Adam. Come and see what desolations it has made upon the earth, and how it has turned the world into a wilderness. "How is the gold become dim, and the most fine gold changed!" What wretched work did sin make! What a black and horrid train of fatal consequences attended its entrance into the world!

Come, my soul, and see how the nature of man is corrupted and vitiated, and lamentably degenerated from its primitive purity and rectitude;—God's image defaced and lost, and Satan's image stamped instead of it;—the understanding blind, and unapt to admit the rays of the divine light: the will stubborn, and unapt to comply with the dictates of the divine law; the affections carnal, and unapt to receive the impressions of the divine love. Come, my soul, and lament the change, for thou thyself feelest from it, and sharest in the sad effects of it; for a nature thus tainted, thus depraved, I brought into the world with me, and carry about with me to this day sad remainders of its corruption. It was a nature by creation, little lower than that of angels, but become by sin, much baser than that of brutes. It was like the Nazarites, "purer than snow, whiter than milk, more ruddy than the rubies, and its polishing was of sapphires; but now its visage is blacker than a coal." Never was beauty so deformed, never was strength so weakened, never was a healthful constitution so spoiled, never was honour so laid in the dust. How is the faithful city become a harlot! Man's nature was planted a choice vine, wholly a right seed; but, alas, it is become "the degenerate plant of a strange vine." I find in myself by sad experience, I am naturally prone to that which is evil, and backward to that which is good. Foolishness is daily breaking out in my life, and by that I perceive it is bound up in my heart: for these things I blush and am ashamed; for these things I tremble and am afraid; "for these things I weep, mine eye, mine eye runs down with tears."

Come, my soul, and see how miserable fallen man is: see him excluded from God's favour, expelled the garden of the Lord, and forbidden to meddle with the tree of life; see how odious he is become to God's holiness, and obnoxious to his justice, and by nature a child of wrath. See how calamitous the state of human life is; with what troops of diseases, disasters, and deaths, in the most horrid and frightful shapes, man is compassed about. Lord, "how are they increased that trouble him!"

See him attacked on every side by the malignant powers of darkness that seek to destroy; see him sentenced for sin to utter darkness, to the devouring fire, to the everlasting burning. "How art thou fallen, O Lucifer, son of the morning!" O what a gulf of misery is man sunk into by sin! Separated from all good to all evil; and his condition in himself helpless and hopeless. A deplorable case! And it is my case by nature: I am of this guilty, exposed, condemned race; undone, undone for ever; as miserable as the curse of heaven, and the flames of hell can make me, if infinite mercy do not interpose. And shall not this affect me? Shall not this afflict me? Shall not these thoughts beget in me a hatred of sin, that evil, that only evil? Shall I ever be reconciled to that which has done so much mischief? Shall I not be quickened hereby to flee to Christ, in whom alone help and salvation is to be had? Is this thy condition, O my soul, thine by nature? And is there a door of hope opened thee by grace? "Up, then, get thee out of this Sodom; escape for thy life, look not behind thee, stay not in all the plain, escape to the mountain," the mountain of holiness, lest thou be consumed.

(II.) Let us set ourselves to think of "the glory of the divine attributes, shining forth in the work of our redemption and salvation." Here is a bright and noble subject, the contemplation and wonder of angels and blessed spirits above, and in the admiring view of which, eternity itself will be short enough to be spent.

Come, then, O my soul, come and think of the kindness and love of God our Saviour, his good-will to man, which designed our redemption, the spring and first wheel of that work of wonder. Herein is love. Though God was happy from eternity before man had a being, and would have been happy to eternity, if man had never been, or had been miserable; though man's nature was mean and despicable; though his crimes were heinous and detestable; though by his disobedience he had forfeited the protection of a prince; though by his ingratitude he had forfeited the kindness of a friend; and though by his perfidiousness he had forfeited the benefits of a covenant; yet the tender mercies of our God moved for his relief. Come and see a world of apostate angels passed by, and left to perish, no Redeemer, no Saviour provided for them; but fallen men pitied and helped, though angels had been more honourable, and would have been more serviceable.

Come and think of God's patience and forbearance exercised towards man: "the long-suffering of our Lord is salvation." Think how much he bears, and how long, with the world, with me, though most provoking. This patience left room for the salvation, and gives hopes of it. "If the Lord had been pleased to kill us," he would have done it before now.

Come, and think especially of the wisdom of God which is so gloriously displayed in the contrivance of the work of our redemption. Here is the wisdom of God " in a mystery, even the hidden wisdom which God ordained before the world for our glory." Think of the measures God has taken, the means he has devised, that the banished might not for ever be expelled from him. Think with wonder how all the divine attributes are by the method pitched upon, secured from damage and reproach, so that one is not glorified by the diminution of the lustre of another. When sin had brought things to that strait, that one would think either God's justice, truth, and holiness, must be eclipsed or clouded, or man's happiness must be for ever lost; infinite wisdom finds out an expedient for the securing both of God's honour, and of man's happiness. It is now no disparagement at all to God's justice to pardon sin, nor to his holiness to be reconciled to sinners; for by the death of Christ justice is satisfied, and by the Spirit of Christ sinners are sanctified. " Mercy and truth here meet together, behold righteousness and peace kiss each other." Be astonished, O heavens, at this, and wonder, O earth. And thou, my soul, that owest all thy joys, and all thy hopes to this contrivance, despairing to find the bottom of this unfathomable fountain of life, sit down at the brink and adore the depth! " O the depth of the wisdom and knowledge of God!"

(III.) Let us set ourselves to think of the "person of the Redeemer, and his glorious undertaking of the work of our salvation." Come, my soul, and think of Christ, who thought of thee: think of him as the eternal Son of God, " the brightness of his Father's glory, and the express image of his person," who lay in his bosom from all eternity, and had an infinite joy and glory with him before the worlds were, and in whom dwells all the fulness of the Godhead; the eternal wisdom, the eternal Word, that has life in himself, and is one with the Father, and who thought it no robbery to be equal with God. He is thy Lord, O my soul, and worship thou him.

Think of him as the Former of all things, without whom was not any thing made that was made. "Thrones and dominions, principalities and powers, all things were created by him, and for him, and he is before all things, and by him all things consist." Let this engage my veneration for him, let this encourage my faith, and hope in him. If I have my being from him, I must consecrate my being to him, and may expect my bliss in him.

Think of him as Emanuel, the Word incarnate, "God manifested in the flesh," clothed with our nature, taking part of flesh and blood, that for us in our nature he might satisfy the justice of God whom we had offended, and break the power of Satan, by whom we were enslaved. Come, my soul, and with an eye of faith, behold the beauties, the transcendent, unparalleled beauties, of the Redeemer. See him, "white and ruddy, fairer than the children of men," perfectly pure and spotless, wise and holy, kind and good; who has the infinite mercies of a God, and withal, the experimental compassions of a man that has been "touched with the feeling of our infirmities." See him by faith, as John saw him in a vision. See him and admire him, as one that in all things has the pre-eminence; none like him, nor any to be compared with him.

Think of him as the undertaker of our redemption, the redemption of the soul, which was so precious, that otherwise it must have ceased for ever. When the sealed book of God's counsels concerning man's redemption was produced, "none in heaven or earth was found worthy to open that book, or to look thereon." When sacrifice and offering for sin would not do, and the blood of bulls and of goats had been tried in vain, and found ineffectual, then said he, "Lo, I come; this ruin shall be under my hands:" alluding to Isa. iii. 6. Come, my soul, and see help laid upon one that is mighty; one chosen out of the people, and every way qualified for the undertaking, able to do the Redeemer's work, and fit to wear the Redeemer's crown. See how willingly he offered himself to the service, how cheerfully he obliged himself to go through with it, and engaged his heart to approach unto God as our Advocate. It is "the voice of thy beloved, O my soul! behold, he cometh leaping upon the mountains, skipping upon the hills," making nothing of the difficulties that lay in his way. "Behold, thy king cometh, thy bridegroom cometh: go forth, my soul, go forth to meet him with thy joyful hosannas, and bid him welcome. Blessed is he that cometh in the name of the Lord."

(IV.) Let us set ourselves to think of the "cross of our Lord Jesus Christ, the dishonours done to him, and the honours done to us by it."—Here is a wide field for our meditations to expatiate in, nor can we determine to know any thing before a sacrament more proper and profitable than Jesus Christ, and him crucified; lifted up from the earth, and drawing all men unto him, as the attractive loadstone of their hearts, and the common centre of their unity. Come then, and behold the man; represent to thyself, O my soul, not to thy fancy, but to thy faith, "the Lamb of God taking away the sins of the world by the sacrifice of himself."

Come and look over the particulars of Christ's sufferings, all the humiliations and mortifications of his life, but especially the pains, agonies, and ignominies of his death. Review the story; thou wilt still find something in it surprising and very affecting; take notice of all the circumstances of his passion, and say, "Never was any sorrow like unto his sorrow." Take notice especially of the disgrace and reproach done him in his sufferings, the shame he was industriously loaded with. This contributed greatly to the satisfaction made by his sufferings. God hath been injured in his glory by sin, and no other way could he be injured; he, therefore, who undertook to make reparation for that injury, not only denied himself in, and divested himself of, the honours due to an incarnate Deity, but, though most innocent and most excellent, voluntarily submitted to the utmost disgraces that could be done to the worst of criminals; thus he "restored that which he took not away." See him, my soul, see him enduring the cross, and despising the shame.

Come and see the purchases of the cross. The blood there shed is the ransom with which we are redeemed from hell; the price with which heaven is bought for us, see it a price of inestimable value: "The topaz of Ethiopia cannot equal it, nor shall it be valued with the gold of Ophir, with the precious onyx, or the sapphire." No, my soul, thou wast not redeemed with such corruptible things. The pardon of sin, the favour of God, the graces of the Spirit, the blessings of the covenant, and eternal life, could not be purchased with silver and gold, but are dearly bought and paid for with the precious blood of the Son of God. All the praise be to the glorious purchaser.

Come and see the victories of the cross; see the Lord Jesus even then a conqueror, when he seemed a captive; then spoiling principalities and powers, when he seemed totally defeated and routed by them. See Christ upon the cross breaking the serpent's head, disarming Satan, triumphing over death and the grave, leading captivity captive, and going forth in that chariot of war, conquering and to conquer.

Think, my soul, think what thou owest to the dying of the Lord Jesus; the privileges of thy way, and the glories of thy home; all thou hast, all thou hopest for that is valuable, they are all precious fruits gathered from this tree of life. Christ's wounds are thy healing, his agonies thy repose, his conflicts thy conquests, his groans thy songs, his pains thine ease, his shame thy glory, his death thy life, his sufferings thy salvation.

(v.) Let us set ourselves to think of the present glories of the exalted Redeemer.—When we meditate on the cross he bore, we must not forget the crown he wears within the veil. Think, my soul, think where he is at the right hand of the Father, far above all principalities and powers, and every name that is named; he is set down upon the throne of the Majesty in the highest heavens. Having obtained eternal redemption for us, he is "entered with his own blood into the holy place." Think how he is attended there with an innumerable company of angels, that continually surround the throne of God and of the Lamb; think of the songs there sung to his praise, the crowns there cast at his feet, and the name he hath there above every name. Think especially what he is doing there: he always appears in the presence of God as the great High Priest of our profession, to intercede for all those that come to God by him; and he attends continually to this very thing: there he is preparing a place for all his followers, and thence he will shortly come to receive them to himself, to behold his glory, and to share in it. Dwell on these thoughts, O my soul, and say as they did who saw his glory in his transfiguration: It is good to be here; here let us make tabernacles. Let these thoughts kindle in thee an earnest desire (shall I call it a holy curiosity?) to see him as he is, face to face. His advancement is thine advantage, as the forerunner he is for me entered. Let the contemplation of the joy he is entered into, and the power he is there girded with, have such an influence upon me, that by faith I may be raised up likewise, and "made to sit together with him in heavenly places."

(VI.) Let us set ourselves to think of the unsearchable riches of the new covenant, made with us in Jesus Christ, and sealed to us in the sacraments.—Peruse this covenant in the several dispensations of it, from the dawning of its day in the first promise, to that noon-day light, which life and immortality are brought to by the gospel. Read over the several articles of it, and see how well ordered it is in all things, so well that it could not be better. Review its promises, which are precious and many, very many, very precious, and sure to all the seed. Search into the hidden wealth that is treasured up in them; dig into these mines; content not thyself with a transient view of these fountains of living water, but bring thy bucket, and draw with joy out of these wells of salvation. "Go, walk about this Zion, this city of God, tell the towers, mark well the bulwarks, consider the palaces, and say, This God, who is our God in covenant, is ours for ever and ever; he will be our guide even unto death."

Stir up thyself, therefore, O my soul, to meditate on the privileges of a justified state; the liberties and immunities, the dignities and advantages, that are conveyed by the charter of pardon. O the blessedness of the man whose iniquities are forgiven! See him secured from the arrests of the law, the curse of God, the evil of affliction, the sting of death, and the damnation of hell. Read with pleasure the triumphs of blessed Paul: (Rom. viii. 33, &c.) Happy thou art, my soul, and all is well with thee, or shall be shortly, if thy sins be pardoned.

Meditate on the honours and comforts of a state of grace. If now I am a child of God, adopted and regenerated, and have received the Spirit of adoption, I have liberty of access to the throne of grace, I have a sanctified use of my creature-comforts, my fellowship is with the Father, and with his Son Jesus Christ; "all is mine, whether Paul, or Apollos, or Cephas, or the world, or life, or death, or things present, or things to come, all are mine." I have meat to eat that the world knows not of, joy that a stranger doth not intermeddle with. Let thoughts of these great privileges work in thee, O my soul, a holy disdain of the pleasures of sense, and the profits of the world; whenever they come in competition with the gains of godliness, and the delights of spiritual life, offer those to them that know no better.

(VII.) Let us set ourselves to think of the communion of saints.—This contributes something to our comfort in communion with Christ, that through him we have fellowship one with another: "So that we, being many, are one bread and one body; for Christ died to gather together in one the children of God that were scattered abroad;" that all might be one in him in whom we all meet, as many members in one head, so making one body; many branches in one root, so making one vine; and many stones on one foundation, so making ône building.

Enlarge thy thoughts, then, O my soul, and let it be a pleasure to thee to think of the relation thou standest in to the whole family, both in heaven and earth, which is named of Jesus Christ; to think that thou art come, in faith, hope, and love, even to the "innumerable company of angels, and to the spirits of just men made perfect." Even these are thy brethren and fellow-servants. Rejoice in thine alliance to them, in their affection to thee, and in the prospect thou hast of being with them shortly, of being with them eternally. Here we sit down with a little handful of weak and imperfect saints, and those mixed with pretenders; but we hope shortly to have a place and a name in the general assembly of the first-born, and to " sit down with Abraham, Isaac, and Jacob, in the kingdom of our Father," with all the saints, and none but saints, and saints made perfect, and so to be together for ever with the Lord.

Please thyself also, O my soul, with thinking of the spiritual communion thou hast in the acts of Christian piety, and in the exercise of Christian charity, with "all that in every place on this earth call on the name of Jesus Christ our Lord, both theirs and ours." Some good Christians there are, that fall within the reach of our personal communion, to whom we give the right hand of fellowship. Others, within the line of our acquantance and correspondence; and many more whom we know not, nor have ever heard of, never saw, nor are ever likely to see in this world; but all these are our "companions in the kingdom and patience of Jesus Christ." They and we are guided by the same rule, animated by the same spirit, conformed to the same image, interested in the same promises, and joined to the same great body; they and we meet daily at the same throne of grace, under the conduct of the same Spirit of adoption, which teaches us all to cry, Abba, Father; and they and we hope to meet shortly at the same throne of glory, under the conduct of the same Jesus, who will gather his elect from the four winds, and present them all together unto the Father. Christ hath prayed, that "all that believe on him may be one;" and therefore we are sure they are so, for the Father heard him always. Let this subject yield us some delightful thoughts here in a scattered world, and a divided church.

(VIII.) Let us set ourselves to think of the happiness of heaven.—A pleasant theme this is, very improvable, and pertinent enough to an ordinance which has so much of heaven in it: if indeed we have heaven in our eye, as our home and rest, and our conversation there, we cannot but have it much upon our hearts. Have we good hope through grace, of being shortly with Christ in the heavenly paradise, where there is fulness of joy and pleasures for evermore,—where we shall see God's glory, and enjoy his love immediately, to our complete and eternal satisfaction? Do we expect that yet a little while, and the veil shall be rent, the shadows of the evening shall be done away, and we shall see as we are seen, and know as we are known? Are we in prospect of a crown of glory that fades not away, an incorruptible, undefiled inheritance?

Raise thy thoughts, then, O my soul, to the joyful contemplation of the glory to be revealed. Arise, then, and survey this land of promise, as Abraham. Go with Moses to the top of Pisgah, and take a view of it by faith. Get a Scripture map of that Canaan, and study it well. Think, my soul, what they see in that world, who always behold the face of the Father, and in it see all truth and brightness, and the perfection of beauty. Think what they have there, who eat of the tree of life, and the hidden manna; whose faculties are enlarged, to take in the full communications of divine love and grace, and who have God himself with them as their God. Think what they are doing there who dwell in God's house, and are still praising him, and rest not day nor night from doing it. Think of the good company that is there, thousands of thousands of blessed angels, and holy souls, with whom we shall have an intimate and undisturbed converse in perfect light and love.

Compare the present state thou art in, my soul, with that thou hopest for; and let it be a pleasure to thee to think, that whatever is here, thy grief and burden shall be there removed and done away for ever. Satan's temptations shall there no more assault thee; thine own corruptions shall there no more ensnare thee; the guilt of sin, and doubts about thy spiritual state, shall there no more terrify and perplex thee; no pain, nor sickness, nor sorrow, shall be an alloy to the enjoyments of that world, as they are to those of this world. All tears shall there be wiped away, even those for sin.

On the other side, whatever is here thy delight and pleasure, shall there be perfected. The knowledge of God, joy in him, and communion with him, are here, as it were, thy running banquets; there, they shall be thy continual feast. The work of grace begun in thee, is that which reconciles thee to thyself, and gives thee some pleasure now in thy reflections upon thyself. This work shall be there completed, and the finishing strokes given to it, by the same skilful and happy hand that began it.

Come now, my soul, and "neglect not the gift that is in thee, but meditate upon these things; give thyself wholly to them." " Be thou in them," as in thy business, as in thine element. Think of the things of the invisible and unchangeable world, till thou findest thyself so affected with them, as even to forget the things that are here below, that are here behind, and look upon them with a holy negligence, that thou mayest, with greater diligence, reach towards "the things that are before, and press towards the mark for the prize of the high calling."

II. We must not only meditate, but we must pray and cry earnestly to God for assistance and acceptance in what we do. When the apostle had reckoned up all the parts of the Christian's armour, he concludes with this, " Praying always." Prayer must gird on the whole armour of God; for, without prayer, all our endeavours are vain and ineffectual. Therefore, in our preparations for the Lord's Supper, time must be spent, and pains taken in prayer, for two reasons:—

1. Because this is a proper means of quickening ourselves, and stirring up our graces.—One duty of religion is of use to dispose and fit us for another; and the most solemn services ought to be approached gradually, and through the outer courts. In prayer, the soul ascends to God, and converses with him; and thereby the mind is prepared to receive the visits of his grace, and habituated to holy exercises. Even the blessed Jesus prepared himself for the offering up of the great sacrifice by prayer, a long prayer in the house, and strong cryings with tears in the garden. Three times was Christ spoken to, while he was here on earth, by voices from heaven, and they all three found him praying.—That at his baptism: "Jesus being baptized, and praying, the heaven was opened."—That at his transfiguration: "As he prayed, the fashion of his countenance was altered."—And that a little before his passion, when he was praying, "Father, glorify thy name," the voice came from heaven, "I have glorified it," &c. Saul of Tarsus prays, and then sees a vision; and afterwards, Cornelius had his vision when he was at prayer, and Peter his. All which instances, and many the like, suggest to us, that communion with God in prayer prepares and disposes the mind for communion with him in other duties.

2. Because this is the appointed way for fetching in that mercy and grace which God has promised, and which we stand in need of.—In God is our help, and from him is our fruit found; and he has promised to help us and to give us "a new heart, to put his Spirit within us, and to cause us to walk in his statutes." "I will yet for all this be inquired of by the house of Israel to do it for them." How can we expect the presence of God with us, if we do not invite him by prayer? Or the power of God upon us, if we do not by prayer derive it from him? The

greatest blessings are promised to the prayer of faith, but God will not give, if we will not ask: why should he?

But what must we pray for, when we draw near to God in this solemn ordinance? Solomon tells us, that both the " preparations of the heart in man, and the answer of the tongue is from the Lord." To him, therefore, we must apply ourselves for both. The whole word of God is of use to direct us in these prayers, and in it the blessed Spirit " helpeth our infirmities, forasmuch as we know not what to pray for," in this or in any other case, as we ought.

1. We must pray that we may be prepared for this solemnity before it comes. Whatever is necessary to qualify us for communion with God in it, is spoken of in Scripture as God's gift; and whatever is the matter of God's promise, must be the matter of our prayers; for promises are given, not only to be the ground of our hope, but also to be the guide of our desire in prayer." Is knowledge necessary? " Out of his mouth cometh knowledge and understanding," and at wisdom's gates we must wait for wisdom's gifts, rejoicing herein " that the Son of God is come, and hath given us an understanding." Is faith necessary? That is not " of ourselves, it is the gift of God." Him, therefore, we must attend, who is both the author and the finisher of our faith. To him we must pray, Lord, increase our faith: Lord, perfect what is lacking in it: Lord, fulfil the work of faith with power. Is love necessary? It is the " Holy Ghost that sheds abroad that love in our hearts, and circumcises our hearts to love the Lord our God." To that heavenly fire we must therefore go for this holy spark, and pray for the breath of the Almighty to blow it up into a flame. Is repentance necessary? It is God that gives repentance, that takes away the stony heart and gives a heart of flesh; and we must beg of him to work that blessed change in us. " Behold the fire and the wood," the ordinance instituted, and all needful provision made for our sacrifice; " but where is the lamb for a burnt-offering?" Where is

the heart to be offered up to God? If God did not provide himself a lamb, the solemnity would fail. To him, therefore, we must go to buy such things as we have need of against the feast, that is, to beg them; for we buy without money and without price: and such buyers shall not be driven out of God's temple, nor slighted there, however they are looked on in men's markets.

2. Pray that our hearts may be enlarged in the duty. It is the gracious promise of God, that he will open rivers in the wilderness, and streams in the desert; and the joint experience of all the saints, that they looked unto him and were lightened: such out-goings of soul therefore towards God, as may receive the incomes of divine strength and comfort, we should earnestly desire and pray for. Pray that God would grace his own institutions with such manifest tokens of his presence as those two disciples had, who reasoned thus for their own conviction, that they had been with Jesus, " Did not our hearts burn within us?" Pray that, by the grace of God, the business of the ordinance may be faithfully done; the work of the day, the sacrament day, in its day, according as the duty of the day requires, (Ezra iii. 4.) Pray that the ends of the ordinance may be sincerely aimed at and happily attained, and the great intention of the institution of it answered; that you may not receive the grace of God therein in vain. O that my heart may be engaged to approach unto God!— so engaged as that nothing may prevail to disengage it. Come, blessed Spirit, and breathe upon these dry bones! Move upon the waters of the ordinances, and produce a new creation! " Awake, O north wind; and come, thou south; and blow upon my garden, that the spices thereof may flow forth. And then let my beloved come into his garden," (his it is, and then it will be fit to be called his,) " and eat his pleasant fruits."

3. Pray that we may be favourably accepted of God, both in the preparation and in the performance. In vain do we worship, if God do not accept us. The

applause of men is but a poor reward, (such as the hypocrites were content with, and put off with,) if we come short of the favour of God. Herein therefore we should labour, this we should be ambitious of as our highest honour, the top of our preferment, "that whether present or absent we may be accepted of the Lord." About this, therefore, we should be very solicitous in our inquiries: "Wherewithal shall I come before the Lord," so as to please him? For this we should be very importunate in our prayers: "O that I knew where I might find him!" O that I might be met at the table of the Lord with a blessing, and not with a breach! O that God would smile upon me there, and bid me welcome! O that the beloved of my soul would show me some token for good there, and say unto me, I am thy salvation! "Son, daughter, be of good cheer; thy sins are forgiven thee. Let him kiss me with the kisses of his mouth, for his love is better than wine." O that it might be a communion indeed between Christ and my soul! That which is in vogue with the most of men is, "Who will show us any good?" But when I am admitted to touch the top of the golden sceptre, this is my petition, this is my request: Lord, lift up the light of thy countenance upon me; and that shall put true gladness into my heart, greater than the joy of harvest.

4. Pray that what is amiss may be pardoned in the blood of Christ. This prayer good Hezekiah has put into our mouths, (God put it into our hearts!) "The good Lord pardon every one that prepareth his heart in sincerity to seek the Lord God of his fathers, "and aims honestly," though he be not cleansed according to the purification of the sanctuary." We cannot but be conscious to ourselves, that in many things we come short of our duty, and wander from it. The rule is strict, it is fit it should be so; and yet no particular rule more strict than that general and fundamental law of God's kingdom, "Thou shalt love the Lord thy God with all thy heart, and soul, and mind, and might." But our own hearts know,

and God, who is greater than our hearts, and knows all things, knows, that we do not come up to the rule, nor "continue in all things that are written in the book of the law to do them." By our deficiencies we become obnoxious to the curse, and should perish by it if we were under the law; but we are encouraged by a penitent believing prayer to sue out our pardon, having an advocate with the Father.

Would we take with us words in these prayers? David's psalms and St. Paul's epistles will furnish us with great variety of acceptable words; words which the Holy Ghost teaches; and other helps of devotion, of which, thanks be to God, we have plenty, may be used to much advantage: and if in these prayers we stir up ourselves to take hold on God, our experience shall be added to that of thousands, that Jacob's God never said to Jacob's seed, "Seek ye me in vain."

CHAPTER VII.

DIRECTIONS IN WHAT FRAME OF SPIRIT WE SHOULD COME TO, AND ATTEND UPON THIS ORDINANCE.

With a fixedness of thought. II. With an easiness and calmness of affection. III. With a holy awe and reverence of the Divine Majesty. IV. With a holy jealousy over ourselves, and an humble sense of our own unworthiness, suspecting ourselves, and abasing ourselves. V. With a gracious confidence, as children to a father. VI. With earnest desires towards God. VII. With raised expectations. VIII. With rejoicing and thanksgiving: two things matter of joy. IX. In charity with all men, and a sincere affection to all good Christians, bearing ill-will to none, and good-will to all.

To make up the wedding garment, which is proper for this wedding feast, it is requisite, not only that we have an habitual temper of mind agreeable to the gospel, but that we have such an actual disposition of spirit as is consonant to the nature and intentions of the ordinance. It is an excellent rule in the Scripture directory for religious worship, " Keep thy foot when thou goest to the house of God;" that is, " Keep thy heart with all diligence." Look well to the motions of thy soul, and observe the steps it takes. When we are to see the goings of our God, our King, in the sanctuary, it concerns us to see to our own goings: " Keep thy foot," that is, do nothing rashly; but, "when thou goest to eat with a ruler, consider diligently what is before thee." It was not enough for the priests under the law that they were washed and dressed in their priestly garments when they were first consecrated, but they must be carefully washed and dressed every time they went in to minister, else they went in at their peril. We are spiritual priests to our God, and must do the office of our priesthood with a due decorum, remembering that this is that which the Lord has said, (God by his grace speak it home to our hearts!) " I will be sanctified in them that come nigh me;" that is, I will be attended as a holy God in a holy manner, "and so before all the people I will be glorified." We then sanctify God in holy duties, when we sanctify ourselves in our approaches to them; that is, when we separate ourselves from every thing that is common or unclean, "from all filthiness both of flesh and spirit," and consecrate ourselves to God's glory as our end, and to his service as our business. If we would have the ordinance sanctified to us for our comfort and benefit, we must thus sanctify ourselves for it. Joshua's command to the people, when they were to follow the ark of the covenant through Jordan, should be still sounding in our ears the night before a sacrament: " Sanctify yourselves, for tomorrow the Lord will do wonders among you." When the God of glory admits such worms, such a generation of vipers as we are, into covenant and communion with himself; when he gives gifts, such gifts, to the rebellious; when by the power of his grace he sanctifies the sinful, and comforts the sorrowful, and gives such holiness and joy as is life from the dead,—surely then he does wonders among us. That we may see these wonders done, and share in the benefit of them—that we may experience them done in our souls, " Jordan driven back at the presence of the Lord, at the presence of the God of Jacob," to open a passage for us into the heavenly Canaan,—let us sanctify ourselves, and earnestly pray to God to sanctify us.

For our help herein, the following directions perhaps may be of some use:—

I. Let us address ourselves to this service with a fixedness of thought.—There is scarcely any instance of the corruption of nature, and the moral impotence which we are brought under by sin, more complained of by serious Christians, than the vanity of the thoughts, and the difficulty of fixing them on that which is good. They are apt to wander after a thousand impertinences; it is no easy matter to gather them in, and keep them employed as they should be; we all find it so by sad experience. " Vain thoughts lodge within us," and are most a hinderance and disturbance to us when good thoughts are invited into the soul, and should be entertained there. When, therefore, we apply ourselves to a religious service, which will find work for all our thoughts, and which presents objects well worthy of our closest contemplation, we are concerned to take pains with ourselves, to get our hearts engaged, and to bring every thought into obedience to the law of this solemnity.

This is a time to set aside the thoughts of every thing that is foreign and unseasonable; and all those foolish speculations which used to be the unprofitable amusement of our idle hours, and the sports and pastimes of our carnal minds; away with them all; clear the court of these vagrants, when the doors are to be opened for the King of glory to come in. Are they thoughts that pretend business, and are as buyers and sellers in the temple? Tell them you have other business to mind; bid them depart for this time, and at a more convenient season you will call for them. Do they pretend urgent business, as Nehemiah's enemies did when they sought to give him a diversion? Give them the repulse that he gave, and like him repeat it as oft as they repeat their solicitations, "I am doing a great work; why should the work cease, while I leave it and come down to you?" Do they pretend friendship, and send in the name of thy mother and thy brethren standing without to speak with thee? Yet dismiss them as Christ did, by giving the preference to better friends. Let not thoughts of those we love best, divert us from thinking of Christ, whom we know we must love better.

This is a time to summon the attendance of all the thoughts, and keep them close to the business we are going about. Suffer none to wander, none to trifle; for here is employment, good employment for them all, and all little enough. Though a perfect fixedness of thought without any distraction during the solemnity, is what I believe none can attain to in this state of imperfection, yet it is what we should desire and aim at, and come to as near as we can. Let us charge our thoughts not to wander; keep a watchful eye upon them, and call them back when they begin to rove; keep them in full employment about that which is proper and pertinent, which will prevent their starting aside to that which is otherwise; come, "bind the sacrifice with cords to the horns of the altar," that it may not be to seek when it should be sacrificed. Be able to say through grace, "O God, my heart is fixed;" though unfixed at other times, yet fixed now. Look up to God for grace to establish the heart and keep it steady; look with sorrow and shame upon its wanderings; shut the door against distractions; watch and pray against temptations; and when those birds of prey come down upon the sacrifices, do as Abraham did, "drive them away." And while you sincerely endeavour to keep your hearts fixed, be not discouraged; the vain thoughts that are disallowed, striven against, and repented of, though they are our hinderance, yet they shall not be our ruin.

II. Let us address ourselves to this service with

an evenness and calmness of affection, free from the disorders and ruffles of passion.—A sedate and quiet spirit, not tossed with the tempests of care and fear, but devolving care on God, and silencing fear by faith; not sinking under the load of temporal burdens, but supporting itself with the hopes of eternal joys; easy itself, because submissive to its God; this is a spirit fit to receive and return divine visits. They were still waters, on the face of which the Spirit moved to produce the world: the Lord was not in the wind, "was not in the earthquake." The prince of the power of the air raises storms, for "he loves to fish in troubled waters;" but the Prince of Peace stills storms and quiets the winds and waves, for he casts his net into a calm sea: "The waters of Siloah run softly," and without noise. And that "river, the streams whereof make glad the city of our God," is none of those, the waters whereof roar and are troubled.

Let us therefore always study to be quiet, and, however we are crossed and disappointed, "let not our hearts be troubled, let them not be cast down and disquieted within us." Let us not create or aggravate our own vexations, nor be put into a disorder by any thing that occurs; but let the peace of God always rule in our hearts, and then that peace will keep them. They whose natural temper is either fretful or fearful, have the more need to double their guard; and when any disturbance begins in the soul, should give diligence to suppress the tumult with all speed, lest the Holy Spirit be thereby provoked to withdraw, and then they will have but uncomfortable sacraments.

But especially let us compose ourselves, when we approach to the table of the Lord. Charge the peace then in the name of the King of kings; command silence when you expect to hear the voice of joy and gladness; stop the mouth of clamorous and noisy passions, banish tumultuous thoughts, "suffer not those evil spirits to speak," but expel them, and let your souls return to God, and repose in him as their rest. Bring not unquiet distempered spirits to a transaction which requires the greatest calmness and serenity possible. Let all intemperate heats be cooled, and the thoughts of that which has made an uproar in the soul be banished, and let a strict charge be given to all about you, to all within you, " by the roes and the hinds of the field," those innocent and pleasant creatures, that they stir not up, nor awake your love, nor give any disturbance to your communion with him.

III. Let us address ourselves to it with a holy awe and reverence of the Divine Majesty.—We ought to be in the fear of the Lord every day, and all the day long, for he is our strict observer wherever we are, and will be the judge of persons and actions, by whose unerring sentence our eternal state will be decided; but in a special manner he is " greatly to be feared in the assemblies of his saints, and to be had in reverence of all them that are about him," and the nearer we approach to him, the more reverent we should be. Angels that always behold God's face, see cause to cover their own. Even then when we are admitted to sit down at God's table, we must remember that we are worshipping at his footstool, and therefore must lay ourselves very low before him, and " in his fear worship towards his holy temple." Let us not rush into the presence of God in a careless manner, as if he were a man like ourselves, nay, so as we would not approach to a prince or a great man; but observe a decorum, " giving to him the glory due unto his name," and taking to ourselves the shame due to ours. If he be a master, where is his fear? We do not worship God acceptably, if we do not worship him " with reverence and godly fear."

1. We must worship him with reverence as a glorious God, a God of infinite perfection and almighty power, who " covers himself with light as with a garment," and yet, as to us, makes darkness his pavilion. Dare we profane the temples of the Holy Ghost, by outward indecencies of carriage and behaviour, the manifest indications of a vain and re-

gardless mind? Dare we allow of low and common thoughts of that God who is over all, blessed for evermore? See him, my soul—see him by faith upon a throne, high and lifted up; not only upon a throne of grace, which encourages thee to come with boldness, but upon a throne of glory and a throne of government, which obliges thee to come with caution. Remember that "God is in heaven, and thou art upon earth; and therefore let thy words be few:" "Be still, and know that he is God," that he is great, and keep thy distance. Let an awful regard to the glories of the eternal God, and the exalted Redeemer, make thee humble and serious, very serious, very humble, in thine approach to this ordinance, and keep thee so during the solemnity.

2. We must also worship him with godly fear, as a holy God, a God whose name is jealous, and who "is a consuming fire." We have reason to fear before him, for we have offended him, and have made ourselves obnoxious to his wrath and curse; and we are but upon our good behaviour, as probationers for his favour. He is not a God that will be mocked, that will be trifled with; if we think to put a cheat upon him, we shall prove in the end to have put the most dangerous cheat upon our own souls. In this act of religion, therefore, as well as in others, we "must work out our salvation with fear and trembling."

IV. Let us come to this ordinance with a holy jealousy over ourselves, and an humble sense of our own unworthiness.—We must sit before the Lord in such a frame as David composed himself into, when he said, "Who am I, O Lord God, and what is my father's house, that thou hast brought me hitherto?" Nothing prepares the soul more for spiritual comforts than humility.

1. It may be that we have reason to suspect ourselves lest we come unworthily. Though we must not cherish such suspicions of our state as will damp our joy in God, and discourage our hope in Christ, and fill us with amazement; nor such as will take off

our chariot-wheels, and keep us standing when we should be going forward; yet we must maintain such a jealousy of ourselves, as will keep us humble, and take us off from all self-conceit and self-confidence; such a jealousy of ourselves, as will keep us watchful, and save us from sinking into carnal security. And now is a proper time to think how many there are that eat bread with Christ, and yet lift up the heel against him: the hand of him that betrays him, perhaps, is with him upon the table; which should put us upon asking, as the disciples did, just before the first sacrament, "Lord, is it I?" Many that eat and drink in Christ's presence, will be rejected and disowned by him in the great day. Have I not some reason to fear lest that be my doom at last?—to fear, lest a promise being left me of entering into rest, I should seem to come short?—to fear, lest, when the King comes in to see the guests, he find me without a wedding garment. Be not too confident, O my soul, lest thou deceive thyself: "Be not high-minded, but fear."

2. However, it is certain we have reason to abase ourselves; for, at the best, we are unworthy to come. If we "are less than the least of God's mercies," how much less are we than the greatest, than this, which includes all? We are unworthy of the crumbs that fall from our Master's table, much more unworthy of the children's bread, and the dainties that are upon the table. Being invited, we may hope to be welcome; but what is there in us that we should be invited? Men invite their friends and acquaintance to their tables, but we were naturally "strangers and enemies in our minds by wicked works," and yet are we invited. Men invite such as they think will, with their quality or merit, grace their tables; but we are more likely to be a reproach to Christ's table, being poor and maimed, halt and blind; and yet are picked up out of the highways and the hedges. Men invite such as they are under obligations to, or have expectations from; but Christ is no way indebted to us, nor can he be benefited by us; our goodness ex-

tends not to him, and yet he invites us. We have much more reason than Mephibosheth had, when he was made a constant guest at David's table, to bow ourselves, and say, "What is thy servant, that thou shouldest look upon such a dead dog as I am?" They who thus humble themselves shall be exalted.

V. Yet let us come to this ordinance with a gracious confidence, as children to a father, to a father's table; not with any confidence in ourselves, but in Christ only.—That slavish fear which represents God as a hard master, rigorous in his demands, and extreme to mark what we do amiss; which straitens our spirits, and subjects us to bondage and torment, must be put off, and striven against; and we must come boldly to the throne of grace, to the table of grace, not as having any thing in ourselves to recommend us, but as having a High Priest, who is touched with the feeling of our infirmities. As a presumptuous rudeness is a provocation to the master of the feast, so a distrustful shyness is displeasing to him; which looks as if we questioned either the sincerity of the invitation, or the sufficiency of the provision.

This is the fault of many good Christians: they come to this sacrament rather like prisoners to the bar, than like friends and children to the table; they come trembling and astonished, and full of confusion. Their apprehensions of the grandeur of the ordinance, and the danger of coming unworthily, run into an extreme, and become a hinderance to the exercise of faith, hope, and love: this extreme we should carefully watch against, because it tends so much to God's dishonour, our own prejudice, and the discouragement of others. Let us remember we have to do with one who is willing to make the best of sincere desires and serious endeavours, though in many things we be defective; and who deals with us in tender mercy, and not in strict justice, and who, though he be out of Christ a consuming fire, yet in Christ is a gracious Father: let us, "therefore, draw near with a true heart, and full assurance of faith." It is related of

Titus the emperor, that when a poor petitioner presented his address to him with a trembling hand, he was much displeased, and asked him, Dost thou present thy petition to thy prince, as if thou wert giving meat to a lion?—Chide thyself for these amazing fears: "Why art thou cast down, O my soul? and why art thou disquieted within me?" If the Spirit undertake to work all my works in me, as the Son hath undertaken to work all my works for me, both the one and the other shall be done effectually: therefore "hope thou in God, for I shall yet praise him."

VI. Let us come to this ordinance with earnest desires towards God and communion with him.—It is a feast, a spiritual feast; and we must come to it with an appetite, a spiritual appetite: for the full soul loathes even the honey-comb, and slights the offer of it; but to the hungry soul, that is sensible of its own needs, every bitter thing is sweet, even the bitterness of repentance, when it is in order to peace and pardon. Our desires towards the world and the flesh must be checked and moderated, and kept under the government of religion and right reason; for we have been too long spending our money for that which is not bread, and which is, at the best, unsatisfying; but our desires towards Christ must be quickened and stirred up. "As the hart, the hunted hart, panteth after the refreshment of the water brook, so earnestly must our souls pant for the living God." The invitation is given, and the promise made to them only that hunger and thirst; they are called to come to the waters, to come and drink, and it is promised to them that they shall be filled. It is very necessary, therefore, that we work upon our hearts the consideration of those things that are proper to kindle this holy fire, and to blow its sparks into a flame. We are then best prepared to receive temporal mercies, when we are most indifferent to them, and content, if the will of God be so, to be without them. "Did I desire a son of my lord?" said the good Shunamite. Here the danger is of being too earnest in our desires, as Rachel: "Give me children, or else I die." But we are then best prepared to receive spiritual mercies, when we are most importunate for them: here the desires cannot be too vehement. In the former case, strong desires evidence the prevalency of sense; but in this they evidence the power of faith, both realizing and valuing the blessings desired. The devout and pious soul " thirsts for God, for the living God, as a thirsty land." It longs, "yea, even faints for the courts of the Lord," and for communion with God in them. It "breaks for the longing it hath unto God's judgments at all times."—Can our souls witness to such desires as these? O that I might have a more intimate acquaintance with God and Christ, and divine things! O that I might have the tokens of God's favour, and fuller assurances of his distinguishing love in Jesus Christ! O that my covenant-interest in him, and relation to him, might be cleared up to me, and that I might have more of the comfort of it! O that I might partake more of the divine grace; and, by its effectual working on my soul, might be made more conformable to the divine will and likeness; more holy, humble, spiritual, heavenly, and more meet for the inheritance! O that I might have the earnest of the Spirit in my heart, sealing me to the day of redemption!

Thus the desire of our souls must be towards the Lord, and towards the remembrance of his name. In this imperfect state, where we are at home in the body, and absent from the Lord, our love to God acts more in holy desires, than in holy delights. It is rather love in motion, like a bird upon the wing, than love at rest, like a bird upon the nest. All those who have the Lord for their God, agree to desire nothing more than God, for they know they have enough in him; but yet still they desire more and more of God; for, till they come to heaven, they will never have enough of him. Come then, my soul, why art thou so cold in thy desires towards those things which are designed for thy peculiar satisfaction, distinct from the body? Why so eager for the meat that perisheth, and so indifferent to that which endures to everlasting life? Hast thou no desire to that which is so necessary to thy support, and without which thou art undone? No desire to that which will contribute so much to thy comfort, and yield thee inexpressible satisfaction? Provision is made in the Lord's Supper of bread to strengthen thee; will not the sense of thine own weakness and emptiness make thee hunger after that? Canst thou be indifferent to that which is the staff of thy life? Provision is made of pleasant food, fat things full of marrow, and wines on the lees; art thou not desirous of dainties, such dainties? Was the tree of knowledge such a temptation, because it was "pleasant to the eye, and a tree to be desired to make one wise," that our first parents would break through the hedge of a divine command, and venture all that was dear to them to come at it? And shall not the tree of life, which we are not only allowed, but commanded to eat of, and the fruit of which will nourish us to life eternal—shall not that appear more pleasant in our eyes, and more to be desired? God, even thine own God, who hath wherewithal to supply all thy needs, and hath promised to be to thee a God all-sufficient, a God that is enough,—he hath said, "Open thy mouth wide and I will fill it;" thou art not straitened in him, be not straitened in thine own desires.

VII. Let us come to this ordinance with raised expectations.—The same faith that enlarges the desire, and draws it out to a holy vehemence, should also elevate the hope, and ripen it to a holy confidence. When we come thirsting to these waters, we need not fear that they will prove like the brooks in summer, which disappoint the weary traveller; for, "when it is hot, they are consumed out of their place." Such are all the broken cisterns of the creature; they perform not what they promise, or rather what we foolishly promise to ourselves from them: no, but these are inexhaustible fountains of living water, in which there is enough for all, though ever so many; enough for each, though ever so needy; enough for me, though most unworthy.

Come, my soul, what dost thou look for at the table of the Lord? The maker of the feast is God himself, who does nothing little or mean, but is "able to do exceeding abundantly above what we are able to ask or think." When he gives, he gives like himself, gives like a king, gives like a God, all things richly to enjoy; considering not what becomes such ungrateful wretches as we are to receive, but what it becomes such a bountiful benefactor as he is to give. A lively faith may expect that which is rich and great from him that is possessor of heaven and earth, and all the wealth of both; and that which is kind and gracious from him that is the "Father of mercies, and the God of all consolation." A lively faith may expect all that is purchased by the blood of Christ from a God who is righteous in all his ways, and all that is promised in the new covenant from a God who cannot lie nor deceive.

The provision in this feast is Christ himself, and all his benefits; all we need to save us from being miserable, and all we can desire to make us happy: and glorious things, no doubt, may be expected from him, in whom "it pleased the Father, that all fulness should dwell." Let our expectations be built upon a right foundation; not any merit of our own, but God's mercy, and Christ's mediation: and then build large, as large as the new covenant in its utmost extent; build high, as high as heaven in all its glory. Come expecting to see that which is most illustrious, and to taste and receive that which is most precious; come expecting that with which you will be abundantly satisfied.

Though what is prepared seems to a carnal eye poor and scanty, like the five loaves set before five thousand men; yet, when Christ has the breaking of those loaves, they shall all eat and be filled. In this ordinance the oil is multiplied, the oil of gladness; it is multiplied in the pouring out, as the widow's oil. Do as she did, therefore: bring empty vessels, bring not a few, they shall all be filled; the expectations of faith shall all be answered; the oil stays not, while there is an empty vessel waiting to be filled. Give faith and hope their full compass, and thou wilt find, as that widow did, there is enough of this oil, this multiplied oil, this oil from the good olive, to pay thy debt, and enough beside for thee and thine to live upon. As we oft wrong ourselves by expecting too much from the world, which is vanity and vexation; so we often wrong ourselves by expecting too little from God, whose "mercy is upon us, according as we hope in him," and who, in exerting his power, and conferring his gifts, still says, "According to your faith be it unto you." The king of Israel lost his advantage against the Syrians, by smiting thrice, and then staying, when he should have smitten five or six times. And we do often, in like manner, prejudice ourselves by the weakness of our faith: we receive little, because we expect little; and are like them among whom "Christ could not do many mighty works, because of their unbelief."

VIII. Let us come to this ordinance with rejoicing and thanksgiving.—These two must go together; for whatever is the matter of our rejoicing, must be the matter of our thanksgiving. Holy joy is the heart of our thankful praise, and thankful praise the language of holy joy; and both these are very seasonable when we are coming to an ordinance, which is instituted both for the honour of the Redeemer, and for the comfort of the redeemed.

Beside the matter of joy and praise with which we are furnished in our attendance on the ordinance, even our approach to it is such an honour, such a favour, as obliges us to "come before his presence with singing, and even to enter into his gates with thanksgiving."—"With gladness and rejoicing shall the royal bride be brought." Those that in their preparations for the ordinance have been "sowing in tears, may not only come again with rejoicing, bringing their sheaves with them," but go with rejoicing to fetch their sheaves, to meet the ark, "lifting up their heads with joy, knowing that their redemption," and the sealing of them to the day of redemption, draws nigh. Let those that are of a sorrowful spirit hearken to this; cheer up and be comforted; "This day is holy unto the Lord your God; mourn not, nor weep." "It is the day that the Lord hath made, and we must rejoice and be glad in it;" and the joy of the Lord will be our strength, and oil to our wheels. All things considered, thou hast a great deal more reason than Haman had, "to go in merrily with the king, to the banquet of wine."

Two things may justly be matter of our rejoicing and thanksgiving in our approach to this ordinance:

1. That God has put such a price as this in our hands to get wisdom; that such an ordinance as this was instituted for our spiritual nourishment and growth in grace; that it is transmitted down to us, is administered among us, and we are invited to it. This is a token for good, in which we have reason to rejoice, and be very thankful for, that our lot is not cast either among those who are strangers to the gospel, and so have not this ordinance at all, or among those who are enemies to the gospel, and have it wretchedly corrupted, and turned into an idolatrous service; but that Wisdom's table is spread among us, and her voice heard in our streets, and we are called to her feasts, we have a nail in God's holy place, a settlement in his house, and stated opportunities of communion with him.—" If the Lord had been pleased to kill us, he would not have shown us such things as these." O what a privilege is it thus to eat and drink in Christ's presence! to sit down under his shadow at his table, with his friends and favourites! that we, who deserved to have been set with the dogs of his flock, should be set with the children of his family, and eat of the children's bread! nay, that we should be numbered among his priests, and eat of the dedicated things! " Bless the Lord, O my soul!"

2. That God hath given us a heart to improve the price in our hands. We have reason to be thankful that he hath not only invited us to this feast, which is a token of his good-will towards us; but that he hath inclined us to accept the invitation, which is the

effect of a good work upon us. Many that are called make light of it, and go their way to their farms and merchandize; and, if we had been left to ourselves, we should have made the same foolish choice, and, in the greatness of our folly, should have gone astray, and wandered endlessly. It was free grace that made us willing in the day of power, and graciously compelled us to come in to the gospel feast; it was distinguishing grace that revealed to us babes, the things that were hid from the wise and prudent; let that grace have the glory, and let us have the joy of this blessed work.

IX. Let us come to this ordinance in charity with all men, and with a sincere affection to all good Christians.—It is a love feast, and if we do not come in love, we come without the wedding garment, and forfeit the comforts of the feast. This is to be seriously thought of when we bring our gift to the altar, as we hope for acceptance there. When we come to the sacrament, we must bring with us ill-will to none, good-will to all, but especially to them who are of the household of faith.

1. We must bear ill-will to none; no, not to those that have been most injurious and provoking to us: though they have affronted us ever so much in our honour, wronged us in our interest, and set themselves to vilify us, and do us mischief, yet we must not hate them, nor entertain any malice towards them; we must not be desirous or studious of revenge, to seek their hurt in any respect, but must from our hearts forgive them, as we ourselves are, and hope to be forgiven of God. We must see to it, that there be not the least degree of enmity to any person in the world lodged in our breast, but carefully purge out all that old leaven; not only lay aside the thoughts of it for the present, but wholly pluck up, and cast out that root of bitterness, "which bears gall and wormwood." Pure hands must, in this ordinance, as well as in prayer, be "lifted up without wrath and doubting." How can we expect that God should be reconciled to us, if we bring not with us a disposition

to be reconciled to our brethren? for our trespasses against God are unspeakably greater than the worst of our brethren's trespasses against us. O that each would apply this caution to themselves! You have a neighbour, that, upon some disgust conceived, you cannot find in your hearts to speak to, nor to speak well of; some one that you have entertained a prejudice against, and would willingly do an ill turn to, if it lay in your power; some one, of whom it may be you are ready to say, you cannot endure the sight. And dare you retain such a spirit when you come to this ordinance? Can you conceal it from God; or do you think you can justify it at his bar, and make it out that you do well to be angry? Let the fear of God's wrath, and the hope of Christ's love, reduce you to a better temper; and when you celebrate the memorial of the dying of the Lord Jesus, be sure you remember this, that he is our peace, and that he died to slay all enmities.

2. We must bear good-will to all, with a particular affection to all good Christians. Christian charity doth not only forbid that which is any way injurious, but it requires that which is kind and friendly.

The desire of our hearts must be towards the welfare of all. If we be indeed solicitous about the salvation of our own souls, we cannot but have a tender concern for the souls of others, and be hearty well-wishers to their salvation likewise; "for this is good and acceptable in the sight of God our Saviour, who will have all men to be saved." True grace hates monopolies. We must thus love those whose wickedness we are bound to hate; and earnestly desire their happiness, even while we industriously decline their fellowship.

But the "delight of our souls must be in the saints that are on the earth, those excellent ones," as David's was. They are precious in God's sight, and honourable, and they should be so in ours; they have fellowship with the Father, and with his Son Jesus Christ: and therefore, by a sincere and affectionate love to them, we also should have fellowship with them. Our hearts will then be comforted, when they are "knit together in love." This love must not be confined to those of our own communion, our own way and denomination: then we love them for our own sakes, because they credit us; not for Christ's sake, because they honour him: but, since God is no respecter of persons, we must not be such. "In every nation, he that fears God, and works righteousness, is accepted of him," and should be so of us. Doubtless, there may be a diversity of apprehensions in the less weighty matters of the law, such as the distinction of meats and days, and diversity of practice accordingly, and yet a sincerity of mutual love, according to the law of Christ. Those who think it is not possible, should be content to speak for themselves only, and must believe there are those who have much satisfaction in being able to say, that they love the image of Christ wherever they see it, and highly value a good man, though not in every thing of their mind. He that casteth out devils in Christ's name must be dear to us, though he follow not us. The differences that are among Christians, though fomented by the malice of Satan for the ruin of love, are permitted by the wisdom of God for the trial of love, that they which are perfect therein may be made manifest. Herein a Christian commendeth his love, when he loves those who differ from him, and joins in affection to those with whom he cannot concur in opinion: this is thankworthy. The kingdom of God is not meat and drink; they that have tasted of the bread of life, and the water of life, know it is not; but it is "righteousness, and peace, and joy in the Holy Ghost: he, therefore, that in these things serveth Christ, is acceptable to God;" and therefore, though he esteem not our days, though he relish not our meats, he should be acceptable and dear to us.

Let us then, in our approach to this sacrament, stir up ourselves to holy love, love without dissimulation; let us bear those on our hearts, whom the great High Priest of our profession bears on his; and, as we are "taught of God to love one another, let us increase therein more and more." Christ's having loved us, is a good reason why we should love him: Christ's having loved our brethren also, is a good reason why we should love them. "Behold how good and how pleasant a thing it is for Christians to be kindly affectioned one towards another," of one heart, and of one soul! there the Lord commands the blessing, and gives earnest of the joys of that world, where love is perfected and reigns eternally.

CHAPTER VIII.

SOME ACCOUNT OF THE AFFECTING SIGHTS THAT ARE TO BE SEEN BY FAITH IN THIS ORDINANCE.

I. In general: Come and see the Lamb that had been slain, opening the seals. II. In particular:—(I.) See the evil of sin. (II.) See the justice of God; in two things. (III.) See the love of Christ; opened in six properties of that love. (IV.) See the conquest of Satan; how Christ conquered Satan in two things. (V.) See the worth of souls; two inferences from that sight. (VI.) See the purchase of the blessings of the new covenant; opened in two things.

CARE being taken, by the grace of God, to compose ourselves into a serious frame of spirit agreeable to the ordinance, we must next apply ourselves to that which is the proper business of it. And the first thing to be done is, to contemplate that which is represented and set before us there. This David aimed at when he coveted to dwell in the house of the Lord all the days of his life, that he might behold the beauty of the Lord; might see his power and his glory. To the natural man, who receives not the things of the Spirit of God, there appears in it nothing surprising, nothing affecting, no form nor comeliness; but to that faith, which is the "substance and evidence of things not seen," there appears a great sight, which, like Moses, it will, with a holy reverence, turn aside now to see. As, therefore, in our preparation for this ordinance, we should pray, with David, "Open thou mine eyes, that I may see the wondrous things of thy law" and gospel; so we should, with Abraham, "lift up our eyes now and look."

When the Lamb that had been slain had taken the book, and was going to open the seals, St. John, who had the honour to be a witness in vision of the solemnity, was loudly called, by one of the four living creatures, to come and see. The same is the call given to us when, in this sacrament, there is a door opened in heaven, and we are bidden to come up hither.

I. In general, we are here called to see the Lamb that had been slain, opening the seals. This is the general idea we are to have of the ordinance. We would have thought ourselves highly favoured indeed, and beloved disciples, if we had seen it in vision, as John did; behold we are all invited to see it in a sacramental representation.

In this ordinance is showed us the Lamb as it had been slain. John the Baptist pointed to him as the Lamb of God, and called upon his followers to behold him;—a Lamb designed for sacrifice, in order to the taking away of the sins of the world, a harmless, spotless Lamb. But John the Divine goes further, and sees him a Lamb slain, now sacrificed for us in the outer court; and not only so, but appearing " in the midst of the throne, and of the four beasts, and of the elders," as if he were newly slain, bleeding afresh, and yet alive, and " lives for evermore," constantly presenting his sacrifice within the veil;— the blood of the Lamb always flowing, that it may still be sprinkled on our consciences, to purify and pacify them, and may still speak in heaven for us, in that prevailing intercession which the Lord Jesus ever lives to make there, in virtue of his satisfaction.

In this ordinance, the Lord's death is shown forth; it is shown forth to us, that it may be shown forth by us. Jesus Christ is here "evidently set forth crucified among us," that we may "all with open face behold, as in a glass, the glory of God in the face of Christ." Thus, as Christ "was the Lamb slain from the foundation of the world," in the types and prophecies of the Old Testament, and the application of his merits to the saints that lived then; so he will be the Lamb slain to the end of the world, in the word and sacraments of the New Testament, and the application of his merits to the saints that are now, and shall be in every age. Still he is seen as a Lamb that had been slain; for this sacrifice does not, like the Old Testament sacrifices, decay and wax old.

This is the sight, the great sight: we are here to see the bush burning, and yet not consumed; for the Lord is in it, his people's God and Saviour. The wounds of this Lamb are here open before us. Come, see in Christ's hands the very print of the nails, see in his side the very mark of the spear. Behold him in his agony, sweating as if it had been "great drops of blood falling to the ground;" then accommodating himself to the work he had undertaken, couching between two burdens, and bowing his shoulder to bear them. Behold him "in his bonds, when the breath of our nostrils, the anointed of the Lord, was taken in their pits," and he was bound that we might go out free. Behold him at the bar prosecuted and condemned as a criminal, because he was made sin for us, and had undertaken to answer for our guilt. Behold him upon the cross, enduring the pain, and despising the shame of the cursed tree. Here is his body broken, his blood shed, his soul poured out unto death; all his sufferings, with all their aggravations, are here, in such a manner as the divine wisdom saw fit, by an instituted ordinance, represented to us, and set before us.

In this ordinance is shown us the Lamb that was slain, opening the seals of the everlasting gospel: not only discovering to us the glories of the divine light, but dispensing to us the graces of divine love; opening the seals of the fountain of life, which had been long as a spring shut up; and rolling away the stone, that from thence we may draw water with joy; opening the seals of the book of life, that things hid from ages and generations might be manifested unto us, and we might know the things which are freely given us of God; opening the seals of God's treasures, "the unsearchable riches of Christ," which should have been sealed up for ever from us, if he had not found out a way to supply and enrich us out of them; opening the seals of heaven's gates, which had been shut and sealed against us, and consecrating for us "a new and living way into the holiest by his own blood." This is a glorious sight, and that which cannot but raise our expectations of something further; this is the principal sight given us in this ordinance: but when we view this accurately, we shall find there is that in it which "eye hath not seen, nor ear heard."

II. In particular, we are here called to see many other things, which we may infer from this general representation of the sufferings of Christ. It is a very fruitful subject, and that which will lead us to the consideration of divers things very profitable. When we come to this sacrament, we should ask ourselves the question, which Christ put to those that had been John's hearers, "What went ye out for to see?" What do we come to the Lord's table to see? We come to see that which, if God gives us the eye of faith to discern it, will be very affecting. Let this voice, therefore, be still sounding in our ears, "Come and see."

(1.) Come and see the evil of sin. This we are concerned to see, that we may be truly humbled for our sins past, and may be firmly engaged by resolution and holy watchfulness against sin for the future. It was for our transgressions that Christ was thus wounded, for our iniquities that he was bruised; "know therefore, O my soul, and see, that it is an evil and bitter thing, that thou hast forsaken the Lord thy God, and that my fear is not in thee, saith the Lord God of hosts." That was a great provocation to God, which nothing would atone for but such a sacrifice; a dangerous disease to us, which nothing would heal but such a medicine. "This is thy wickedness, because it is bitter, because it reacheth unto thine heart."

Here sin appears sin, and by the cross of Christ, as well as by the command of God, it becomes exceeding sinful. The malignity of its nature was very great, and more than we can conceive or express; for it had made such a breach between God and man, as none less than he who was both God and man could repair; none less than he durst undertake to be made sin for us, to become surety for that debt, and intercessor for such offenders. It was impossible that the blood of bulls and goats should take away sin; the stain was too deep to be washed out so: "sacrifice and offering God did not desire," would not accept as sufficient to purge us from it; no, the Son of God himself must come to "put away sin by the sacrifice of himself," or it will for ever separate between God and us.

Here sin appears death, and in the cross of Christ shows itself exceeding hurtful. Behold, my soul, and see what mischief sin makes, by observing how dear it cost the Redeemer, when he undertook to satisfy for it; how he sweated and groaned, bled and died, when the "Lord laid upon him the iniquities of us all;" look on sin through this glass, and it will appear in its true colour, black and bloody! nothing can be more so. The fatal consequences of sin are seen more in the sufferings of Christ, than in all the calamities that it has brought upon the world of mankind. O what a painful, what a shameful thing is sin, which put our Lord Jesus to so much pain, to so much shame, when he bore our "sins in his own body upon the tree!"

See this, my soul, with application: it was thy sin, thy own iniquity, that lay so heavy upon the Lord Jesus, when he cried out, "My soul is exceeding sorrowful, even unto death." It was thy pride and passion, thy worldliness and uncleanness, the carnal mind in thee, which is enmity against God, that crowned him with thorns, and nailed him to the cross, and laid him for a time under the sense of God's withdrawings from him. Is this so? And shall I ever again make a mock at sin? ever again make a light matter of that of which Christ made so great a matter? God forbid! " Is it a small thing to weary men, but have I by my sins wearied my God also?" " Have I made him thus to serve, and thus to suffer by my sins?" and shall I ever be reconciled to sin again? or shall I ever think a favourable thought of it any more? No: by the grace of God I never will. The carnal pleasure, and worldly profit that sin can promise, will never balance the pain and shame to which it put my Redeemer.

Meditate revenge, my soul, a holy revenge, such a revenge as will be no breach of the law of charity; such a revenge as is one of the fruits of godly sorrow. If sin was the death of Christ, why should not I be the death of sin? When David lamented Saul and Jonathan, who were slain by the archers of the Philistines, it is said, " He taught the children of Judah the use of the bow," that they might avenge the death of their princes upon their enemies. Let us thence receive instruction.—Did sin, did my sin crucify Christ? And shall not I crucify it? If it be asked, Why, what evil has it done? say, It cost the blood of the Son of God to expiate it: and therefore, cry out so much the more, " Crucify it, crucify it." And thus all that are Christ's, have in some measure crucified the flesh. As Christ died for sin, so we must die to sin.

(II.) Come and see the justice of God. Many ways the great Judge of the world has made it to appear that he hates sin; and, both by the judgments of his mouth in the written word, and the judgments of his hand in the course of his providence, he has revealed " his wrath from heaven against all ungodliness and unrighteousness of men." It is true, that he is gracious and merciful; but it is as true, that " God is jealous, and the Lord revengeth." God, even our God, is a consuming fire, and will reckon for the violation of his laws, and the injuries done to his crown and dignity. The tenor of the Scripture, from the second of Genesis to the last of Revelation, proves this, "The soul that sinneth, it shall die." In many remarkable punishments of sin, even in this life, it is written as with a sunbeam, so that he that runs may read, That the Lord is righteous.

But never did the justice of God appear so conspicuous, so illustrious, as in the death and sufferings of Jesus Christ set before us in this ordinance. Here his "righteousness is like the great mountains, though his judgments are a great deep." Come and see the holy God, showing his displeasure against sin in the death of Christ, more than in the ruin of angels, the drowning of the old world, the burning of Sodom, and the destruction of Jerusalem: nay, more than in the torments of hell, all things considered.

God manifested his justice, in demanding such satisfaction for sin, as Christ was to make by the blood of his cross. Hereby he made it to appear how great the provocation was which was done him by the sin of man, that, not only such an excellent person must be chosen to intercede for us, but his sufferings and death must be insisted on to atone for us. Sin being committed against an infinite Majesty, seems by this to have in it a kind of infinite malignity, that the remission of it could not be procured, but by a satisfaction of infinite value. If mere mercy had pardoned sin, without any provision made to answer the demands of injured justice, God had declared his goodness; but, when Jesus Christ is set forth to be a propitiation for sin, and God is pleased to put himself to so vast an expense for the saving of the honour of his government in the forgiveness of sin, this declares his righteousness; it declares, "I say, at this time, his righteousness." See what an emphasis the apostle lays upon this.

Sin hath wronged God in his honour, for he cannot otherwise be wronged by any of his creatures. In breaking the law, we dishonour God; we sin and come short of his glory. For this wrong, satisfaction must be made: that which first offers, is the eternal ruin of the sinner; let the sentence of the law be executed, and thereby God may get him honour upon us, in lieu of that he should have had from us. But can no expedient be found out to satisfy God, and yet save the sinner? Is it not possible to offer an equivalent? "Will the Lord be pleased with thousands of rams, or ten thousands of rivers of oil? Shall we give our first-born for our transgression, the fruit of our body for the sin of our soul?" No; these are not tantamount: no submissions, sorrows, supplications, services, or sufferings of ours, can be looked upon as a valuable consideration for the righteous God to proceed upon, in forgiving such injuries, and restoring such criminals to his favour. The best we do is imperfect; the utmost we can do is already owing. Here, therefore, the Lord Jesus interposes, undertakes to make a full reparation of the injury done to God's glory by sin; clothes himself with our nature, and becomes surety for us, as Paul for Onesimus: "If they have wronged thee, or owe thee aught, put that on mine account; I have written it with mine own hand, with mine own blood I will repay it." He was made sin for us, a curse for us, an offering for our sin. He "bore our sins in his own body on the tree;" and thus the justice of God was not only satisfied, but greatly glorified. Come and see how bright it shines here.

God manifested his justice, in dealing as he did with him who undertook to make satisfaction. Having "laid upon him the iniquity of us all, he laid it home to him; for it pleased the Lord to bruise him, and put him to grief. He was not only despised and rejected of men, who knew him not, but he was stricken, smitten of God and afflicted." The ancient way in which God testified his acceptance of sacrifices, was by consuming them with fire from heaven. The wrath of God, which the offerers deserved should have fallen upon them, fell upon the offering; and so the destruction of the sacrifice was the escape of the sinner. Christ becoming a sacrifice for us, the fire of God's wrath descended upon him, which troubled his soul, put him into an agony, and made him cry out, "My God, my God, why hast thou forsaken me?" "Come, then, and behold the goodness and severity of God." "Christ being made sin for us, God did not spare him." "By the determinate counsel and foreknowledge of God, he was delivered to them who, with wicked hands, crucified and slew him." "Awake, O sword," the sword of divine justice, furbished and bathed in heaven!—awake "against my Shepherd, and against the man that is my fellow, saith the Lord of hosts; smite the Shepherd."

Let us look on the sufferings of Christ, and say, as he himself hath taught us, "If this be done in the green tree, what shall be done in the dry?" What was done to him, shows what should have been done to us, if Christ had not interposed, and what will be done to us if we reject him. If this were done to the Son of God's love, what shall be done to the generation of his wrath? If this were done to one that had but sin imputed to him, who, as he had no corruptions of his own for Satan's temptations to fasten upon, so he had no guilt of his own for God's wrath to fasten upon, who was as a green tree, not apt to take fire; what shall be done to those who have sin inherent in them, which makes them as a dry tree, combustible and proper fuel for the fire of God's wrath? If this were done to one that had done so much good, what shall be done to us that have done so little? If the Lord Jesus himself was put into an agony by the things that were done to him, was sorrowful, and very heavy, "can our hearts endure, or can our hands be strong, when God shall deal with us?" "Who would set the briers and thorns against him in battle?" From the sufferings of Christ, we may easily infer what a "fearful thing it is to fall into the hands of the living God."

(III.) Come and see the love of Christ. This is that which, with a peculiar regard, we are to observe and contemplate in this ordinance: where we see Christ, and him crucified, we cannot but see the love of Christ, which passeth knowledge. When Christ did but drop a tear over the grave of Lazarus, the Jews said, "See how he loved him!" Much more reason have we to say, when we commemorate the shedding of his blood for us, "See how he loved us!" Greater love hath no man than this, to lay down his life for his friend. Thus Christ hath loved us; nay, he laid down his life for us when we were enemies. Herein is love—love without precedent, love without parallel. Come and see the wonders of this love.

It was free love.—Christ gave himself for us; and what more free than a gift? It was free, for it was unasked: nothing cried for this mercy, but our own misery; when no eye pitied us, of his own good will he relieved us, "said to us, when we were in our blood, Live; yea, he said to us, Live." That was a time of love indeed. It was free, for it was unmerited: there was nothing in us desirable, nothing promising; the relation we stood in to God as creatures, did but aggravate our rebellion, and make us the more obnoxious. As he could not obtain any advantage by our happiness, so he would not have sustained any damage by our misery. If there was no profit in our blood, yet for certain there would have been no loss by it; no, but the reasons of his love were fetched from within himself, as God's love of Israel was. He loved them, because he would love them. It was free, for it was unforced: he willingly offered himself. Here am I, send me. This sacrifice was bound to the horns of the altar, only with the cords of his own love.

It was distinguishing love.—It was good-will to fallen man, and not to fallen angels. He did not lay hold on a world of sinking angels; as their tree fell, so it lies, and so it is like to lie for ever: but on the seed of Abraham he taketh hold. The nature of angels was more excellent than that of man, their place in the creation higher, their capacity for honouring God greater; and yet they were passed by. Man that sinned, was pitied and helped; while angels that sinned, were not so much as spared. The deplorable state of devils, serves as a foil to set off the blessed state of the ransomed of the Lord.

It was condescending love.—Never did love humble itself, and stoop so low as the love of Christ did. It was great condescension, that he should fix his love upon creatures so mean, " man that is a worm, the son of man that is a worm;" so near a-kin to the brutal part of the creation, especially since the fall, that one would think he should rather be the scorn than the love of the spiritual and purely intellectual world: yet this is the creature that is chosen to be the darling of heaven, and in whom Wisdom's delights are. But especially that, in prosecution of this love, he should humble himself as he did: humble himself to the earth in his incarnation; humble himself into the earth in the meanness of his life; humble himself into the earth, when he went to the grave, the place where mankind appears under the greatest mortification and disgrace.

It was expensive love.—His washing the feet of his disciples is spoken of as an act of love to them; and that was condescending love, but not costly like this. He loved us, and bought us, and paid dear for us, that we might be unto him a purchased people. Because he loved Israel, he gave "men for them, and people for their life, even Egypt for their ransom." But because he loved us, he gave himself for us, even his own blood for the ransom of our souls.

It was strong love, strong as death, and which many waters could not quench.—This was the greatness of his strength, in which the Redeemer travelled, who is mighty to save; it was strong to break through great difficulties, and trample upon the discouragements that lay in his way. When he had this baptism of blood to be baptized with, it was love that said, " How am I straitened till it be accomplished!" It was love that said, " With desire have I desired to eat this passover," which he knew was to be his last. It was the strength of his love that reconciled him to the bitter cup which was put into his hand, and made him wave his petition, "that it might pass from him;" which, for ought we know, if he had insisted upon it, had been granted, and the work undone.

It was an everlasting love.—It was from everlasting in the counsels of it, and will be to everlasting in the consequences of it, Not like our love, which comes up in a night and perishes in a night. He loved to the end, and went on with his undertaking till he said, "It is finished." Never was there such a constant lover as the blessed Jesus, whose gifts and callings are without repentance.

(iv.) Come and see the conquest of Satan. And this is a very pleasing sight to all those who through grace are turned from the power of Satan unto God, as it was to the Israelites, when they had newly shaken off the Egyptian yoke, to see their task-masters and pursuers dead upon the sea-shore. Come and see our Joshua discomfiting the Amalekites; our David, with a sling and a stone, vanquishing that proud Goliath, who not only himself basely deserted, but then boldly defied the armies of the living God. Come and see, not Michael and his angels, but Michael himself; Michael our Prince, who trode the wine-press alone, entering the lists with the dragon and his angels, and giving them an effectual overthrow; the seed of the woman, though bruised in the heel, yet breaking the serpent's head, according to that ancient promise made unto the fathers. Come and see the great Redeemer, not only making peace with earth, but making war with hell; dispossessing the strong man armed, "spoiling principalities and powers, making a show of them openly, and triumphing over them in his cross."

(v.) Come and see Christ triumphing over Satan at his death. Though the war was in heaven, yet some fruits of the victory even then appeared on earth. Though, when Christ was in the extremity of his sufferings, there was darkness over all the land, which gave the powers of darkness all the advantage they could wish for; yet he beat the enemy upon his own ground. Satan, some think, terrified Christ into his agony; but then he kept possession of his own soul, and steadily adhered to his Father's will, and to his own undertaking: so he baffled Satan. Satan put it into the heart of Judas to betray him; but in the immediate ruin of Judas, who presently went and hanged himself, Christ triumphed over Satan, and made a show of him openly. Satan tempted Peter to deny Christ, desiring to have him, that he might sift him as wheat; but, by the speedy repentance of Peter, who, upon a look from Christ, went out and wept bitterly, Christ triumphed over Satan, and baffled him in his designs. Satan was ready to swallow up the thief upon the cross; but Christ rescued him from the gates of hell, and raised him to the glories of heaven, and thereby spoiled Satan, who was as a lion disappointed of his prey.

Come and see Christ triumphing over Satan by his death; the true Samson, that did more towards the ruin of the Philistines dying than living: having by his life and doctrine destroyed the works of the devil, at length by his death "he destroyed the devil himself, that had the power of death." In him was fulfilled the blessing of the tribe of Gad: "A troop shall overcome him, but he shall overcome at the last;" and "through him that loved us we are conquerors, yea, more than conquerors."

Christ, by dying, made atonement for sin, and so conquered Satan. By the merit of his death he satisfied God's justice for the sins of all that should believe in him; and if the judge remit the sentence, the executioner has nothing to do with the prisoner. We were ready to fall under the curse, to be made an anathema, that is, to be delivered unto Satan; Christ said, Upon me be the curse: this blotted out the handwriting that was against us, took it out of the way, nailed it to the cross; and so Satan is spoiled;—Who shall condemn? It is Christ that died. When God forgives the iniquity of his people, he brings back their captivity. If we shall not come into condemnation, we are saved from coming into execution.

Christ, by dying, sealed the gospel of grace, and purchased the Spirit of grace; and so conquered Satan. The Spirit acting by the gospel as the instrument, and the gospel animated by the Spirit as the principal, are become "mighty to the pulling down of Satan's strong holds." Thus a foundation is laid for a believer's victory over the temptations and terrors of the wicked one. Christ's victory over Satan is our victory, and we overcome him "by the blood of the Lamb." Thus kings of armies did flee apace, and even they that tarried at home, and did themselves contribute nothing to the victory, yet "divided the spoil." Christ, having thus trodden Satan under our feet, calls to us, as Joshua to the captains of Israel, "Come near, put your feet upon the necks of these kings." "Resist the devil and he will flee from you," for he is a conquered enemy.

(vi.) Come and see the worth of souls.—We judge of the value of a thing, by the price which a wise man that understands it gives for it. He that made souls, and had reason to know them, provided for their redemption, not "corruptible things as silver and gold, but the precious blood of his own Son." It was not a purchase made hastily, for it was the contrivance of infinite wisdom from eternity; it was not made for necessity, for he neither needed us nor could he be benefited by us; but thus he was pleased to teach us what account we should make of our own souls, and their salvation and happiness. The incarnation of Christ put a great honour upon the human nature: never was it so dignified, as when it was taken into union with the divine nature in the person of Immanuel. But the death and sufferings of Christ add much more to its value, for he laid down his own life to be a ransom of ours, when nothing else was sufficient to answer the price. Lord, what is man that he should be thus visited, thus regarded! —that the Son of God should not only dwell among us, but die for us!

Now, let us see this, and learn how to put a value upon our own souls. Not so as to advance our conceit of ourselves,—nothing can be more humbling and abasing, than to see our lives sold by our own folly, and redeemed by the merit of another; but so as to increase our concern for ourselves, and our own spiritual interests. Shall the souls, the precious souls, upon which Christ put such a value, and paid such a price for, debase and undervalue themselves so far as to become slaves to Satan, and drudges to the world and the flesh? We are bought with a price; and therefore we not only injure the purchaser's right to us, if we alienate ourselves to another, but we reproach his wisdom in paying such a price, if we alienate ourselves for a thing of nought. It is the apostle's argument against uncleanness, and against making ourselves the servants of men. Christ having purchased our souls at such a rate, we disparage them if we stake them to the trifles of the world, or pawn them for the base and sordid pleasures of sin. Shall that birthright be sold for a mess of pottage, which Christ bought with his own blood? No; while we live, let our souls be our darlings, (Ps. xxii. 20,) for his sake to whom they were so dear. If Christ died and suffered so much to save our souls, let us not hazard the losing of them, though it be to gain the whole world.

Let us see this, and learn how to put a value upon the souls of others. This forbids us to do any thing that may turn to the prejudice of the souls of others, by drawing them to sin, or discouraging them in that which is good. The apostle lays a great stress upon this argument, against the abuse of our Christian liberty, to the offence of others—" Destroy not him with thy meat for whom Christ died." Shall not we deny ourselves and our own satisfaction, rather than occasion guilt or grief to them for whom Christ humbled himself, even to the death of the cross? Shall we slight those upon whom Christ put such a value? Shall we set those with the dogs of our flock, whom

Christ purchased with his own blood, and set among the lambs of his flock? God forbid.

This also commands us to do all we can for the spiritual welfare and salvation of the souls of others. Did Christ think them worth his blood? and shall not we think them worth our care and pains? Shall not we willingly do our utmost to save a soul from death, and thereby hide a multitude of sins, when Christ did so much, and suffered so much, to make it possible? Shall not we pour out our prayers for them for whom Christ poured out his soul unto death, and bear them upon our hearts whom Christ laid so near his? Blessed Paul, in consideration hereof, not only made himself the servant of all, to please them for their edification, but was willing to be "offered upon the sacrifice and service of their faith," and so to fill up what was behind of the afflictions of Christ for his body's sake. And if we be at any time called upon even to lay down our lives for the brethren, we must remember that in that, as well as in washing their feet, Christ has left us an example.

(VII.) Come and see the purchase of the blessings of the new covenant.—The blood of Christ was not only the ransom of our forfeited lives, and the redemption of our souls from everlasting misery; but it was the valuable consideration upon which the grant of eternal life and happiness is grounded. Christ's death is our life; that is, it is not only our salvation from death, but it is the fountain of all our joys, and the foundation of all our hopes. All the comforts we have in possession, and all we have in prospect; all the privileges of our way, and all those of our home, are the blessed fruits of that accursed tree on which our Redeemer died.

See the blood of Christ, the spring from whence all the blessings of the covenant flow. That is the price of all our pardons, "we have redemption through his blood, even the forgiveness of sins:" without the shedding of blood, that precious blood, there had been no remission. That is the purchase of the divine favour, which is our life; we are made accepted only in the beloved. Peace is made, a covenant of peace settled, and peace secured to all the sons of peace, by the blood of his cross, and not otherwise. That is the price paid for the "purchased possession, that they which are called may receive the promise of eternal inheritance." Christ was made a curse for us, not only to redeem us from the curse of the law, but that we through him might inherit the blessing. Thus, "out of the eater comes forth meat, and out of the strong sweetness." Behold, he shows us a mystery.

See the blood of Christ, the stream in which all the blessings of the covenant flow to us. The blood of Christ, as it is exhibited to us in this ordinance, is the vehicle, the channel of conveyance by which all graces and comforts descend from heaven to earth. "This cup is the new testament in the blood of Christ," and so it becomes a cup of blessing, a cup of consolation, a cup of salvation. All the hidden manna comes to us in this dew. It is the blood of Christ speaking for us, that pacifies an offended God: it is the blood of Christ sprinkled on us, that purifies a defiled conscience. As it was the "blood of Jesus that consecrated for us the new and living way," and opened the kingdom of heaven to all believers; so it is by that blood that we have boldness "to enter into the holiest."

(VIII.) Come and see how much we owe to the death of Christ, the rich purchases he made for us, that he might cause us to inherit substance, and might fill our treasures.—Let this increase our esteem of the love of Christ, which was not only so very expensive to himself, but so very advantageous to us. Let this also enhance the value of covenant blessings in our eyes. The blessings of this life we owe to the bounty of God's providence, but spiritual blessings in heavenly things we owe to the blood of his Son. Let these, therefore, be to us more precious than rubies, —let these always have a preference,—let us be willing to part with any thing, rather than hazard the favour of God, the comforts of the Spirit, and life eternal, remembering what these cost,—let us never make light of wisdom's preparations, when we see at what rate they were bought in. To them who believe they are precious, for they know they were purchased by the precious blood of Christ, which we undervalue as a common thing, if we prefer farms and merchandize before heaven and the present earnests of it.

CHAPTER IX.

SOME ACCOUNT OF THE PRECIOUS BENEFITS WHICH ARE TO BE RECEIVED BY FAITH IN THIS ORDINANCE.

I. The pardon and forgiveness of our sins; a renewed pardon of daily trespasses, and a confirmed pardon of all trespasses. II. The adoption of sons; the privileges of adoption, and the Spirit of adoption. III. Peace and satisfaction to our minds; opened in two things. IV. Supplies of grace, confirming gracious habits, quickening gracious acts; instances of both. V. The earnests of eternal bliss and joy, the assurances of it, and the foretastes of it.

In the Lord's Supper, we are not only to "show the Lord's death," and see what is to be seen in it, as many who, when he was upon the cross, stood afar off beholding;—no; we must there be more than spectators—we must eat of the sacrifice, and "so partake of the altar." The bread which came down from heaven was not designed merely for showbread, bread to be looked upon; but for household bread, bread to be fed upon, bread to strengthen our hearts, and wine to make them glad; and wisdom's invitation is, "Come, eat of my bread, and drink of the wine that I have mingled." Christ's feeding great multitudes miraculously, more than once, when he was here upon earth, was (as his other miracles) significant of the spiritual provision he makes in the everlasting gospel, for the support and satisfaction of those that leave all to follow him. If we do not all eat, and be not all filled abundantly with the goodness of his house, it is our own fault. Let us not then straiten and starve ourselves, for the Master of the feast has not stinted us; he has not only invited us, and made provision for our entertainment, but he calls to us as one that bids us hearty welcome — "Eat, O friends! drink, yea, drink abundantly, O beloved!"

All people are for what they can get: here is something to be got in this ordinance, if it be rightly improved, which will turn to our account infinitely more than the "merchandize of silver, or the gain of fine gold." Christ and all his benefits are here not only set before us, not only offered to us, but settled upon us, under certain provisos and limitations; so that a believer, who sincerely consents to the covenant, receives some of the present benefit of it, in and by this ordinance, both in the comfortable experience of communion with God in grace, and the comfortable expectation of the vision and fruition of God in glory.

Gospel ordinances in general, and this in particular, which is the seal of gospel promises, are wells of salvation, out of which we may draw water with joy; breasts of consolation, from which we may suck and be satisfied; golden pipes, through which the oil of grace is derived from the good olive, to keep our lamps burning. We receive the grace of God herein in vain, if we take not what is here tendered—gospel blessings upon gospel terms. We are here to receive Christ Jesus the Lord, and since "with him God freely gives us all things," we must with him by faith take what he gives—"all spiritual blessings in heavenly things by Christ Jesus."

I. Here we may receive the pardon and forgiveness of our sins. This is that great blessing of the new covenant, which makes way for all other blessings, by taking down that wall of partition which separated between us and God, and hinders good things from us: it is the matter of that promise which comes in as a reason for all the rest—I will do so and so for them, "for I will be merciful to their unrighteousness." This is that great blessing which Christ died to purchase for us: his blood was shed for many, for the remission of sins; and perhaps he intimated this to be in a special manner designed by him in his sufferings, when the first word we find recorded that he spoke, after he was nailed to the cross, was, "Father, forgive them;" which seems to look not only to those that had an immediate hand in his death, but to those that are remotely accessary to it, as all sinners are, though they know not what they do.

The everlasting gospel is an act of indemnity—an act of oblivion we may call it, for it is promised that our sins and iniquities he will remember no more: it is indeed an act of grace; repentance and remission of sins is by it published in Christ's name to all nations. It is proclaimed to the rebels, that, if they will lay down their arms, acknowledge their offence, return to their allegiance, approve themselves good subjects for the future, and make the merits of him whom the Father hath appointed to be the Mediator, their plea in suing out their pardon, the offended Prince will be reconciled to them, their attainder shall be reversed, and they shall not only be restored to all the privileges of subjects, but advanced to the honours and advantages of favourites. Now it concerns us all to be able to make it out that we are entitled to the benefit of this act, that we are qualified, according to the tenor of it, for the favour intended by it; and if we be so indeed, in the Lord's Supper we receive that pardon to us in particular, which in the gospel is proclaimed to all in general. We do here receive the atonement, as the expression is. God hath received it for the securing of his honour, and we receive it for the securing of our happiness and comfort; we claim the benefit of it, and desire to be justified and accepted of God for the sake of it.

This sacrament should therefore be received with

a heart thus lifting up itself to God: "Lord, I am a sinner, a great sinner, I have done very foolishly; forfeited thy favour, incurred thy displeasure, and deserve to be for ever abandoned by thee. But Christ died; yea rather, is risen again, hath finished transgression, made an end of sin, made reconciliation for iniquity, and brought in an everlasting righteousness; he gave his life a ransom for many, and if for many, why not for me? In him a free and full remission is promised to all penitent, obedient believers; by him all that believe are justified, and to them there is no condemnation. Thou, even thou, art he that blottest out their transgressions for thine own sake, and art gracious and merciful; nay, thou art faithful and just to forgive them their sins. Lord, I repent,—I believe, and take the benefit of those promises, those exceeding great and precious promises, which are to my soul as life from the dead. I flee to this city of refuge, I take hold of the horns of this altar; here I humbly receive the forgiveness of my sins, through Jesus Christ, the great propitiation, to whom I entirely owe it, and to whom I acknowledge myself infinitely indebted for it, and under the highest obligations imaginable to love him, and live to him. He is the Lord our righteousness, so accept I him: let him be made of God to me righteousness, and I have enough; I am happy for ever."

Every time we come to the Lord's Supper, we come to receive the remission of sins; that is,

1. A renewed pardon of daily trespasses.—In many things we offend daily, and even he that is washed, that is, in a justified state, needs to wash his feet; and, blessed be God, there is a fountain opened for us to wash in, and encouragement given to pray for daily pardon as duly as we do for daily bread. We have to do with a God that multiplies pardon. Lord, the guilt of such a sin lies upon me like a heavy burden; I have lamented it, confessed it, renewed my covenant against it, and now in this ordinance I receive the forgiveness of that sin: and here it is said to my soul, "The Lord hath put away thy

sin, thou shalt not die." Many a fault I have been overtaken in since I was last with the Lord at his table; and, having repented of them, I desire to apply the blood of Christ to my soul, in a particular manner, for the forgiveness of them.

2. A confirmed pardon of all trespasses.—I come here to receive further assurances of the forgiveness of my sins, and further comfort arising from those assurances. I come to hear again that voice of joy and gladness, which has made many a broken bone to rejoice—" Son, daughter, be of good cheer; thy sins are forgiven thee:" I come for the father's kiss to a returning prodigal, which seals his pardon, so as to silence his doubts and fears. When God would by his prophets speak comfortably to Zion, thus he saith—" Thy warfare is accomplished, thine iniquity is pardoned." And the inhabitant shall not say, " I am sick;" that is, he shall see no cause to complain of any outward calamity, if his iniquity be forgiven. O that I might here have the white stone of absolution, and my pardon written more legibly! O that Christ would say to me, as he did to that woman to whom much was already forgiven, " Thy sins are forgiven!" This is what I come to receive, O let me not go away without it.

II. Here we may receive adoption of sons. The covenant of grace not only frees us from the doom of criminals, but advances us to the dignity of children: Christ redeemed us from the curse of the law, in order to this, that " we might receive the adoption of sons." The children's bread given us in this ordinance is, as it were, livery and seisin, to assure us of our adoption upon the terms of the gospel, that if we will take God in Christ to be to us a Father, to rule and dispose of us, and to be feared and honoured by us, he will take us to be his sons and daughters. " Behold, what manner of love is this!" Be astonished, O heavens! and wonder, O earth! Never was there such compassionate, such condescending love! God here seals us the grant both of the privileges of adoption, and the Spirit of adoption.

Here is a grant of the privileges of adoption sealed to us.—Here we are called the children of God, and he calls himself our Father, and encourages us to call himself so. " Seemeth it to you a light thing," saith David, " to be a king's son-in-law, seeing I am a poor man, and lightly esteemed?" And shall it not seem to us a great thing, an honour infinitely above all those which the world can pretend to confer, for us who are worms of the earth, and a generation of vipers, children of disobedience and wrath by nature, to be the adopted children of the King of kings? " This honour have all the saints." Nor is it an empty title that is here granted us, but real advantages of unspeakable value.

The eternal God here saith it, and seals it to every true believer: Fear not, I will be a Father to thee, an ever-loving, ever-living Father: leave it to me to provide for thee; on me let all thy burdens be cast; with me let all thy cares be left, and to me let all thy requests be made known; "the young lions shall lack and suffer hunger," but thou shalt want nothing that is good for thee, nothing that is fit for thee; my wisdom shall be thy guide, my power thy support, and " underneath thee the everlasting arms. As the tender father pities his children, so will I pity thee, and spare thee as a man spareth his son that serves him." Thou shalt have my blessing and love, the smiles of my face, and the kisses of my mouth, and in the arms of my grace will I carry thee to glory, as the nursing father doth the sucking child. Does any thing grieve thee? Whither shouldst thou go with thy complaint, but to thy Father? saying to him as that child, " My head, my head;" and thou shalt find that "as one whom his mother comforteth, so will the Lord thy God comfort thee." Does any thing terrify thee? " Be not afraid, for I am thy God; when thou passest through the waters, I will be with thee; and through the rivers, they shall not overflow thee." Art thou in doubt? Consult me, and " I will instruct thee in the way that thou shouldst go: I will guide thee with mine eye." Acknowledge me, and I will direct thy steps. Dost thou offend? Is there foolishness bound up in thy heart? Thou must expect fatherly correction: "I will chasten thee with the rod of men, and with the stripes of the children of men; but my loving-kindness will I not utterly take from thee;" thine afflictions shall not only consist with, but flow from covenant love; and but for a season, when need is, shalt thou be in heaviness.

"I will be a father to thee; and, son, thou shalt be ever with me, and all that I have is thine; whether Paul, or Apollos, or Cephas, or the world, or life, or death, or things present, or things to come, all are thine," as far as is necessary to thine happiness; nor shall any thing ever be able to separate thee from my love. I will be a father to thee, and then Christ shall be thy elder brother, the prophet, priest, and king of the family, as the first-born among many brethren. Angels shall be thy guard: with the greatest care and tenderness shall they bear thee up in their arms, as ministering spirits charged to attend the heirs of salvation.

Providence shall be thy protector, and the disposer of all thine affairs for the best; so that whatever happens, thou mayest be sure it shall be made to work for thy good, though as yet thou canst not see how or which way. The assurances of thy Father's love to thee, in his promises and communion with him in his ordinances, shall be thy daily bread, thy continual feast, the manna that shall be rained upon thee, the water out of the rock that shall follow thee in this wilderness, till thou come to Canaan.

Now art thou a child of God, but it doth not yet appear what thou shalt be. When thou wast predestinated to the adoption of a son, thou wast designed for the inheritance of a son; if a child, then an heir. Thy present maintenance shall be honourable and comfortable, and such as is fit for thee in thy minority, while thou art under tutors and governors; but what is now laid out upon thee is nothing, in comparison with what is laid up for thee; an inheritance incorruptible, undefiled, and that fades not away. If

God be thy Father, no less than a crown, a kingdom, shall be thy portion, and heaven thy home, where thou shalt be for ever with him. In thy Father's house there are many mansions, and one for thee, if thou be his dutiful child. It is thy Father's good pleasure to give thee the kingdom.

Here is a grant of the Spirit of adoption sealed to us.—As the giving of Christ for us was the great promise of the Old Testament, which was fulfilled in the fulness of time, so the giving of the Spirit to us is the great promise of the New Testament, and a promise that is sure to all the seed: this promise of the Father, which we have heard of Christ, we in this ordinance wait for, and it follows upon the former; for, wherever God gives the privileges of children, he will give the nature and disposition of children; regeneration always attends adoption—" because ye are sons, God hath sent forth the Spirit of his Son into your hearts." Great encouragement we have to ask this gift, from the relation of a Father, wherein God stands towards us: if earthly parents "know how to give good gifts to their children," such as are needful and proper for them, " much more shall our heavenly Father give the Holy Spirit to them that ask him." He will give the Spirit to teach his children, and, as their tutor, to lead them into all truth; to govern his children, and, as the best of guardians, to dispose their affections, while Providence disposes their affairs for the best. He will give his Spirit to renew and sanctify them, and make them meet for his service in this world, and his kingdom in a better; to be the guide of their way, and the witness of their adoption, and to seal them to the day of redemption.

An earnest of this grant of the Spirit to all believers in this ordinance, Christ gave, when, in his first visit he made to his disciples after his resurrection, having showed them his hands and his side, his pierced hands, his pierced side, (which in effect he does to us in this sacrament,) he breathed on them, and said unto them, " Receive ye the Holy Ghost." What he said to them, he says to all his disciples, making them an offer of this inestimable gift, and bestowing it effectually on all believers, who are all "sealed with that Holy Spirit of promise." Receive then the Holy Ghost, in the receiving of this bread and wine; the graces of the Spirit, as bread to strengthen the heart; his comforts, as wine to make it glad. Be willing and desirous to receive the Holy Ghost, let the soul and all its powers be put under his operations and influences: "Lift up your heads, O ye gates, and be lifted up, ye everlasting doors, and then this King of Glory shall come in," to all that invite him and will bid him welcome.

"But will God in very deed thus dwell with men," with such men upon the earth? And shall they become temples of the Holy Ghost? Shall he come upon them? Shall the power of the Highest overshadow them? Shall Christ be formed in me, a holy thing? Say, then, my soul, say as the blessed virgin did, Here I am, "be it unto me according to thy word." I acknowledge myself unworthy the being of a man, having so often acted more like a brute, much more unworthy the dignity of a son; I have been an undutiful, rebellious prodigal; I deserve to be turned out of doors, abandoned and disinherited, and forbidden my Father's house and table. But who shall set bounds to infinite mercy, and to the compassions of the Everlasting Father? If, notwithstanding this, he will yet again take me into his family, and clothe me with the best robe; though it is too great a favour for me to receive, who am a child of disobedience, yet it is not too great for him to give, who is the Father of mercies. To thee, therefore, O God, I give up myself, and I will "from this time cry unto thee, My Father, thou art the guide of my youth." Though I deserve not to be owned as a hired servant, I desire and hope to be owned as an adopted son. Be it unto thy servant according to thy promise.

III. Here we may receive peace and satisfaction in our minds.—This is one of the precious legacies Christ has left to all his followers; and it is here in this ordinance paid, or secured to be paid, to all those that are ready and willing to receive it: "Peace I leave with you, my peace I give unto you;" such a peace as the world can neither give nor take away. This is the repose of the soul in God, our reconciliation to ourselves, arising from the sense of our reconciliation to God, the conscience being thus fully purged from dead works, which not only defile, but disturb and disquiet us. When the "Spirit is poured out on high, then the work of righteousness is peace, and the effect of righteousness, quietness and assurance for ever." The guilt of sin lays the foundation of trouble and uneasiness; where that is removed by pardoning mercy, there is ground for peace: but there must be a further act of the divine grace to put us in the actual possession of that peace; when he who alone can open the ear to comfort, as well as discipline, makes us to hear joy and gladness, then the storm ceases, and there is a calm. The mind that was disturbed with the dread of God's wrath, is quieted with the tokens of his favour and love.

This we should have in our eye at the Lord's table: here I am waiting to hear what God the Lord will speak, and hoping that he, who speaks peace to his people and to his saints, will speak that peace to me, who make it the top of my ambition to answer the character, and have the lot, of his people and saints. This peace we may here expect to receive for two reasons:

Because this ordinance is a seal of the promise of peace; in it God assures us that his thoughts towards us are thoughts of peace, and then ours towards ourselves may be so. We are here among his people, whom he has promised to bless with peace, and we may apply that promise to ourselves, plead it, and humbly claim the benefit of it. This is that rest to the soul which our Master has promised to all those that come to him, and take his yoke upon them; and this promise, among the rest, is here ratified, as yea and amen in Christ.

The covenant of grace is indeed a covenant of peace, in the ever-blessed soil of which "light is sown for the righteous, and gladness for the upright in heart." And this covenant of peace is that which eternal truth hath said, shall never be removed, but shall stand firm as a rock, when the "everlasting mountains shall melt" like wax, and the "perpetual hills shall bow." Has God so far consulted my present repose, as well as my future bliss, that he has provided not only for the satisfaction of his own justice, but for the satisfaction of my conscience; and shall I indulge my own disturbance, and refuse to be comforted? No; welcome the promised peace, the calm so long wished for, the desired haven of a troubled spirit, tossed with tempest. Come, my soul, and take possession of this Canaan; by faith enter into this rest, and let not thine own unbelief exclude thee. If the God of peace himself speak peace, though with a still small voice, let that silence the most noisy and clamorous objections of doubts and fears; and, if he give quietness, let not them make trouble.

Because this ordinance is an instituted means of obtaining the peace promised. As the sacrifice was ordained to make atonement for the soul, so the feast upon the sacrifice was intended for the satisfaction of the soul concerning the atonement made, to remove that amazement and terror which arose from the consciousness of guilt. This ordinance is a feast appointed for that purpose. God doth here not only assure us of the truth of his promise to us, but gives us an opportunity of solemnizing our engagements to him, and sealing ourselves to be his, which is appointed not to satisfy him, (he that knows all things knows if we love him,) but to satisfy ourselves, that, thus taking hold of the hope set before us, we may have strong consolation. The blood of Christ is in this ordinance sprinkled upon the conscience, to pacify that, having been already sprinkled upon the mercy-seat, to make atonement there, so making the comers thereunto perfect.

When the Lord Jesus appeared to his disciples after his resurrection, the first word he said to them was, "Peace be unto you;" and he saith the same to us in this ordinance, Peace be unto this house, peace to this heart. But the disciples of Christ, like those that are apt to be terrified "and affrighted, supposing that they have seen a spirit," or apparition, fearing that it is but all a delusion, it is too good news to be true; what have they to do with peace, think they, while their corruptions, follies, and infirmities are so many? But Christ, by this sacrament, checks those fears; as there, "Why are ye troubled; and why do thoughts arise in your hearts? Behold my hands and my feet!" There is that in the marks of the nails, which is sufficient to stop the mouth of unbelief, and to heal the wounds of a broken and contrite spirit. There is merit enough in Christ, though in us there is nothing but meanness and unworthiness. Such considerations this ordinance offers, as have often been found effectual, by the grace of God, to create the fruit of the lips, peace, and to restore comfort to the mourners. In it Christ saith again, " Peace be unto you," as he did unto the disciples. And sometimes a mighty power has gone along with that word to lay a storm, as it did with that, (Mark iv. 39.) "Peace, be still;" so that the soul so calmed, so quieted, has gone away, and said with wonder, "What manner of man is this, for even the winds and the seas obey him!"

IV. Here we may receive supplies of grace.—Jesus Christ is, in this ordinance, made of God to all believers, not only righteousness, but sanctification; so we must receive him; and having received him, so we must walk in him. It is certain we have as much need of the influences of the Spirit to furnish us for our duties, as we have of the merit of Christ to atone for our sins; and as much need of divine grace, to carry on the good work, as to begin it. We are in ourselves not only ungodly, but without strength, impotent in that which is good, and inclined to that which is evil; and in the Lord alone have we both righteousness and strength. If, therefore, we have it in him, hither we must come, to have it from him: for gospel ordinances, and this particularly, are the means of grace, and the ordinary vehicle in which grace is conveyed to the souls of believers. Though God is not tied to them, we are, and must attend with an expectation to receive grace from God by them, and an entire submission of soul to the operation and conduct of that grace. This ordinance is as the pool of Bethesda, which our weak and impotent souls must lie down by, waiting for the moving of the waters, as those that know there is a healing virtue in them by which we may experience benefit as well as others. Here, therefore, we must set ourselves, expecting and desiring the effectual workings of God's free grace in us, attending at wisdom's gates for wisdom's gifts, and endeavouring to improve the ordinance to this end.

From the fulness that is in Jesus Christ, in whom " it pleased the Father that all fulness should dwell," we are here waiting to receive grace for grace, that is " abundance of grace, and of the gift of righteousness." Where there is true grace, there is need of more, for the best are sanctified but in part; and there is a desire of more, forgetting the things which are behind, and reaching forth to those which are before, pressing towards perfection; and there is a promise of more, for to him that hath shall be given; and " he that hath clean hands shall be stronger and stronger." Therefore, in a sense of our own necessities, and a dependence on God's promises, we must by faith receive and apply to ourselves the grace offered us. "What things soever we desire," according to the will of God, "if we believe that we receive them," our Saviour has told us, " we shall have them." "According to thy faith, be it unto thee."

Reach forth a hand of faith, therefore, and receive the promised grace, both for the confirming of gracious habits, and for the quickening of gracious acts.

1. Let us here receive grace for the confirming of gracious habits, that they may be more deeply rooted. We are conscious to ourselves of great weak-

ness in grace: it is like a grain of mustard seed, as a bruised reed, and smoking flax;—we are weak in our knowledge, and apt to mistake; weak in our affections, and apt to cool; weak in our resolutions, and apt to waver. How weak is my heart! But here is bread that strengthens man's heart, signifying that grace of God, which confirms the principles, and invigorates the powers of the spiritual and divine life in the souls of the faithful. Come, my soul, come eat of this bread, and it shall strengthen thee: though perhaps thou mayest not be immediately sensible of this strength received; the improvement of habits is not suddenly discerned; yet, through this grace, thou shalt find hereafter, that thy path has been like the shining light, which shines more and more.

We find there is much lacking in our faith, in our love, and every grace; here, therefore, we must desire and hope, and prepare to receive from Christ such gifts of the Holy Ghost as will be mighty, through God, to increase our faith, that its discoveries of divine things may be more clear and distinct, and its assurances of the truth of them more certain and confident; that its consent to the covenant may be more free and resolved, and its complacency in the covenant more sweet and delightful. And that which thus increases our faith will be effectual to inflame our love, and make that strong as death, in its desires towards God, and resolutions for him. We must here wait to be strengthened with all might, by his Spirit in the inner man, unto all patience in suffering for him, and diligence in doing for him, and both with joyfulness. We here put ourselves under the happy influence of that great and glorious power, which works mightily in them that believe.

2. Let us here receive grace for the quickening of gracious acts, that they may be more strongly exerted; we come to this throne of grace, this mercy-seat, this table of our God, that here we may not only obtain mercy to pardon, but may find "grace to help in every time of need," grace to excite us to, to direct us in, and thoroughly furnish us for every good

word and work, according as the duty of every day requires. It was a very encouraging word which Christ said to Paul, when he prayed for the removal of that messenger of Satan which was sent to buffet him: "My grace is sufficient for thee;" and all true believers may take the comfort of it: what was said to him is said to every person, whatever the exigence of the case is; they that commit themselves to the grace of God, with a sincere resolution in every thing to submit to the conduct and government of that grace, shall be enabled to do all things through Christ strengthening them.

3. Let a lively faith here descend to particulars, and receive this grace with application to the various occurrences of the Christian life. When I go about any duty of solemn worship, I find I am not sufficient of myself for it, not so much as to think one good thought of myself, much less such a chain of good thoughts as is necessary to an acceptable prayer, to the profitable reading and hearing of the word, and the right sanctification of the Lord's day; but all our sufficiency for these services is of God, and of his grace. That grace I here receive according to the promise, and will always go forth, and go on in the strength of it.

When an opportunity offers itself of doing good to others, to their bodies, by relieving their necessities, or contributing any way to their comfort and support; or to their souls by seasonable advice, instruction, reproof, or other good discourse; we must depend on this grace for ability to do it prudently, faithfully, and successfully, and so as to be accepted of God in it. I find I want wisdom for these and such like services, and for the ordering of all my affairs; and whither shall I go for it but to wisdom's feasts, whose preparations are not only good for food, and pleasant to the eye, but greatly to be desired to make one wise? Here therefore I receive "Christ Jesus the Lord, as made of God unto me wisdom;" wisdom dwelling with prudence; wisdom to understand my way, that wisdom in which every doubtful case is profitable to direct. Having many a time prayed Solomon's prayer, for a wise and understanding heart, I here receive the sealed grant in answer to it: "wisdom and knowledge are given thee," so much as shall be sufficient for thee in thy place and station, to guide thee in glorifying God, so that thou mayest not come short of enjoying him.

When we are assaulted with temptations to sin, we find how weak and ineffectual our resistance has often been; here, therefore, we receive grace to fortify us against all those assaults, that we may not be foiled and overcome by them. All that in this sacrament list themselves under the banner of the Captain of our salvation, and engage themselves as his faithful soldiers in a holy war against the world, the flesh, and the devil, may here be furnished with the whole armour of God, and that power of his might, as it is called, wherewith they shall be able to stand and withstand in the evil day. I now receive from God and his grace, strength against such a sin that has oft prevailed over me, such temptation that has oft been too hard for me; "now, therefore, O God, strengthen my hands." Through God I shall do valiantly.

When we are burdened with affliction, we find it hard to bear up: we faint in the day of adversity, which is a sign our strength is small; we grieve too much, and are full of fears in a day of trouble, our hearts many a time are ready to fail us; hither therefore we come to receive grace sufficient for our support under the calamities of this present time, that, whatever we lose, we may not lose our comfort, and whatever we suffer we may not sink;—grace to enable us, whatever happens, to keep possession of our own souls, by keeping up our hope and joy in God; that, when flesh and heart fail, we may find God the strength of our heart; and if he be so, "as our day is, so shall our strength be." Such assurances are here given to all believers of God's presence with them in all their afflictions, and of the concurrence of all for their good, that, being thus encouraged, they have all the reason in the world to say, Welcome the will of God; nothing can come amiss.

We know not how we may be called on to bear our testimony to the truths and ways of God in suffering for righteousness' sake; we are bid to count upon them, and to prepare for them. We must in this ordinance faithfully promise, that however we may be tried, we will never forsake Christ, nor turn from following after him; though we should die with him, yet will we not deny him. But we have no reason to confide in any strength of our own, for the making good of this promise; nor can we pretend to such a degree of resolution, steadiness, and presence of mind, as will enable us to encounter the difficulties we may meet with. Peter, when he shamed himself, warned us to take heed lest we fall, when we think we stand. Here, therefore, we must receive strength for such trials, that we may overcome them by the blood of the Lamb, and by not loving our lives unto the death, and that the prospect of none of these things may move us.

4. How near our great change may be we cannot tell, perhaps nearer than we imagine: we are not sure that we shall live to see another opportunity of this kind; but this we are sure of, that it is a serious thing to die: it is a work we never did, and when we come to do it, we shall need a strength we never had. In this sacrament, therefore, from the death of Christ, we must fetch in grace to prepare us for death, and to carry us safely and comfortably through that dark and dismal valley. I depend not only on the providence of God, to order the circumstances of my removal hence for the best to me, but upon the grace of God to take out the sting of death, and then to reconcile me to the stroke of death, and to enable me to meet death's harbinger, and bear its agonies, not only with the constancy and patience that becomes a wise man, but with the hope and joy that becomes a good Christian.

V. Here we may receive the earnests of eternal

bliss and joy.—Heaven is the crown and centre of all the promises, and the perfection of all the good contained in them; all the blessings of the new covenant have a tendency to this, and are in order to it. Are we predestinated? It is to the inheritance of sons. Called? It is to his kingdom and glory. Sanctified? It is that we may be made meet for the inheritance, and wrought to the self-same thing. This, therefore, we should have in our eye, in our covenant and communion with God; that eternal life which God who cannot lie promises. We must receive the Spirit in his graces and comforts, as the earnest of our inheritance. They that deal with God, must deal upon trust, for a happiness in reversion, a recompense of reward to come; must forsake a world in sight and present, for a world out of sight and future. All believers consent to this; they lay up their treasure in heaven, and hope for what they see not. This they depend upon; and in prospect of it they are willing to labour and suffer, to deny themselves, and take up their cross, knowing that heaven will make amends for all: though they may be losers for Christ, they shall not be losers by him in the end; this is the bargain. In the Lord's Supper, Christ gives us earnest upon this bargain, and what we receive there, we receive as earnest. An earnest not only confirms the bargain and secures the performance of it, but is itself part of the payment, though but a small part in comparison with the full sum.

We here receive the earnest of our inheritance; that is,

We here receive the assurance of it. The royal grant of it is here sealed and delivered by the King of kings. God here says to me as he did to Abraham, "Lift up thine eyes now, and look from the place where thou art." Take a view of the heavenly Canaan, that land which eternally flows with better things than milk and honey,—Immanuel's land. Open the eye of faith, and behold the pleasures and glories of that world, as they are described in Scripture, such as eye hath not seen, nor ear heard; and know of a surety that all the land which thou seest, and that which is infinitely more and better than thou canst conceive, to thee will I give it, to thee for ever. "Fear not, little flock," fear not ye little ones of the flock, "it is your Father's good pleasure to give you the kingdom." Follow Christ and serve him, and you shall be for ever with him; continue with him now in his temptations, and you shall shortly share with him in his glories. Only be faithful unto death, and the crown of life is as sure to you, as if it were already upon your heads. Here is livery and seizin upon the deed. Take this and eat it, take this and drink it: in token of this, "I will be to thee a God;" that is, a perfect and everlasting happiness, such as shall answer the vast extent and compass of that great word. "But now they desire a better country, that is, a heavenly: wherefore God is not ashamed to be called their God, for he hath prepared for them a city."

Come now, my soul, and accept the security offered. The inheritance secured is unspeakably rich and invaluable; the losses and sufferings of this present time are not worthy to be compared with it; the title is good, it is a purchased possession, he that grants it has power over all flesh, that he should give eternal life. The assurances are unquestionably valid, not only the word and oath, but the writing and seal of the eternal God, in the Scriptures and sacraments: here is that, my soul, which thou mayest venture thyself upon, and venture thine all for; do it then, do it with a holy boldness. Lay hold on eternal life, lay fast hold on it, and keep thy hold. Look up, my soul, look as high as heaven, the highest heaven; look forward, my soul, look as far forward as eternity, and let eternal life, eternal joy, eternal glory, be thine aim in thy religion, and resolve to take up with nothing short of these. God has been "willing more abundantly to show to the heirs of promise the immutability of his counsel," and therefore has thus confirmed it, so as to leave no room for doubting, that by all these "immutable things, in which it is impossible for God to lie, we might have strong consolation, who have fled for refuge to lay hold on the hope set before us." Take him at his word, then, and build thy hope upon it. Be not faithless, but believing; be not careless, but industrious. Here is a happiness worth striving for; "run with patience the race that is set before thee," with this prize in thine eye.

We receive the foretastes of it.—We have in this ordinance, not only a ratification of the promise of the heavenly Canaan, but a pattern or specimen given us of the fruits of that land, like the bunch of grapes which was brought from the valley of Eshcol to the Israelites in the wilderness; a view given us of that land of promise, like that which Moses had of the land of Canaan from the top of Pisgah. As the law was a type and figure of the Messiah's kingdom on earth, so the gospel is of his kingdom in heaven; both are "shadows of good things to come," like the map of a rich and large country in a sheet of paper. Our future happiness is, in this sacrament, not only sealed to us, but shown to us; and we here taste something of the pleasures of that better country. In this ordinance we have a sight of Christ, he is evidently set forth before us; and what is heaven, but to see him as he is, and to be for ever beholding his glory? We are here receiving the pledges and tokens of Christ's love to us, and returning the protestations and expressions of our love to him; and what is heaven but an eternal interchanging of love between a holy God and holy souls? We are here praising and blessing the Redeemer, celebrating his honour, and giving him the glory of his achievements; and what is that but the work of heaven? It is what the inhabitants of that world are doing now, and what we hope to be doing with them to eternity. We are here in spiritual communion with all the saints coming in faith, hope, and love, to the general assembly and church of the first-born; and what is heaven but that in perfection? In a word, heaven is a feast, and so is this; only this is a running banquet, that is an everlasting feast.

Come, my soul, and see a door here opened in heaven; look in at that door now, by which thou hopest to enter shortly. Let this ordinance do something of the work of heaven upon thee, God having provided in it something of the pleasures of heaven for thee. Heaven will for ever part between thee and sin; let this ordinance, therefore, set thee at a greater distance from it. Heaven will fill thee with the love of God; in this ordinance, therefore, let that love be shed abroad in thine heart. In heaven thou shalt enter into the joy of the Lord; let that joy now enter into thee, and be thy strength and thy song. Heaven will be perfect holiness; let this ordinance make thee more holy, and more conformable to the image of the holy Jesus; heaven will be everlasting rest; here, therefore, return to God as thy rest, O my soul, and repose thyself in him. Let every sacrament be to thee a heaven upon earth, and each of these days of the Son of man, as one of the days of heaven.

CHAPTER X.

HELPS FOR THE EXCITING OF THOSE PIOUS AND DEVOUT AFFECTIONS WHICH SHOULD BE WORKING IN US WHILE WE ATTEND THIS ORDINANCE.

I. Here we must be sorry for sin; three things here to excite this sorrow. II. Confiding in Christ, in his power, in his promise. III. Delighting in God; three things to be thought of with pleasure. IV. Admiring the mysteries and miracles of redeeming love; seven things instanced as marvellous. V. Caring what we shall render; seven things which we must render.

WONDERFUL sights are here to be seen, where the Lord's death is shown forth; precious benefits are here to be had, where the covenant of grace is sealed; the transaction is very solemn, very serious, nothing more so on this side death. But what impressions must be made hereby upon our souls? How must we stand affected while this is doing? Is this service only a show, at which we may be unconcerned spectators? Or is it a market-place, in which we may stand all the day idle? No, by no means; here is work to be done, heart-work, such as requires a very close application of mind, and a great liveliness and vigour of spirit, and in which all that is within us should be employed, and all little enough. Here is that to be done which calls for fixed thoughts and warm affections, which needs them, and well deserves them. What sensible movings of affection we should aim at, is not easy to direct; tempers vary; some are soon moved, and much moved with every thing that affects them: from such it may be expected that their passions, which are strong at other times, should not be weak at this ordinance: and yet, no doubt, there are others whose natural temper is happily more calm and sedate, who are not conscious to themselves of such stirring of affections as some experience at this ordinance, and yet have as comfortable communion with God, as good evidence of the truth and growth of grace, and as much real benefit by the ordinance, as those that think themselves even transported by it. The deepest rivers are scarce perceived to move, and make the least noise. On the other hand, there may be much heat where there is little light, and strong passions where there are very weak resolutions. Like the waters of a land flood, which make a great show, but are shallow and soon gone. We must not, therefore, build a good opinion of our spiritual state upon the vehemence of our affection. A romance may represent a tragical story so pathetically, as to make a great impression upon the minds of some, who yet know the whole matter to be both feigned and foreign; bodily exercise, if that be all, profits little. And, on the other hand, there may be a true and strong faith, informing the judgment, bowing the will, and commanding the affections, and purifying the heart and life, where yet there are not any transports, or pathetical expressions. There may be true joy, where the mouth is not filled with laughter, nor the tongue with singing; and true sorrow where yet the eye doth not run down with tears. They whose hearts are firmly fixed for God, may take the comfort of that, though they do not find their hearts sensibly flowing out towards him.

And yet in this sacrament, where it is designed that the eye should affect the heart, we must not rest in the bare contemplation of what is here set before us, but the consideration thereof must make an impression upon our spirits, which should be turned as wax to the seal. If what is here done do not affect us for the present, it will not be likely to influence us afterwards; for we retain the remembrance of things better by our affections, than by our notions: "I shall never forget thy precepts, when by them thou hast quickened me." Here, therefore, let us stir up the gift that is in us, endeavouring to affect ourselves with the great things of God and our souls; and let us pray to God to affect us with them by his Spirit and grace, and to testify his acceptance of the sacrifice of a devoted heart, which we are to offer, by kindling it with this holy fire from heaven. "Awake, O north wind! and come thou south, and blow upon my garden." Come, thou blessed Spirit, and move upon these waters, these dead waters, to set them a-moving in rivers of living water: come and breathe upon these dry bones, that they may live. O that I might now be in the mount with God! That I might be so taken up with the things of the Spirit, and the other world, that for the time I may even forget that I am yet in the body, and in this world! O that I might now be soaring upward, upward towards God, pressing forward, forward toward heaven, as one not slothful in business, but fervent in spirit, serving the Lord, for here it is no time to trifle!

Let us then see, in some particulars, how we should be affected, when we are attending on the Lord in this solemnity, and in what channels these waters of the sanctuary should run, that we may take our work before us, and apply our minds to the consideration of those things that are proper to excite those affections.

I. Here we must be sorrowful for sin, after a godly sort, and blushing before God at the thought of it. Penitential grief and shame are not at all unsuitable to this ordinance, though it is intended for our joy and honour, but excellent preparatives for the benefit and comfort of it. Here we should be, like Ephraim, bemoaning ourselves; like Job, abhorring ourselves, renewing those sorrowful reflections we made upon our own follies, when we were preparing for this service, and keeping the fountain of repentance still open, still flowing. Our sorrow for sin needs not hinder our joy in God, and therefore our joy in God must not forbid our sorrow for sin.

Our near approach to God in this ordinance, should excite and increase our holy shame and sorrow. When we see what an honour we are advanced to, what a favour we are admitted to, it is seasonable to reflect upon our own unworthiness, by reason of the guilt of sin, and our own unfitness, by reason of the power of sin, to draw near to God. A man's deformity and defilement is never such a mortification to him, as when he comes into the presence of those that are comely, clean, and fashionable; and when we are conscious to ourselves, that we have dealt basely and disingenuously with one we are under the highest obligations to love and honour, an interview with the person offended cannot but renew our grief.

I am here drawing nigh to God, not only treading his courts with Christians at large, but sitting down at his table with select disciples; but when I consider how pure and holy he is, and how vile and sinful I am, I am ashamed, and blush to lift up my face before him. To me belongs shame and confusion of face. I have many a time heard of God by the hearing of the ear, but now I am taken to sit down with him at his table. Mine eyes see him, see the King in his beauty; wherefore I abhor myself, and repent in dust and ashes.—What a fool, what a wretch have I been, to offend a God who appears so holy in the eyes of all who draw nigh unto him, and so great to all them that are about him? Wo is me, for I am undone, lost and undone for ever, if there were not a Mediator between me and God, because I am a man of unclean lips, and an unclean heart. Now I perceive it, and my own degeneracy and danger by reason of it, for mine eyes have seen the King, the Lord of hosts. I have reason to be ashamed to see one to whom I am so unlike, and afraid to see one to whom I am so obnoxious. The higher we are advanced by the free grace of God, the more reason we shall see to abase ourselves, and cry, God be merciful to us, sinners!

A sight of Christ crucified should increase, excite our penitential shame and sorrow, and that evangelical repentance, in which there is an eye to the cross of Christ. It is prophesied, nay, it is promised, as a blessed effect of the pouring out of the Spirit, in gospel times, "upon the house of David, and the inhabitants of Jerusalem, that they shall look on him whom they have pierced, and shall mourn." Here we see Christ pierced for our sins, nay, pierced by our sins: our sins were the cause of his death, and the grief of his heart. The Jews and Romans crucified Christ; but, as David killed Uriah with his letter, and Ahab killed Naboth with his seal; so the hand-writing that was against us for our sins, nailed Christ to the cross, and so he nailed it to the cross. We had eaten the sour grapes, and his teeth were set on edge. Can we see him thus suffering for us, and shall we not suffer with him? Was he in such pain for us, and shall not we be in pain for him? Was his soul exceeding sorrowful, even unto death, and shall not ours be exceeding sorrowful, when that is the way to life? Come, my soul, see by faith the holy Jesus made sin for thee; the glory of heaven made a reproach of men for thee; his Father's joy made a man of sorrow for thy transgressions; see thy sins burdening him when he sweat, spitting upon him, and buffeting him, and putting him to open shame; crowning him with thorns, and piercing his hands and his side; and let this melt and break this hard and rocky heart of thine, and dissolve it into tears of godly sorrow. Look on Christ dying; and weep not for him, (though they who have any thing of ingenuousness and good nature, will see reason enough to weep for an innocent sufferer,) but weep for thyself, and thine own sins; for them be in bitterness, as one that is in bitterness for an only son.

Add to this, that our sins have not only pierced him, as they were the cause of his death, but as they have been the reproach of his holy name, and the grief of his Holy Spirit. Thus we have crucified him afresh, by doing that which he has often declared to be a vexation and dishonour to him, as far as the joys and glories of his present state can admit. The consideration of this should greatly humble us; nothing goes nearer to the quick with a true penitent, nor touches him in a more tender part than this: "They shall remember me among the nations whither they shall be carried captives, because I am broken with their whorish heart, which hath departed from me." A strange expression, that the great God should reckon himself broken by the sins of his people! No wonder it follows, they "shall loathe themselves for the evils which they have committed." Can we look upon an humbled, broken Christ, with an unhumbled, unbroken heart? Do our sins grieve him, and shall they not grieve us? Come, my soul, and sit down by the cross of Christ, as a true mourner; let it make thee weep to see him weep, and bleed to see him bleed. That heart is frozen hard indeed, which these considerations will not thaw.

The gracious offer here made us, of peace and pardon, should excite and increase our godly sorrow and shame. This is a gospel motive; "Repent, for the kingdom of heaven is at hand;" that is, the promise of pardon upon repentance is published and sealed, and whoever will, may come and take the benefit of it. The terrors of the law are of use to startle us, and put us into a horror for sin, as those that are afraid of God; but the grace of the gospel contributes more to an ingenuous repentance, and makes us more ashamed of ourselves. This rends the heart, to consider God so gracious and merciful, so slow to anger, and ready to forgive. Let this loving-kindness melt thee, O my soul! and make thee to relent more tenderly than ever. Wretch that I have been, to spit in the face, and spurn at the bowels, of such mercy and love, by my wilful sin! to despise the riches of gospel grace! I am ashamed, yea even confounded, because I do bear the reproach of my youth. Doth God meet thee thus with tenders of reconciliation? Doth the party offended make the first motion of agreement? Shall such an undutiful, disobedient, prodigal son as I have been, be embraced and kissed, and clothed with the best robe? This kindness overcomes me. Now, it cuts me to the heart, and humbles me to the dust, to think of my former rebellions; they never appeared so heinous, so vile, as they do now I see them pardoned. The more certain I am that I shall not be ruined by them, the more reason I see to be humbled for them. When God promised to establish his covenant with repenting Israel, he adds, "that thou mayest remember, and be confounded, and never open thy mouth any more, because of thy shame, when I am pacified toward thee." To see God provoked, causes a holy trembling; but to see God pacified, causes a holy blushing. The day of atonement, when the sins of Israel were to be sent to a land of forgetfulness, must be a day to afflict the soul. The blood of Christ will be the more healing and comforting to the soul, for its bleeding afresh thus upon every remembrance of sin.

II. Here we must be confiding on Christ Jesus, and relying on him alone, for life and salvation. When we mourn for sin, blessed be God, we do not sorrow as those that have no hope; true penitents are perplexed, but not in despair; cast down, but not destroyed. Faith in Christ turns even their sorrows into joy, gives them their vineyards from thence, and even the valley of Achor (of trouble for sin) for a door of hope. We have not only an all-sufficient happiness to hope for, but an all-sufficient Saviour to hope in. Here, therefore, let us exercise and encourage that hope; let us trust in the name of the Lord Jesus, and stay ourselves upon him; come up out of this wilderness, leaning upon our Beloved. Come, my soul, weary as thou art, and rest in Christ; cast thy burden upon him, and he shall sustain thee; commit thy way to him, and thy thoughts shall certainly be established; commit thyself to him, and it shall be well with thee; he will keep, through his own name, that which thou committest to him.

Commit thyself to him, as the scholar commits himself to his teacher, to be instructed, with a resolution to take his word for the truth of what he teaches; as the patient commits himself to the physician to be cured, with a resolution to take whatever he prescribes, and punctually to observe his orders; as the client commits himself to his counsel, to draw his plea, and to bring him off when he is judged, with a resolution to do all things as he shall advise; as the traveller commits himself to his guide, to be directed in his way, with a resolution to follow his conduct; as the orphan commits himself to his guardian, to be governed and disposed of at his discretion, with a resolution to comply with him. Thus must we commit ourselves to Christ.

We must confide in his power, trusting in him as one that can help and save us. He has an incontestable authority, is a Saviour by office, sanctified and sealed, and sent into the world for this purpose; help is laid upon him. We may well offer to trust him with our part of this great concern, which is the securing of our happiness; for God trusted him with his part of it, the securing of his honour, and declared himself well pleased in him. He has likewise an unquestionable ability to save to the uttermost; he is mighty to save, and every way qualified for the undertaking; he is skilful, for treasures of wisdom and knowledge are hid in him; he is solvent, for there is in him an inexhaustible fulness of merit and grace, sufficient to bear all our burdens, and to supply all our needs. We must commit ourselves, and the great affairs of our salvation unto him, with a full assurance that he is "able to keep what we commit to him against that day," that great day, which will try the foundation of every man's work. We must confide in his promise, trusting in him as one that will certainly help and save us, on the terms proposed. We may take his word for it, and this is the word which he has spoken—"Him that cometh unto me I will in nowise cast out;" a double negative, " I will not, no, I will not." He is engaged for us in the covenant of redemption, and engaged to us in the covenant of grace, and in both he is the Amen, the faithful witness. On this, therefore, we must rely, the word on which he has caused us to hope. God has spoken in his holiness, that he will accept us in the Beloved, and in that " I will rejoice; I will divide Shechem; Gilead is mine, and Manasseh is mine." Pardon is mine, and peace mine, and Christ mine, and heaven mine: " for faithful is he that promised, who also will do it."

Come then, my soul, come thou, and all thy concerns, into this ark, and there thou shalt be safe when the deluge comes; flee, flee to this city of refuge, and in it thou shalt be secured from the avenger of blood. Quit all other shelters; for every thing but Christ is a "refuge of lies, which the hail will sweep away." There is not salvation in any other but in him; trust him for it therefore, and depend upon him only. Reach hither thy finger, and, in this ordinance, "behold his hands; reach hither thy hand, and thrust it into his side," and say, as Thomas did, " My Lord, and my God!" Here I cast anchor, here I rest my soul. " It is Christ that died, yea rather that is risen again, and is, and will be, the author of eternal salvation to all them that obey him." To him I entirely give up myself, to be ruled, and taught, and saved by him; and in him I have a full satisfaction. I will draw near to God for mercy and grace, in a dependence upon him as my righteousness; I will go forth, and go on, in the way of my duty, in a dependence upon him as my strength; I will shortly venture into the invisible, unchangeable world, in a dependence upon him as the "captain of my salvation;" who is able to bring many sons to glory, and as willing as he is able. "Lord, I believe; help thou my unbelief."

Having thus committed thyself, my soul, to the Lord Jesus, comfort thyself in him. Please thyself with the thoughts of having disposed of thyself so well, and of having lodged the great concern of thy salvation in so good a hand; now "return to thy rest, O my soul," and be easy. Every good Christian may by faith triumph as the prophet does, pointing at Christ: "The Lord God will help me, therefore shall I not be confounded, therefore have I set my face like a flint," in a holy defiance of Satan and all the powers of darkness; "and I know that I shall not be ashamed. He is near that justifieth me, who will contend with me?" Take the Bible, turn to the 8th of the Romans, and read from verse 31, to the end of the chapter; if ever blessed Paul rode in a triumphant chariot on this side heaven, it was when he wrote these lines, "What shall we then say to these things," &c. Apply those comforts to thyself; "O my soul, thou hast said of the Lord, he is my Lord; rejoice in him, then, and be exceeding glad. Thy Redeemer is mighty, and he rides upon the heavens for thy help, and in his excellency on the sky— "Do thou, then, ride upon the high places of the earth, and suck honey out of this rock, and oil out of this flinty rock." Having made sure of thy interest in Christ, live in a continual dependence upon him; and being satisfied of his love, be satisfied with it: thou hast enough, and needest no more.

III. Here we must be delighting in God, and solacing ourselves in his favour.—If we had not a Christ to hope in, being guilty and corrupt, we could not have a God to rejoice in; but, having an Advocate with the Father, so good a plea as Christ dying, and so good a pleader as Christ interceding, we may not only "come boldly to the throne of grace, but may sit down under the shadow of it with delight, and behold the beauty of the Lord." That God who is love, and the God of love, here shows us his "marvellous loving-kindness; causeth his goodness to pass before us; proclaims his name gracious and merciful." Here he gives us his love, and thereby invites us to give him ours. It is a love-feast, the love of Christ is here commemorated, the love of God here offered; and the frame of our spirits is disagreeable, and a jar in the harmony, if our hearts be not here going out in love to God, the chief good, and our felicity. They that come hither with holy desires, must refresh themselves here with holy delights. If we must "rejoice in the Lord always," much more now; for a feast was made for laughter, and so was this for spiritual joy; if ever "wisdom's ways be ways of pleasantness," surely they must be so when we come to "eat of her bread, and to drink of the wine which she hath mingled."

Put thyself then, my soul, into a pleasant frame; let the joy of the Lord be thy strength, and let this ordinance "put a new song into thy mouth." Come and hear the voice of joy and gladness.

Let it be a pleasure to thee to think, "that there is a God, and that he is such a one as he hath revealed himself to be." The being and attributes of God are a terror to those that are unjustified and unsanctified; nothing can be more so: they are willing to believe "there is no God, or that he is altogether such a one as themselves," because they heartily wish there were none, or one that they could be at peace with, and yet continue their league with sin: but to those who, through grace, partake of a divine nature themselves, nothing is more agreeable, nothing more acceptable, than the thoughts of God's nature and infinite perfections. Delight thyself, therefore, in thinking that there is an infinite and eternal Spirit, who is self-existent and self-sufficient, the best of beings, and the first of causes; the highest of powers, and the richest and kindest of friends and benefactors; the fountain of being and fountain of bliss; the "Father of lights, the Father of mercies." Love to think of him whom thou canst not see, and yet canst not but know; who is not far from thee, and yet between thee and him there is an infinite, awful distance. Let these thoughts be thy nourishment and refreshment.

Let it be a pleasure to thee to think of "the obligations thou liest under to this God as the Creator." He that is the former of my body, and the Father of my spirit, in whom I live, and move, and have my being, is upon that account my rightful owner, my sovereign ruler, whom I am bound to serve. Because he made me, and not I myself, therefore I am not mine own, but his. Please thyself, my soul, with this thought, that thou art not thine own, but his that made thee; nor left to thine own will, but bound up to his; not made for thyself, but designed to be to him for a name and a praise. Noble powers are then intended for a noble purpose. Delight thyself in him, as the felicity and end of thy being, who is the fountain and cause of it. Were I to choose, I would not be mine own master, my own carver, mine own centre; no, I would not, it is better as it is. I love to think of the eternal God, as the just director of all my actions, to whom I am accountable, and the wise disposer of all my affairs, to whom I must submit. I love to think of him as my chief good, who, having made me, is alone able to make me happy; and as my highest end, "of whom and through whom, and to whom, are all things."

Let it be a pleasure to thee "to think of the covenant relations wherein this God stands to thee in Jesus Christ." This is especially to be our delight in this sealing ordinance: though the sacrament directs us immediately to Christ, yet through him it leads us to the Father. He died, "the just for the unjust, that he might bring us to God." To God therefore we must go as our end and rest, by Christ as our way; to God as a Father, by Christ as Mediator.

Come then, my soul, and see with joy and the highest satisfaction, the God that made thee entering into covenant with thee, and engaging to make thee happy. Hear him saying to thee, my soul, "I am thy salvation, thy shield," and not only thy bountiful rewarder, but "thine exceeding great reward;" I am and will be to thee a God all-sufficient; a God that is enough. "Fear thou not, for I am with thee," wherever thou art; "be not dismayed, for I am thy God;" whatever thou wantest, whatever thou losest, call me God, even thine own God. When thou art weak, I will strengthen thee, yea, when thou art helpless, I will help thee; yea, when thou art ready to sink, "I will uphold thee with the right hand of my righteousness." The God that cannot lie has said it, and here seals it to thee, "I will never leave thee nor forsake thee." Let this be to thee, my soul, the voice of joy and gladness, making even broken bones to rejoice. Encourage thyself in the Lord thy God. He is thy Shepherd, thou shalt not want any thing that is good for thee. "Thy Maker is thy husband, the Lord of hosts is his name;" and as the bridegroom rejoices over the bride, so shall thy God rejoice over thee. He shall rest in his love to thee: rest then in thy love to him, and rejoice in him always. The Lord is thy lawgiver, thy king that will save thee: swear allegiance to him, then, with gladness and loud hosannas. "Let Israel rejoice in him that made him, (that new-made him;) let the children of Zion be joyful in their King." What wouldst thou more? This God is thy God for ever and ever.

Stir up thyself, my soul, to take the comfort which is here offered thee. Let this strengthen the weak hands, let it confirm the feeble knees. If God be indeed the "health of thy countenance and thy God, why art thou cast down, why art thou disquieted?" Die not for thirst when there is such a fountain of living waters near thee, but draw water with joy out of these wells of salvation. Shiver not for cold when there is such a reviving, quickening heat in these promises; but say with pleasure, "Ah, I am warm,

I have seen the fire!" Faint not for hunger, now thou art at a feast of fat things, but be abundantly satisfied with the goodness of God's house. The God whose wrath and frowns thou hast incurred, here favours thee and smiles on thee; let this therefore give thee a joy greater than the joy of harvest, and far surpassing what they have that divide the spoil. Though thou canst not reach to holy raptures, yet compose thyself to a holy rest. Delight thyself always in the Lord, especially at this ordinance, and, by thus taking the comfort of what thou hast received, thou qualifiest thyself to receive more; for then he shall give thee the desire of thy heart. The way to have thy heart's desire is to make God thy heart's delight. Triumph in his love, and thine interest in him: his benignity is better than life, let it be to thee sweeter than life itself. "Behold, God is my Saviour, God is my salvation; I will trust and not be afraid: for the Lord Jehovah is my strength, and therefore my song: the strength of my heart and my portion for ever." When thou comest to the altar of God, call him, "God thy exceeding joy"— "thy God, thy glory."

IV. Here we must be admiring the mysteries and miracles of redeeming love.—They that worshipped the beast are said to wonder after him, so must they that worship the Lamb, for he hath done marvellous things. We have reason to say that we were fearfully and wonderfully made; but without doubt, we were more fearfully and wonderfully redeemed. We were made with a word, but we were bought with a price: stand still, then, and see the salvation of the Lord, see it with admiration. Affect thyself, my soul, with a pleasing wonder, while thou art seeing this great sight. The everlasting gospel is here magnified and made honourable, let it be so in thine eyes; call it the glorious gospel of the blessed God. Let us take a view of some of the marvellous things which are done in the work of our redemption.

1. The contrivance of the salvation is marvellous.—It would have for ever puzzled the wisdom of

angels and men, to have found out such a method of salvation as might effectually satisfy God's justice, and yet secure man's happiness; save the life of the law-breaker, and yet maintain the honour of the law-maker. This is that mystery which the angels desire to look into, and of which the most piercing eye of those inquisitive spirits, that see by the light of the upper world, will not be able to eternity to discern the bottom. O the depth of this hidden wisdom!

2. The purposes of God's love concerning it from eternity are marvellous.—Be astonished, O my soul, at this, that the God who was infinitely happy in the contemplation and enjoyment of himself and his own perfections, should yet entertain thoughts of love towards a remnant of mankind, and towards thee amongst the rest, and design such favours for them, such favours for thee, before the worlds were! "How precious should these thoughts be unto us, for how great is the sum of them!"

3. The choice of the person who should undertake it is marvellous;—the Son of his love, that in parting with him for us he might commend his love;—the eternal Wisdom, the eternal Word, that he might effectually accomplish this great design, and might not fail nor be discouraged; a person every way fit, both to do the Redeemer's work, and to wear the Redeemer's crown. It is spoken of as an admirable invention—" I have found a ransom;" and, " I have found David my servant." On earth there was not his like, nor in heaven either.

4. The Redeemer's consent to the undertaking is marvellous.—Considering his own dignity and self-sufficiency, our unworthiness and obnoxiousness, the difficulty of the service, and the ill requitals he foresaw from an ungrateful world, we have reason to admire that he should be so free, so forward to it; and should say, " Lo, I come: here am I, send me." Never was there such a miracle of love and pity; verily it passeth knowledge.

5. The carrying on of his undertaking in his humi-

liation is marvellous.—His name was wonderful. His appearance in the world, from first to last, was a continued series of wonders; without controversy, great was this mystery of godliness. The bringing of the first begotten into the world was attended with the adorations of wondering angels. His doctrine and miracles, while he was in the world, were admirable; they that heard the one, and saw the other, were beyond measure astonished. But his going out of the world was the greatest wonder of all: it made the earth to shake, the rocks to rend, and the sun to cover his face. Never was there such a martyr, never such a sacrifice, never such a paradox of love as that was. "God forbid that we should glory, save in the cross of Christ," which is so much the wisdom of God and the power of God.

6. *The honours of his exalted state are marvellous.*—He that was made a little lower than the angels, a worm and no man, is now the Lord of angels. One in our nature is advanced to the highest honours, invested with the highest powers, having an incontestable authority to execute judgment, even for this reason, that he is the son of man; not only though he is so, but because he is so. This is the Lord's doing, and it is, and should be, marvellous in our eyes.

7. *The covenant of grace, made also with us in him, is marvellous.*—The terms of the covenant are wonderful, reasonable, and easy; the treasures of the covenant are wonderful, rich, and valuable. The covenant itself is well ordered in all things, and sure; admirably well, both for the glory of God, and the comfort of all believers. God in it "showeth us his marvellous loving kindness," and we answer not the design of the discovery, if we do not admire it. Other things, the more they are known the less they are wondered at; but the riches of redeeming love appear more admirable to those that are best acquainted with them.

V. Here we must be caring what we shall render to him that has thus loved us. This wondrous love is love to us; and not only gives the greatest encouragements to us to come to God for mercy and peace, but lays the strongest engagements upon us to walk with God in duty and obedience. We are bound in conscience, bound in honour and in gratitude, to love him, and to live to him who loved us and died for us. This concern should much affect us, and lie very near our hearts, how we may answer the intentions of this love!

We should be affected with a jealous fear, lest we prove ungrateful, and, like Hezekiah, "render not again according to the benefit done unto us." We cannot but know something, by sad experience, of the treachery and deceitfulness of our own hearts, and how apt they are to start aside like a broken bow; and therefore we have no reason to presume upon our own strength and sufficiency. We are told of many who eat and drink in Christ's presence, and yet are found at last unfaithful to him; and what if I should prove one of those? This thought is not suggested here to alarm any that tremble at God's word, or to weaken the hands and sadden the hearts of those that are truly willing, though very weak; but to awaken those that slumber, and humble those that are wise in their own conceit. Distrust thyself, O my soul, that thou mayest trust in Christ only; fear thine own strength, that thou mayest hope in his. He that has done these great things for thee, must be applied to and depended on to work those great things in thee, which are required of thee. Go forth, therefore, and go on in his strength. If the same that grants us those favours, give us not wherewithal to make suitable returns for them, we shall perish for ever in our ingratitude.

We should be filled with serious desires to know and do our duty, in return for that great love wherewith we are loved. The affections of a grateful mind are very proper to be working in us at this ordinance. Does not even nature teach us to be grateful to our friends and benefactors? Let us be so to Christ then, the best of friends, and kindest of benefactors.

Come, my soul, here I see how much I am indebted, and how I owe my life, my joy, and hope, and all, to the blessed Jesus: and is it not time to ask with holy David, "What shall I render unto the Lord for all his benefits towards me?" Shall I not take the cup of salvation, as he does, with this thought, "What shall I render?" Let David's answer to that question, which we find in the 116th Psalm, be mine.

"I love the Lord," (ver. 1.) Love is the loadstone of love; even the publicans love those that love them. Lord, thou hast loved me with an everlasting love; from everlasting in the counsels of it, to everlasting in the consequences of it: and shall not my heart, with this loving kindness, be drawn to thee? Lord, I love thee; the world and the flesh shall never have my love more: I have loved them too much, I have loved them too long; the best affections of my soul shall now be consecrated to thee, O God, to thee, O blessed Jesus! "Whom have I in heaven but thee? Lord, thou knowest all things; thou knowest that I I love thee." It is my sorrow and shame that I am so weak and defective in my love to thee: what a wretched heart have I, that I can think, and speak, and hear, and see so much of thy love to me, and be so little affected with it! So low in my thoughts of thee, so cool in my desires towards thee, so unsteady in my resolutions for thee! Lord, pity me, Lord, help me! for yet I love thee, I love to love thee. • I earnestly desire to love thee better, and long to be where love shall be made perfect.

"I will offer to thee the sacrifice of thanksgiving," (ver. 17.) As love is the heart of praise, so praise is the language of love. What shall I render? I must render to all their due; tribute to whom tribute is due; the tribute of praise to God, to whom it is due. We do not accommodate ourselves to this thanksgiving feast, if we do not attend it with hearts enlarged in thanksgiving: this cup of salvation must be a cup of blessing; in it we must bless God, because in it God blesses us. Thankful acknowledgments of God's favour to us are but poor returns for rich receivings; yet they are such as God will accept, if they come from an upright heart. "Bless the Lord, therefore, O my soul, and let all that is within me bless his holy name." Speak well of him who hath done well for thee. Thank him for all his gifts both of nature and grace, especially for Jesus Christ, the spring of all. "As long as I live, I will bless the Lord, yea, I will praise my God while I have my being;" for he is the God of my life, and the author of my well-being: and when I have no life, no being on earth, I hope to have a better life, a better being in a better world, and to be doing this work for ever in a better manner.

"O Lord, truly I am thy servant, I am thy servant." (ver. 16.) I acknowledge myself already bound to be so, and further oblige myself by solemn promise to approve myself so. What shall I render? Lord, I render myself to thee, my whole self, body and soul and spirit, not in compliment, but in truth and sincerity; I own myself thy servant, to obey thy commands, to be at thy disposal, and to be serviceable to thine honour and interest: it will be my credit and ease, my safety and happiness, to be under thy government; make me as one of thy hired servants.

"I will call upon the name of the Lord." (ver. 13.) This is an immediate answer to that question, What shall I render? and it is a surprising answer. It is uncommon among men to make petitions for further favours, or returns for former favours; yet such a return as this, the God that delights to hear prayers will be well pleased with. Is God my Father? I will apply myself to him as a child, and call him Abba, Father. Have I an advocate with the Father? Then I will come boldly to the throne of grace. Are there such exceeding great and precious promises made me, and sealed to me? Then will I never lose the benefit of them for want of putting them in suit. As I will love God the better, so I will love prayer the better as long as I live; and having given myself unto God, I will give myself unto prayer, as David did, till I come to the world of everlasting praise.

"Return unto thy rest, O my soul." (ver. 7.) The God who has pleasure in the prosperity of his servants, would have them easy to themselves; and that they can never be, but by reposing in him; this, therefore, we must render. It is work that has its own wages: honour God by resting in him, please him by being well pleased in him. Having received so much from him, let us own that we have enough in him, and that we can go nowhere but to him with any hopes of satisfaction. Lord, whither shall we go? He has the words of eternal life.

"I will walk before the Lord in the land of the living." (verse 9.) A holy life, though it cannot profit God, yet glorifies him; and therefore it is insisted upon as a necessary return for the favours we have received from God. While I am here in the land of the living, I will walk by faith, having mine eyes ever towards the Lord, to see him as he reveals himself, hoping that shortly in that land above, which is truly the land of the living, I shall walk by sight, having mine eyes ever upon the Lord, to see him as he is. God has here sealed to be to me a God all-sufficient: here therefore I seal to him, according to the tenor of the covenant, that, his grace enabling me, I will "walk before him and be upright."

"I will pay my vows unto the Lord." (ver. 14, 18.) Those that receive the blessings of the covenant, must be willing, not only to come, but always to abide under the bonds of the covenant. Here we must make vows, and then go away and make them good. More of this in the next chapter.

CHAPTER XI.

DIRECTIONS CONCERNING THE SOLEMN VOWS WE ARE TO MAKE TO GOD IN THIS ORDINANCE.

Four reasons why, at the Lord's Supper, we must make vows. I. We must, by solemn vows, bind ourselves up from all sin; largely opened in five things. II. We must bind ourselves up to all duty. To the duties of religion in general; opened in four things. To some duties of religion especially; opened in four things. Duties which we have most neglected, which we have experienced most benefit by, which we have most opportunity for; and the duties of our respective callings and relations.

A RELIGIOUS vow is a bond upon the soul; so it is described, Numb. xxx. 2, where he that vows a vow unto the Lord, is said thereby to bind his soul with a bond. It is a solemn promise, by which we voluntarily oblige ourselves to God and duty, as a "willing people in the day of his power." The cords of a man, and bonds of love, wherewith God draws us and holds us to himself, call upon us by our own act and deed to bind ourselves; and these vows also are cords of a man, for they are highly reasonable; and bonds of love, for to the renewed soul they are an easy yoke, and a light burden.

From all the other parts of our work at the Lord's table, we may infer that this is one part of it: we must there make solemn vows to God, that we will diligently and faithfully serve him.

We are here to renew our repentance for sin, and it becomes penitents to make vows. When we profess ourselves sorry for what we have done amiss, it is very natural and necessary to add, that we will not offend any more as we have done; "if I have done iniquity, I will do so no more." We mock God when we say we repent that we have done foolishly, if we do not at the same time resolve that we will never return again to folly. Times of affliction are proper times to make vows; and what is repentance but self-affliction? Trouble for sin was not the least of that trouble which David was in, when his lips uttered those vows of which he spoke so feelingly: "I will go into thy house with burnt-offerings; I will pay thee my vows, which my lips have uttered, and my mouth hath spoken, when I was in trouble." Probably it was under this penitential affliction that he "sware unto the Lord, and vowed unto the mighty God of Jacob, that he would find a place for the ark." Vows against sin, resulting from sorrow for sin, shall not be rejected as extorted by the rack, but graciously accepted as the genuine language of a broken heart, and fruits meet for repentance.

We are here to ask and receive mercy from God, and it becomes petitioners to make vows. When Jacob found himself in special need of God's gracious presence, he vowed a vow, and set up a stone, for a memorial of it. And Hannah, when she prayed for a particular mercy, vowed a vow, that the comfort she prayed for should be consecrated to God. Great and precious things we are here waiting to receive from God; and therefore, though we cannot offer any thing as a valuable consideration for his favours, yet it becomes us to promise such suitable returns as we are capable of making. When God encourages us to seek to him for grace, we must engage ourselves not to receive his grace in vain, but to improve and employ for him what we have from him.

We are here to give God thanks for his favours to us; now, it becomes us in our thanksgivings to make vows, and to offer to God, not only the calves of our lips, but the works of our hands. Jonah's mariners, when they offered a sacrifice of praise to the Lord for a calm after a storm, as an appendix to that sacrifice, made vows. The most acceptable vows are those which take rise from gratitude, and which are drawn from us by the mercies of God. Here I see what great things God has done for my soul, and what greater things he designs for me: shall I not therefore freely bind myself to that, which he has by such endearing ties bound me to?

We are here to join ourselves to the Lord in an

everlasting covenant; and it is requisite that our general covenant be explained and confirmed by particular vows. When we present ourselves to God as a living sacrifice, with these cords we must bind that sacrifice to the horns of the altar: and, while we experience in ourselves such a bent to backslide, we shall find all the arts of obligation little enough to be used with our own souls. As it is not enough to confess sin in the gross, saying, I have sinned, but we must enter into the detail of our transgressions, saying, with David, " I have done this evil;" so it is not enough in our covenanting with God, that we engage ourselves in the general to be his; but we must descend to particulars in our covenants, as God does in his commands, that thereby we may the more effectually both bind ourselves to duty, and remind ourselves of duty. If the people must distinctly say Amen to every curse pronounced on Mount Ebal, much more to every precept delivered on Mount Horeb.

Come then, my soul, thou hast now thy hand upon the book to be sworn; thou art lifting up thy hand to the most high God, the possessor of heaven and earth; think what thou art doing, and adjust the particulars, that this may not become a rash oath, inconsiderately taken. God is here confirming his promises to us by an oath, to show the immutability of his counsels of love to us. Here, therefore, we must confirm our promise to him by an oath, to walk in God's law, and to " observe and do all the commandments of the Lord our God." Some of the oriental writers tell us, that the most solemn oath which the patriarchs before the flood used, was, by the blood of Abel, and we are sure that the blood of Jesus is infinitely more sacred, and speaks much greater and much better things than that of Abel. Let us therefore testify our value for that blood, and secure to ourselves the blessings purchased by it, by our sincere and faithful dealing with God in that covenant, of which this is the blood.

The command of the eternal God is, that we " cease

to do evil, and learn to do well; that we put off the old man, and put on the new." And our vows to God must accordingly be against all sin, and to all duty; and under each of these heads we must be particular, according as the case is.

I. We must here, by a solemn vow, bind ourselves against all sin; so as not only to break our league with it, but to enter into league against it. The putting away of the strange wives, in Ezra's time, was not the work of one day or two, but a work of time; and therefore Ezra, when he had the people under convictions, and saw them weeping sore for their sin in marrying them, very prudently bound them, by a solemn covenant, that they would put them away. If ever we conceive an aversion to sin, surely it is at the table of the Lord; and therefore we should improve that opportunity to invigorate our resolutions against it, that the remembrance of those resolutions may quicken our resistance of it, when the sensible impressions we are under from it are become less lively. Thus we must, by a solemn vow, cast away from us all our transgressions, saying, with Ephraim, "What have I to do any more with idols?"

We must solemnly vow that we will not indulge or allow ourselves in any sin. Though sin may remain, it shall not reign; though those Canaanites be in the land, yet we will not be tributaries to them. However it may usurp and oppress as a tyrant, it shall never be owned as a rightful prince, nor have a peaceful and undisturbed dominion. I may be in some particular instances, through the surprise of temptations, led into captivity by it; but I am fully resolved, through Christ, never to join in affinity with it, never espouse its cause, never plead for it, nor strike in with its interest.

Bind thyself with this bond, O my soul, that though, through the remainders of corruptions, thou canst not say thou hast no sin; yet, through the beginnings of grace, thou wilt be able to say thou lovest none. That thou wilt give no countenance or connivance to any sin; no, not to secret sins, which, though they shame thee not before men, yet shame thee before God and thine own conscience; no, not to heart sins, those first-born of the corrupt nature, the beginning of its strength. Vain thoughts may intrude, and force a lodging in me, but I will never invite them, never bid them welcome, nor court their stay. Corrupt affections may disturb me, but they shall never have the quiet and peaceable possession of me: no, whatever wars against my soul, by the grace of God, I will war against it, hoping in due time to get the dominion, and have the yoke broken from off my neck, when "judgment shall be brought forth unto victory," and grace perfected in glory.

We must solemnly vow, that we will never yield to any gross sin, such as lying, injustice, uncleanness, drunkenness, profanation of God's name, and such like, which are not the spots of God's children. Though all the high places be not taken away, yet there shall be no remains of Baal, or of Baal's priests and altars in my soul. However my own heart may be spotted by sins of infirmity, and may need to be daily washed, yet, by the grace of God, I will never spot my profession, nor stain the credit of that by open and scandalous sin. I have no reason to be ashamed of the gospel, and therefore it shall be my constant endeavour, not to be in any thing a shame to the gospel; it is an honour to me, I will never be a dishonour to it; I will never do any thing, by the grace of God I will not, which may give just occasion to the enemies of the Lord to blaspheme that worthy name by which I am called. So shall it appear, that I am upright, if I be innocent from these great transgressions.

We must solemnly vow, that with a particular care we will keep ourselves from our own iniquity. That sin, with which, in our penitent reflections, our own consciences did most charge us, and reproach us for, that sin we must in a special manner renew our resolutions against. Was it pride? Was it passion? Was it distrust of God, or love of the world? Was it an unclean fancy, or an idle tongue?—Whatever it was, let the spiritual force be mustered and drawn out against that. The instructions which Samuel gave to Israel, when they were lamenting after the Lord, are observable to this purpose—" If ye do return to the Lord with all your hearts," and would be accepted of him therein, " then put away the strange gods and Ashtaroth." Was not Ashtaroth one of the strange gods or goddesses? Yes; but that is particularly mentioned, because it had been a beloved idol, dearer than the rest, that especially must be put away. Thus, in our covenanting with God, we must engage against all sin, but in particular, against that which, by reason of the temper of our minds, the constitution of our bodies, or the circumstances of our outward affairs, does most easily beset us, and we are most prone to.

Knowest thou thine ownself, O my soul? If thou dost, thou "knowest thine own sickness, and thine own sore,". that is, thine own iniquity: bring that hither and slay it; let not thine eyes spare, neither do thou pity it. Hide it not, excuse it not, stipulate not for leave to reserve it as Naaman did for his house of Rimmon; though it hath been to thee as a right eye, as a right hand, as thy guide and thine acquaintance, it hath been a false guide, an ill acquaintance, pluck it out, cut it off, and cast it from thee. Now come and fortify thy resolutions in the strength of Christ against that; fetch in help from heaven against that; be vigorous in thy resistance of that, and how many soever its advantages are against thee, yet despair not of a victory at last.

We must solemnly vow, that we will abstain from all appearance of evil; not only from that which is manifestly sin, and which carries the evidences of its own malignity written on its forehead, but from that which looks like sin, and borders upon it. Wisdom is here profitable to direct, so that we may not on the one hand indulge a scrupulous conscience, and yet on the other hand may preserve a tender conscience. Far be it from us to make that to be sin which God hath not made so; and yet in doubtful cases it must be our care and covenant to keep the safer side, and to be cautious of that which looks suspicious; "he that walks uprightly walks surely." What we find to be either a snare to us, and an occasion of sin, or a blemish to us, and an occasion of scandal, or a terror to us in the reflection, and an occasion of grief or fear, it may do well expressly to resolve against, though we be not very clear that it is in itself sinful, nor dare censure it as evil in others; provided that this vow be made with such limitations that it may not afterwards prove an entanglement to us, when, either by the improvement of our knowledge, or the change of our circumstances, it ceases to have in it an appearance of evil.

And art thou willing, my soul, to come under this bond? Wilt thou put far from thee the accursed thing? Wilt thou in this ordinance make a covenant with thine eyes, and oblige them not to look on the wine when it is red, nor to look on a woman to lust after her? Wilt thou shun sin as the plague, and engage thyself, not only never to embrace that adulteress, but never to come nigh the door of her house? Thy vow being like that of the Nazarite, not to drink of this intoxicating wine; let it be then like his, not to eat any thing that cometh of the vine, "from the kernel to the husk." Abandon sin and all its appurtenances; cast out Tobiah and all his stuff. Resolve to deny thyself in that which is most desirable, rather than give Satan any advantage; to abridge thyself even in that which is lawful, rather than come within the confines of sin, or bring thyself into danger of that which is unlawful. "Happy is the man that feareth always."

We must solemnly vow, that we will have no fellowship "with the unfruitful works of darkness, neither be partakers of other men's sins." We live in a corrupt and degenerate age, in which iniquity greatly abounds. Our business is not to judge others; to their own masters they stand or fall, but our care must be, to preserve ourselves, and the purity and peace of our own minds; our covenant therefore must be, that we will never "walk in the counsel of the ungodly, nor stand in the way of sinners." When David engaged himself to keep the commandments of his God, pursuant to that engagement, he said to evil-doers, " Depart from me." And St. Peter reminded his new converts of the necessity of this care; —" Save yourselves from this untoward generation."

Let the Psalmist's vow be mine then. Having hated the congregation of evil-doers, such as drunkards, swearers, filthy talkers, and scoffers at godliness, " I will not sit with the wicked." Though I cannot avoid being sometimes in the sight and hearing of such, yet I will never take those for my chosen companions and bosom friends in this world, with whom I should dread to have my portion in the other world. Religion in rags shall be always valued by me, and profaneness in robes despised. Having chosen God for my God, his people shall always be my people; " Lord, gather not my soul with sinners." If thou art in good earnest for heaven, resolved to swim against the stream, thou wilt find that sober singularity is an excellent guard to serious piety. On all that glory let there be this defence.

II. We must here by a solemn vow, bind ourselves up to all duty. It is not enough that we depart from evil, but we must do good; that we separate ourselves from the service of sin, and shake off Satan's iron yoke; but we must devote ourselves to the service of Christ, and put our necks under the sweet and easy yoke of God's commandments, with a solemn promise faithfully to draw in that yoke all our days. We need not bind ourselves to more than we are already bound to by the divine law, either expressly or by consequence; either as primary duties or secondary, in order to them. We are not called to lay upon ourselves any other burden than necessary things, and they are not heavy burdens, nor grievous to be borne; but we must bind ourselves faster and by additional ties, to that which we are already bound to.

We must, by a solemn vow, oblige ourselves to all the duties of religion in general.—Jacob's vow must be ours, "Then the Lord shall be my God." Having avouched him for mine, I will fear him and love him, delight in him and depend upon him, worship him and glorify him, as my Lord and my God. Having owned him as mine, I will ever eye him as mine, and "walk in his name." David's vow must be ours; that we will "keep God's righteous judgments;" that we will keep in them as our way, keep to them as our rule; that we will keep them as the apple of our eye, keep them always unto the end.

In the strength of the grace of Jesus Christ, we must here solemnly promise and vow,

(1.) That we will make religion our business.—It is our great business in this world, to serve the honour of him that made us, and secure the happiness we were made for: this we must mind as our business, and not, as most do, make a by-business of it. Religion must be our calling; the calling we resolve to live in, and hope to live by: in the services of it we must be constant and diligent, and as in our element. Other things must give way to it, and be made, as much as may be, serviceable to it. And this must be our covenant with God here, that, however we have trifled hitherto, henceforward we will mind religion as the one thing needful, and not be slothful in the business of it, but fervent in spirit, serving the Lord. And art thou willing, my soul, thus to devote thyself entirely to the service of thy God? Shall that engage thy cares, fill thy thoughts, command thy time, and give law to the whole man? Let this matter be settled then, in this day's vows, and resolve to live and die by it.

(2.) That we will make conscience of inside godliness.—Having in our covenant given God our hearts, which is what he demands, we must resolve to employ them for him; for without doubt, he is a Jew, he is a Christian, that is one inwardly; and that is circumcision, that is baptism, that is true and pure religion, "which is of the heart, in the spirit, and not in the letter;"—that we are really, what we are inwardly: and they only are the true worshippers, that worship God in the spirit. This is the power of godliness, without which the form is but a carcass, but a shadow. "The king's daughter is all glorious within." This, therefore, we must resolve in the strength of the grace of God, that we will keep our hearts with all diligence, keep them fixed, fixed upon God; that the desire of our souls shall ever be towards God; our hearts shall be lifted up to God in every prayer, and their doors and gates thrown open to admit his word; and that our constant care shall be about the "hidden man of the heart, in that which is not corruptible;" so approving ourselves to God in our integrity, in every thing we do in religion.

(3.) That we will live a life of communion with God.—Without controversy, great is this mystery of godliness; if there be a heaven upon earth, certainly this is it, by faith to set the Lord always before us, having an eye to him with suitable affections, as the first cause, and last end, of all things that concern us; and so having communion with him in providence as well as ordinances. When we receive the common comforts of every day from his hand with love and thankfulness; and bear the common crosses and disappointments of every day, as ordered by his will, with patience and submission; when we commit every day's care to him, and manage every day's business and converse for him, having a constant habitual regard to God in the settled principles of the divine life, and frequent actual out-goings of soul towards him in pious ejaculations, the genuine expressions of devout affections; then we live a life of communion with God. Did we know by experience, what it is to live such a life as this, we would not exchange the pleasures of it, for the peculiar treasures of kings and provinces.

Engage thyself, then, my soul, elevate thyself to this spiritual and divine life, that every day may be thus with thee a communion-day, and thy constant fellowship may be with the Father, and with his Son, Jesus Christ, by the Spirit. Let me resolve henceforward to live, more than I have hitherto done, a life of complacency in God, in his beauty, bounty, and benignity; a life of dependence upon God, upon his power, providence, and promise; a life of devotedness to God, to the command of his word, to the conduct of his Spirit, and the disposal of his providence; and thus to walk with God in all holy conversation.

(4.) That we will keep heaven in our eye, and take up with nothing short of it.—We are made for another world, and we must resolve to set our hearts upon that world, and have it always in our eye; seeking the things that are above, and slighting things below in comparison with them, as those that are born from heaven, and bound to heaven. Bind thyself, my soul, with this bond, that, "forgetting the things that are behind, as one that hath not yet attained, neither is already perfect," thou wilt reach forth to those things that are before, "pressing forwards towards the mark, for the prize of the high calling." My treasure is in heaven—my head, and hope, and home, are there: I shall never be well till I am there; there, therefore, shall my heart be, and to that recompense of reward I will ever have respect; with an eye to that joy and glory set before me in the other world, I will, by the grace of God, patiently run the race of godliness set before me in this world.

2. We must, by a solemn vow, oblige ourselves to some duties of religion in particular.—As it is good to engage ourselves by covenant against particular sins, that, by the help of resolution, our resistance of them may be invigorated; so it is good to engage ourselves to particular duties, that we may be quickened diligently to apply ourselves to them, and may see our work before us.

(1.) We should particularly oblige ourselves to those duties, with the neglect of which our own consciences have charged us. We have known that good which our own hearts tell us we have not done; we find upon reflection, it may be, that we have not been constant in our secret devotion, that we have not done that good in our families which we should have done; we have been barren in good discourse, careless of our duty to the souls of others, backward to works of charity, unfurnished for and indisposed to religious exercises; in these, or other things, wherein we are conscious to ourselves that we have been defective, we must covenant for the future to be more circumspect and industrious, that our works may be found filled up before God. When the Jews in Nehemiah's time made a sure covenant, wrote it, and sealed to it, they inserted particular articles, relating to those branches of God's service which had been neglected, and made ordinances for themselves, according to the ordinances that God had given them; so should we do, as an evidence of the sincerity of our repentance for our former omissions, both of duty and in duty. That work of our Lord, wherein we have been most wanting, in that we must covenant to abound most, that we may redeem the time.

(2.) We should particularly oblige ourselves to those duties which we have found by experience to contribute most to the support and advancement of the life and power of godliness in our hearts. They that have carefully observed themselves, perhaps can tell what those religious exercises are, which they have found to be most serviceable to the prosperity of their souls, and by which they have reaped most spiritual benefit and advantage. Have our hearts been most enlarged in secret devotion? Has God sometimes met us in our closets with special comforts, and the unusual manifestations of himself to our souls? Let us from thence take an indication, and covenant to be more and longer alone in secret communion with God. Have public ordinances been to us as green pastures, and have we sat down by them with delight? Let us resolve to be so much the more diligent in our attendance on them, and wait more closely at those gates where we have so often been abundantly satisfied. Though one duty must never be allowed to trench upon another, yet those duties which we have found to be the most effectual means of increasing our acquaintance with God, confirming our faith in Christ, and furthering us in our way to heaven, we should, with a peculiar care, engage ourselves to.

Though God has strictly commanded us the great and necessary acts of religious worship, yet, for the trial of our holy ingenuity and zeal, he has left it to us to determine many of the circumstances. That even instituted sacrifices may be in some respects free-will offerings, he has commanded us to pray and read the Scriptures, but has not told us just how often and how long we must pray and read. Here, therefore, it is proper for us to bind ourselves to that which will best answer the intention of the command in general, best agree with the circumstances we are in, and best advance the interests of our souls; in which we must take heed, on the one hand, that we indulge not spiritual sloth, by contenting ourselves with the least proportions of time that may be, much less by confining ourselves to them; and, on the other hand, that we make not religious exercises a task and burden to ourselves, by binding ourselves to that, at all times, which, in an extraordinary fervour of devotion, is easy and little enough. In making resolutions of this kind, we ought to be cautious, and not hasty to utter any thing before God, that we may not afterwards say before the angel, "It was an error." Though such is the decay of Christian zeal in the age we live in, that few need this caution, yet it must be inserted, "because it is a snare to a man to devour that which is holy, and after vows to make inquiry."

(3.) We should particularly oblige ourselves to those duties by which we have opportunities of glorifying God, adorning our profession, and doing good in our places. We are not born for ourselves, nor bought for ourselves; we are born for God, and bought for Christ: and both as men and as Christians, we are members one of another, and we ought to sit down and consider how we may trade with the talent with which we are intrusted, though it be but one, to the glory of our Creator, the honour of our Redeemer, and the good of our brethren. The liberal and pious devise liberal and pious things, and oblige themselves to them. Think then, my soul, not only what must I do, but what may I do for God, who has done such great things for me? How may I be serviceable to the interests of God's kingdom among men? What can I do to promote the strength and beauty of the church, and the welfare of precious souls? And if we have thought of any thing of this kind that falls within the sphere of our activity, though but a low and narrow sphere, it may do well, when we find ourselves in a good frame at the table of the Lord, by a solemn vow, with due caution, to oblige ourselves to it, that we may not leave room for a treacherous heart to start back. Thus Jacob, for the perpetuating the memory of God's favour to him, made it a part of his vow—" This stone which I have set for a pillar, shall be God's house." Thus Hannah vowed, that if God would give her a son, she would give him to the Lord. It is one of the rules prescribed concerning cost or pains bestowed for pious and charitable uses—" Every man according as he purposeth in his heart, so let him give, so let him do." Now, lest that purpose should fail and come to nothing, it is good, when the matter of it is well digested, to bring it to a head in a solemn promise, that the tempter seeing us steadfastly resolved, may cease soliciting us to alter our purpose.

(4.) We should particularly oblige ourselves to the duties of our respective callings and relations. Much of Christian obedience lies in these instances; and in them we are especially called to serve God and our generation, and should therefore bind ourselves to do so.

They that are in places of public trust and power, should here oblige themselves, by a solemn vow, to be faithful to the trust reposed in them, and to use their power for the public good. They that rule over men, must here covenant that they will be just, ruling in the fear of God. Their oaths must here

be ratified, and David's promise must be theirs—
"When I shall receive the congregation, I will judge
uprightly." This ought to be seriously considered
by all those who receive this holy sacrament at their
admission into the magistracy. When publicans and
soldiers submitted to the baptism of John, and thereby
obliged themselves to live a holy life, they asked
and received of John instructions how to discharge
the duty of their respective employments; for, when
we vow to keep God's commandments, though we
must have a universal respect to them all, yet we
must have a special regard to those precepts which
relate to the calling wherein we are called, whatever
it is.

The stewards of the mysteries of God, when they
administer this ordinance to others, receive it themselves
as an obligation upon them to stir up the gift
that is in them, that they may make full proof of
their ministry. Their ordination vows are repeated
and confirmed in every sacrament, and they are
again sworn to be true to Christ and souls. He that
ministereth about holy things, must here oblige himself
to "wait on his ministering; he that teacheth,
on teaching; he that exhorteth, on exhortation."

Governors of families must here oblige themselves,
as David did, to walk before their houses in a perfect
way, with a perfect heart; and they must affix this
seal to Joshua's resolution, that, whatever others do,
"they and their houses will serve the Lord." Here
they must consecrate to God a church in their house,
and bind themselves to set up, and always to keep
up, both an altar and a throne for God in their habitation,
that they may approve themselves the spiritual
seed of faithful Abraham, who was famous for
family religion. And inferior relations must here
oblige themselves to do the duty they owe to their
superiors: children to be dutiful to their parents, servants
to be obedient to their masters; yea, all of us
to be subject one to another. They that are under
the yoke, as the apostle speaks, may here make the
yoke they are under easy to them, by obliging them-

selves to draw in it from a principle of duty to God, and gratitude to Christ, which will both sanctify and sweeten the hardest services and submission.

Whatever our employments are, and our dealings with men, we must here promise and avow, that we will be strictly just and honest in them; that whatever temptations we may be under to the contrary at any time, we will make conscience of "rendering to all their due, and of speaking the truth from the heart; that we will walk uprightly, and work righteousness, despise the gain of oppression, and shake our hand from holding of bribes;" knowing that they who do so "shall dwell on high, their place of defence shall be the munition of rocks, bread shall be given them, and their water shall be sure." We find it upon record, to the honour of Christ's holy religion, when it was first planted in the world, that Pliny, a heathen magistrate, and a persecutor of Christianity, giving an account to the Emperor Trajan, of what he had discovered concerning the Christians, in an epistle yet extant, acknowledges, that in their religious assemblies they bound themselves by a "sacrament," that is, by an oath, not to do any thing evil; that they would not rob or steal, or commit adultery; that they would never be false to any trust reposed in them, never deny any thing that was put into their hands to keep; and the like. The same is still the true intent and meaning of this service; it is the bond of a covenant, added to the bond of a command, that we "do justly, love mercy, and walk humbly with our God."

Come then, my soul, come under these bonds, come willingly and cheerfully under them. He that bears an honest mind does not startle at assurances; be not afraid to promise that which thou art already bound to do; for these vows will rather facilitate thy duty, than add to the difficulty of it; the faster thou findest thyself fixed to that which is good, the less there will be of uneasy hesitation and wavering concerning it, and the less danger of being tempted from it.

Only remember, that all these vows must be made with an entire dependence upon the strength and grace of Jesus Christ, to enable us to make them good. We have a great deal of reason to distrust ourselves, so weak and treacherous are our hearts. Peter betrayed himself by confiding in himself, when he said, "Though I should die with thee, yet will I not deny thee." But we have encouragement enough to trust in Christ: in his name therefore let us make our vows, in his grace let us be strong; surely " in the Lord alone have we righteousness and strength;" he is the surety of the covenant for both parties: into his custody, therefore, and under the protection of his grace, let us put our souls, and we shall find he is able to keep what we commit to him.

CHAPTER XII.

DIRECTIONS CONCERNING THE FRAME OF OUR SPIRITS WHEN WE COME AWAY FROM THIS ORDINANCE.

I. We must come from this ordinance admiring the condescension of the divine grace to us; considering our meanness by nature, and our vileness by sin. II. Lamenting our manifold defects, either trembling, or at least blushing. III. Rejoicing in Christ, and the great love wherewith he has loved us; expressing itself in praises to God, and encouragements to ourselves. IV. Much quickening to every good work. V. With a watchful fear of Satan's wiles, and a firm resolution to stand our ground against them. Let us therefore fear, and therefore fix. VI. Praying that God will fulfil his promises to us, and enable us to fulfil ours to him. VII. With a charitable disposition, to love our fellow Christians, to give to the poor, and forgive injuries. VIII. Longing for heaven. Our complaints and our comforts should make us long for heaven.

THEY that have fellowship with the Father, and with his Son Jesus Christ, at the table of the Lord, whose hearts are enlarged to send forth the workings of pious and devout affections towards God, and to take in the communication of divine light, life, and love from him, cannot but say, as Peter did upon the holy mount, "Lord, it is good for us to be here; here let us make tabernacles." They sit down under the refreshing shadow of this ordinance with delight, and its fruit is sweet unto their taste. Here they could dwell all the days of their life, beholding the beauty of the Lord, and inquiring in his temple. But it is not a continual feast: we must come down from this mountain; these sweet and precious minutes are soon numbered and finished; supper is ended, thanks are returned, the guests are dismissed with a blessing, the hymn is sung, and we go out to the Mount of Olives; even in this Jerusalem, the city of our solemnities, we have not a continuing city. Jacob has an opportunity of wrestling with the angel for a while, but he must "let him go, for the day breaks," and he has a family to look after, a journey to prosecute, and the affairs thereof call for his attendance. We must not be always at the Lord's table; the high priest himself must not be always within the veil, he must go out again to the people when his service is performed. Now, it ought to be as much our care to return in a right manner from the ordinance, as to approach in a right manner to it. That caution is here needful: "Look to yourselves, that we lose not those things which we have wrought," "which we have gained,"—so some read it. Have we in this ordinance wrought any thing, or gained any thing that is good? We are concerned to see to it, that we do not undo what we have wrought, and let slip what we have gained.

When the solemnity is done, our work is not done; still we must be pressing forwards in our duty. This perhaps is the mystery of that law in Ezekiel's temple service, that they should not return from worshipping before the Lord, in the solemn feasts, "through the same gate by which they entered in, but by that over against it." Forgetting those things which are behind, still we must reach forth to those things which are before.

Let us inquire, then, What is to be done, at our

coming away from the ordinance, for the preserving and improving of the impressions of it?

I. We should come from this ordinance, admiring the condescension of the divine grace to us.—Great are the honours which have here been done us, and the favours to which here we have been admitted: the God who made us has taken us into covenant and communion with himself; the King of kings has entertained us at his table, and there we have been feasted with the dainties of heaven, abundantly satisfied with the goodness of his house; exceeding great and precious promises have been here sealed to us, and earnests given us of the eternal inheritance: now, if we know ourselves, this cannot but be the matter of our wonder, our joyful, and yet awful wonder.

Considering our meanness by nature, we have reason to wonder that the great God should thus advance us. Higher than heaven is above the earth, is God above us; between heaven and earth there is, though a vast, yet only a finite distance; but between God and man there is an infinite disproportion. "What is man, then, (man that is a worm, and the son of man that is a worm,) that he should be thus visited and regarded, thus dignified and preferred?" That favour done to Israel sounds great: "Man did eat angels' food;" but here man is feasted with that which was never angels' food, the "flesh and blood of the Son of man," which gives life to the world. Solomon himself stood amazed at God's condescending to take possession of that magnificent temple he had built; "but will God in very deed dwell with men on the earth?" And, which is more, shall men on the earth dwell in God, and make the Most High their habitation? If great men look with respect upon those that are much their inferiors, it is because they expect to receive honour and advantage by them; "but can a man be profitable unto God?" No, he cannot; "our goodness extendeth not unto him." He was from eternity happy without us, and would have been so to eternity, if we had never been, or had been miserable; but we are undone, undone for ever, if his goodness extends not to us: he needs not our services, but we need his favours; men adopt others because they are childless, but God adopts us purely because we are fatherless. It was no excellency in us that recommended us to his love, but poverty and misery made us proper objects of his pity.

Come then, my soul, and compose thyself as king David did, when, having received a gracious message from heaven, assuring him of God's kind intentions to him and his family, he went in, and with a great fixedness of mind sat before the Lord; and say, as he said, "Who am I, O Lord God, and what is my house, that thou hast brought me hitherto?" That I should be so kindly invited to the table of the Lord, and so splendidly treated there? That one so mean and worthless as I am, the poorest dunghill-worm that ever called God Father, should be placed among the children, and fed with the children's bread? And yet, as if this were a "small thing in thy sight, O Lord God, thou hast spoken also concerning thy servant for a great while to come," even as far as eternity itself reaches; and thus "thou hast regarded me according to the estate of a man of high degree," though I am nothing, yea, less than nothing, and vanity. "And is this the manner of men, O Lord God?" Could men expect thus to be favoured? No; but thou givest to men, not according to their poverty, but according to thy riches in glory. Do great men use to condescend thus? No; it is usual with them to take state upon them, and to oblige their inferiors to keep their distance; but we have to do with one that is God, and not man; whose thoughts of love are as much above ours, as his thoughts of wisdom are; and therefore, as it follows there, "What can David say more unto thee?" What account can I give of this unaccountable favour? "It is for thy word's sake, and according to thine own heart," for the performance of thy purposes and promises, that "thou hast done all these great things, to make thy servant know them."

Considering our vileness by sin, we have yet more reason to wonder that the holy God should thus favour us. We are not only worms of the earth, below his cognizance, but a generation of vipers, obnoxious to his curse; not only unworthy of his love and favour, but worthy of his wrath and displeasure. How is it, then, that we are brought so near unto him, who deserved to have been sentenced to an eternal separation from him? He has said, "The foolish shall not stand in his sight." Foolish we know we are, and yet we are called to sit at his table, being through Christ reconciled to him, and brought into covenant with him. Justice might have set us as criminals at his bar; but behold, mercy sets us as children at his board: and it is a miracle of mercy, mercy that is the wonder of angels, and will be the eternal transport of glorified saints. See how much we owe to the Redeemer, by whom we have access into this grace.

Let me therefore set myself, and stir up myself, to admire it; I have more reason to say than Mephibosheth had, when David took him to eat bread, at his table continually, "What is thy servant, that thou shouldest look upon such a dead dog as I am?" I am less than the least of God's mercies, and yet he hath not withheld the greatest from me! I have forfeited the comforts of my own table, and yet I am feasted with the comforts of the Lord's table! I deserve to have had the cup of the Lord's indignation put into my hand, and to have drunk the dregs of it; but behold, I have been treated with the cup of salvation! Were ever traitors made favourites? Such traitors made such favourites? Who can sufficiently admire the love of the Redeemer, who "received gifts for men, yea, even for the rebellious also," upon their return to their allegiance, "that the Lord God might dwell among them?"[1] And have I shared in these gifts, notwithstanding my rebellions? This is the Lord's doing, and it is marvellous. Whence is this to me, that not the mother of my Lord, but my Lord himself should come to me?

that he should thus prevent me, thus distinguish me with his favours? "Lord! how is it that thou wilt manifest thyself to me, and not unto the world?"

II. We should come from this ordinance lamenting our own manifold defects and infirmities in our attendance upon God in it.—When we look back upon the solemnity, we find, that as we cannot speak well enough of God and of his grace, so we cannot speak ill enough of ourselves, and of the folly and treachery of our own hearts. Now, conscience, thou art charged in God's name to do thine office, and to accomplish a diligent search; review the workings of thy soul in this ordinance distinctly and impartially.

And if upon search thou findest cause to suspect that all has been done in hypocrisy, then set thy soul a trembling; for its condition is sad, and highly dangerous. If I have been here pretending to join myself in a covenant with God, while I continue in league with the world and the flesh; pretending to receive the pardon of my sins, when I never repented of them, nor designed to forsake them; I have but deceived myself, and have reason to fear that I shall perish at last with a lie in my right hand. While this conviction is fresh and sensible, let care be taken to mend the matter; and, blessed be God, it may be mended. Have I reason to fear that my heart is not right in the sight of God, and that therefore I have no part nor lot in the matter, but am in the gall of bitterness, and bond of iniquity? I must then take the advice which Peter gave to Simon Magus, when he perceived that to be his condition, after he had received the sacrament of baptism: "Repent, therefore, of this thy wickedness, and pray God, if perhaps the thought of thine heart may be forgiven thee." Let that be done with a double care after the ordinance, which should have been done before.

But if upon search thou findest that there has been, through grace, truth in the inward part; yet set thy soul a blushing, for it has not been cleansed according to the purification of the sanctuary. When we would do good, evil is present with us; our wine is mixed with water, and our gold with dross; and who is there that "doeth good, and sinneth not" even in his doing good? We find, by sad experience, that the sons of God never come together but Satan comes also among them, and stands at their right hand to resist them; and that, wherever we go, we carry about with us the remainders of corruption, a body of death, which inclines us to that which is evil, and indisposes us to that which is good. If the spirit be willing, yet, alas! the flesh is weak, and we cannot do the things that we would.

O what reason have I to be ashamed of myself, and blush to lift up my face before God, when I review the frame of my heart during my attendance on this ordinance! How short have I come of doing my duty, according as the work of the day required! My thoughts should have been fixed, and the subjects presented to them to fix upon, were curious enough to engage them, and copious enough to employ them; and yet they went with the fool's eyes unto the ends of the earth, and wandered after a thousand impertinencies. A little thing served to give them a diversion from the contemplation of the great things set before me. My affections should have been raised and elevated, but they were low and flat, and little moved; if sometimes they seemed to soar upwards, yet they soon sunk down again, and the things which remained were ready to die. My desires were cold and indifferent, my faith weak and inactive; nor were there any workings of soul in me proportionable to the weightiness of the transaction. Through my own dulness, deadness, and inadvertency, I lost a deal of time out of a little, and slipped much of that which might have been done and got there, if I had been close and diligent.

This thought forbids us to entertain a good conceit of ourselves, and our own performances, or to build any confidence upon our own merit. While we are conscious to ourselves of so much infirmity cleaving to our best services, we must acknowledge that boasting is for ever excluded; we have nothing to glory of before God, nor can we challenge a reward as of debt, but must ascribe all to free grace. What good there is in us, is all of God, and he must have the honour of it; but there is also much amiss, which is all of ourselves; and we must take the shame of it, lamenting those sad effects of the remainder of sin in us, which we feel to our loss, when we draw nigh to God in holy ordinances.

This thought obliges us, likewise, to rely on Christ alone for acceptance with God in all our religious duties: he is that great and gracious High Priest, who "bears the iniquity of the holy things, which the children of Israel hallow in their holy gifts," that, notwithstanding that iniquity when it is repented of, "the gifts may be accepted before the Lord." Of his righteousness therefore we must make mention, even of his only; for the most spiritual sacrifices are acceptable to God only through him. 1 Pet. ii. 5.

III. We should come from this ordinance rejoicing in Jesus Christ, and in that great love wherewith he has loved us.—From this feast we should go to our tents, as the people went from Solomon's feast of dedication, "joyful and glad in heart, for all the goodness that the Lord hath done by David his servant, for Israel his people." They that went forth weeping, must come back rejoicing, as they have cause, if they "bring their sheaves with them." Has God here lifted up the light of his countenance upon us? That should "put gladness into our hearts." Have we here lifted up our souls to God, and joined ourselves to him in an everlasting covenant? We have reason, with the baptized eunuch, to "go on our way rejoicing." The day of our espousals should be the day "of the gladness of our hearts." This cup of blessing was designed to be a cup of consolation, and its wine ordained to make glad man's heart, to make glad the heart of the new man; having therefore drunk of this cup, let our souls "make their boast in the Lord, and sing in his ways, and call him their exceeding joy."

Let this holy joy give check to carnal mirth; for

having seen so much reason to rejoice in Christ Jesus, we deceive ourselves, if we rejoice in a thing of nought: we are not forbidden to rejoice, but our joy must be turned into the right channel, and our mirth sanctified, which will suppress and silence the laughter that is mad. The frothiness of a vain mind must be cured by a religious cheerfulness, as well as by a religious seriousness.

Let it give check also to the sorrow of the world, and that inordinate grief for outward crosses, which sinks the spirits, dries the bones, and works death. Why art thou cast down? and why disquieted for a light affliction, which is but for a moment? when even that is so far from doing thee any real prejudice, that it works for thee a far more exceeding and eternal weight of glory. Learn, my soul, to sit down upon the ruins of all thy creature-comforts, by a withered fig-tree, a fruitless vine, and a blasted crop, and even then to sing to the praise and glory of God, as the God of thy salvation. When thou art full, enjoy God in all; when thou art empty, enjoy all in God.

Let this holy joy express itself in praises to God, and encouragements to ourselves.

Let it express itself in the thankful acknowledgment of the favours we have received from God. As spiritual joy must be the heart and soul of divine praise, so divine praise must be the breath and speech of spiritual joy. Whatever makes us joyful, must make us thankful. Do we come from this ordinance easy and pleasant, and greatly refreshed with the goodness of God's house? Let the high praises of God then be in our mouths, and in our hearts. This is a proper time for us to be engaged with great fixedness, and enlarged with great fluency in his service. If we must give thanks for the mercies we receive at our own table, which relate only to a perishing body and a dying life, much more ought we to give thanks for the mercies we receive at God's table, which relate to an immortal soul and eternal life.

"When thou hast eaten, and art full, then thou shalt bless the Lord thy God, for the good land which he hath given thee." Bless him for a Canaan on earth, a land of light, and a valley of vision, in which God is known, and his name great; and for the comfortable lot thou hast in that land, a name among God's people, and a nail in his holy place, a portion in Immanuel's land; bless him for a Canaan in heaven which he has given thee the promise and prospect of, that land flowing with milk and honey. Rejoice in hope of that, and sing in hope.

"Bless the Lord, O my soul, and let all that is within thee," all thy thoughts, and all thy powers, be employed in blessing his holy name; and all little enough. O give thanks unto the Lord, for he is good; good to all, good to Israel, good to me. " I will mention the loving-kindnesses of the Lord, and the praises of the Lord, according to all that the Lord hath bestowed on us." Give glory to the exalted Redeemer, and mention to his praise the great things he has done for us. " Worthy is the Lamb that was slain," to take the book, and open the seals; worthy to wear the crown, and sway the sceptre for ever; worthy to receive blessing, and honour, and glory and power; worthy to be adored by the innumerable company of angels, and the spirits of just men made perfect; worthy to be attended with the constant praises of the universal church; worthy of the innermost and uppermost place of my heart, of the best affections I can consecrate to his praise, and the best services I can do to his name; for he was slain, and has " redeemed us to God by his blood; and has made us to our God kings and priests. He has loved us, and washed us from our sins in his own blood;" a note of praise, which the angels themselves cannot sing, though they have many a song to which we are strangers. " He loved me, and gave himself for me," to satisfy for my sin, and to obtain eternal redemption for me. Blessed, and for ever blessed, be the great and holy name of the Lord Jesus—that name which is as ointment poured forth—

that name which is above every name, which is worthy of, and yet "exalted far above, all blessing and praise."

And whenever we confess that Jesus Christ is Lord, let it always be done to the glory of God the Father. His kindness and love to man was the original spring, and first wheel in the work of our redemption. It was he that "gave his only-begotten Son, delivered him up for us all, and who was in Christ reconciling the world unto himself;" glory, therefore, eternal glory be unto God in the highest, for in Christ there is on earth eternal peace and good-will towards men. God hath in Christ glorified himself, we must therefore in Christ glorify him, and make all our joys and praises to centre in him. In the day of our rejoicing, this must be the burden of all our songs, Blessed be God for Jesus Christ; thanks be unto God for this unspeakable gift, the foundation of all other gifts.

Let this holy joy speak encouragement to ourselves, cheerfully to proceed in our Christian course. The comfort we have had in our covenant relation to God, and interest in Christ, should put a sweetness into all our enjoyments, and sanctify them to us. We must see the love of God in them, and taste that he is gracious, and this must make them comforts indeed to us; see the curse removed from them, see a blessing going along with them, and then "go thy way, eat thy bread with joy, and drink thy wine with a merry heart, for God now accepteth thy works." Have we good ground to hope, that through grace our works are accepted of God? If we sincerely aim at God's acceptance, make that our end, and labour for it, with an eye to Christ as Mediator, we may hope that our persons and performances are accepted; if we accept of God's works, accept the disposals of his providence, and the offers of his grace, with an humble acquiescence in both, that will be a good evidence, that he accepts our works. And if so, we have reason to rejoice with joy unspeakable and full of glory. "Eat thy bread with joy," for it is thy Father's gift, the bread wherewith the Lord thy God feeds thee in this wilderness, through which he is leading thee to the land of promise; "drink thy wine with a merry heart," remembering Christ's love more than wine; what thou hast, though mean and scanty, thou hast it with the blessing of God, which will make the little thou hast "better than the riches of many wicked."

Rejoice in the Lord now, O my soul, rejoice in him always; having kept this feast with gladness, as Hezekiah and his people did, carry with thee some of the comforts of God's table to thine own, and there eat thy meat with gladness, as the primitive Christians did. Live a life of holy cheerfulness, and the joy of the Lord will be thy strength.

IV. We should come from this ordinance much quickened to every good work.—Seeing ourselves compassed about here with so great a cloud of witnesses, bound by so many engagements, invited by so many encouragements, and obliged to God and godliness by so many ties of duty, interest, and gratitude; let us "lay aside every weight, and the sin that most easily besets us," whatever it is, especially the evil heart of unbelief, which is our great hinderance, and "let us run with patience the race that is set before us, looking unto Jesus." Let the covenant we have renewed, and the comforts we have received, make us more ready to every good duty, and more lively in it; more active and zealous for the glory of God, the service of our generation, and the welfare and prosperity of our own souls. From what we have seen and done here, we may fetch powerful considerations to shame us out of our slothfulness and our backwardness to that which is good, and to stir us up to the utmost diligence in our Master's work.

When Jacob had received a gracious visit from God, and had made a solemn vow to him, it follows, "Then Jacob went on his way." The original phrase is observable: "Then Jacob lift up his feet." After that comfortable night he had at Bethel, knowing himself to be in the way of his duty, he proceeded with a great deal of cheerfulness, that strengthened the weak hands, and confirmed the feeble knees. Thus should our communion with God in the Lord's Supper enlarge our hearts to run the way of God's commandments. After such an ordinance we should lift up our feet in the way of God; that is, as it is said of Jehoshaphat, we should lift up our hearts in those ways, abiding and abounding in the work of the Lord.

Rouse up thyself now, my soul, from thy spiritual slumber: up, and be doing, for the Lord is with thee. Awake, awake, put on thy strength, put forth thy strength, that thou mayest push on thy holy war, thy holy work with vigour; shake thyself from the dust, to which thou hast too much cleaved; loose thyself from the bands of thy neck, with which thou hast been too much clogged. Meditate more fixedly, pray more earnestly, resist sin more resolutely, keep Sabbaths more cheerfully, do good more readily. Thou hast heard the sound of a going in the tops of the mulberry trees, plain indications of the presence of God with thee, therefore now thou shalt bestir thyself. Let the comforts of this ordinance employ thy wings, that thou mayest soar upward, upward towards God; let them oil thy wheels, that thou mayest press forward, forward towards heaven: let God's gifts to thee stir up his gifts in thee.

V. We should come from this ordinance with a watchful fear of Satan's wiles, and a firm resolution to stand our ground against them.—Whatever comfort and enlargement we have had in this ordinance, still we must remember, that we are but girding on the harness, and therefore we have no reason to boast or be secure, as though we had it put off. When we return to the world again, we must remember that we go among snares, and must provide accordingly; it is our wisdom so to do.

1. Let us therefore fear. He that travels with a rich treasure about him, is in most danger of being robbed. The ship that is richly laden, is the pirate's

prize. If we come away from the Lord's table replenished with the goodness of God's house, and the riches of his covenant, we must expect the assaults of our spiritual enemies, and not be secure. A strong guard was constantly kept upon the temple, and there needs one upon the living temples. The mystical song represents the bed which is Solomon's, thus surrounded by valiant men of the valiant of Israel, " because of fear in the night." The Holy Ghost thus signifying, that believers in this world are in a military state, and the followers of Christ must be his soldiers. They that work the good work of faith, must fight the good fight of faith.

We must always stand upon our guard, for the goodman of the house knows not at what hour the thief will come; but this we know, that immediately after our Saviour was baptized, and owned by a voice from heaven, " he was led into the wilderness to be tempted of the devil." And immediately after he had administered the Lord's Supper to his disciples, he told them plainly, " Satan hath desired to have you," he has challenged you, " that he may sift you as wheat;" and what he said to them, he says to all—" Watch and pray, that ye enter not into temptation." We must then double our guard against temptations to rash anger, and study to be more than ordinarily meek and quiet, lest, by the tumults and transports of passion, the Holy Spirit be tempted to withdraw. If we have in this ordinance, received Christ Jesus the Lord, let a strict charge be given, like that of the spouse, " by the roes, and by the hinds of the field, that nothing be said, nothing done to stir up or awake our love until he please." Peace being spoken, peace made, let us be afraid of every thing that may give disturbance to it. We should also watch against the inroads of worldly cares and fears, lest they make a descent upon us after a sacrament, and spoil us of the comforts we have there received.

But with a particular care we must watch against the workings of spiritual pride, after a sacrament.

When our Lord Jesus first instituted this ordinance, and made his disciples partakers of it, they were so elevated with the honour of it, that, not content to be all thus great, a contest immediately arose among them, which of them should be greatest. And when St. Paul had been in the third heavens, he was in danger of being "exalted above measure with the abundance of the revelations." We therefore have cause to fear lest this dead fly spoil all our precious ointment, and to keep a very strict and jealous eye upon our own hearts, that they be not lifted up with pride, "lest we fall into the condemnation of the devil." Let us dread the first risings of self-conceit, and suppress them; for, "What have we that we have not received? And if we have received it, why then do we boast?"

2. Let us therefore fix; and let our hearts be established with the grace here received. What we have done in this ordinance, we must go away firmly resolved to abide by all our days. I am now fixed immovably for Christ and holiness, against sin and Satan. The matter is settled, never to be called in question again, "I will serve the Lord." The bargain is struck, the knot is tied, the debate is come up to a final resolve; and here I fix, as one steadfastly resolved, with purpose of heart to cleave unto the Lord. No room is left to parley with a temptation; I am a Christian, a confirmed Christian, and, by the grace of God, a Christian I will live and die; and therefore, "get thee behind me, Satan, thou art an offence unto me." My resolutions, in which before I wavered and was unsteady, are now come to a head, and are as a nail in a sure place; I am now at a point, "I have opened my mouth unto the Lord, and I cannot go back;" and therefore, by the grace of God, I am determined to go forward, and not so much as look back, or wish for a discharge from those engagements. "I have chosen the way of truth, and therefore in thy strength, Lord, I will stick to thy testimonies." Now my foot stands in an even place, well shod with the preparation of the gospel of peace.

I am now like a strong man refreshed with wine, resolved to resist the devil, that he may flee from me, and never yield to him.

VI. We should come from this ordinance praying; lifting up our hearts to God in ejaculatory petitions; and retiring, as soon as may be, for solemn prayer.—Not only before, and in the duty, but after it, we have occasion to offer up our desires to God, and bring in strength and grace from him.

Two things we should be humbly earnest with God in prayer for, after this solemnity, and we are furnished from the mouth of holy David with very emphatical and expressive petitions for them both. We may therefore take with us these words in addressing God:—

1. We must pray that God will fulfil to us those promises which he was graciously pleased to seal to us in this ordinance. David prayed for this: "Now, Lord, let the thing that thou hast spoken concerning thy servant, and concerning his house, be established for ever, and do as thou hast said." God's promises in the word are designed to be our pleas in prayer; and we receive the grace of God in them in vain, if we do not make that use of them, and sue out the benefits conveyed and secured by them. These are talents to be traded with, and improved as the guide of our desires, and the ground of our faith in prayer, and we must not hide them in a napkin. Having here taken hold of the covenant, thus we must take hold on God for covenant mercies. "Lord, remember the word unto thy servant, upon which thou hast caused me to hope." Thou hast not only given me the word to hope in, but the heart to hope in it. It is a hope of thy own raising, and thou wilt not destroy, by a disappointment, the work of thy own hands.

Come, therefore, O my soul, come order thy cause before him, and fill thy mouth with arguments. Lord, is not this the word which thou hast spoken, "Sin shall not have dominion over you, the God of peace shall tread Satan under your feet: There shall no temptation take you, but such as is common to men, and the faithful God will never suffer you to be tempted above what you are able?" Lord, be it unto thy servant according to these words. Is not this the word which thou hast spoken, "That all things shall work for good to them that love thee; that thou wilt be to them a God all-sufficient, their shield, and their exceeding great reward; that thou wilt give them grace and glory, and withhold no good thing from them; that thou wilt never fail them, nor forsake them?" Now, Lord, let those words which thou hast spoken concerning thy servant (and many other the like,) be established for ever, and do as thou hast said; for they are the words upon which thou hast caused me to hope.

2. We must pray, that he will enable us to fulfil those promises which we have made to him in this ordinance. David's prayer for this is, " O Lord God of Abraham, Isaac, and of Israel, our fathers, keep this for ever in the imagination of the thoughts of the hearts of thy people, and prepare, or confirm their hearts unto thee." Have there been some good affections, good desires, and good resolutions in the imagination of the thoughts of our hearts at this ordinance, some good impressions made upon us, and some good expressions drawn from us by it? We cannot but be sensible how apt we are to lose the good we have wrought, and therefore it is our wisdom by prayer to commit the keeping of it to God, and earnestly to beg of him effectual grace, thoroughly to furnish us for every good word and work, and thoroughly to fortify us against every evil word and work. We made our promises in the strength of the grace of God, that strength we must therefore pray for, that we may be able to make good our promises. Lord, maintain thine own interest in my soul; let thy name be ever hallowed there, thy kingdom come, and thy will be done in my heart, as it is done in heaven.

When we come away from this ordinance, we return to a cooling, tempting, distracting world; as when Moses came down from the mount, where he had been with God, he found the camp of Israel dancing before the golden calf to his great disturbance. In the midst of such sorrows and such snares as we are compassed about with here, we shall find it no easy matter to preserve the peace and grace which we hope we have obtained at the Lord's table; we must therefore put ourselves under the divine protection. Methinks it was with an affecting air of tenderness, that Christ said concerning his disciples, when he was leaving them, " Now I am no more in the world," the days of my temptation are at an end; "but these are in the world," they have their trial yet before them. What then shall I do for them? " Holy Father, keep through thine own name them which thou hast given me." That prayer of his was both the great example, and the great encouragement of our prayers. Now, at the close of a sacrament, it is seasonable thus to address ourselves to God: I have not yet put off this body; I am not yet clear of this world; yet I am a traveller exposed to thieves, yet I am a soldier exposed to enemies. Holy Father, keep through thine own name the graces and comforts thou hast given me; for they are thine. Mine own hands are not sufficient for me; O let thy grace be so, to preserve me to thy heavenly kingdom.

Immediately after the first administration of the Lord's Supper, our Saviour, when he had told Peter of Satan's design upon him, added this comfortable word, " I have prayed for thee, that thy faith fail not;" and that is it which we must pray for, that this faith, which we think is so strong in the day of its advantage, may not prove weak in the day of its trial; for, as they who would have the benefit of the Spirit's operation, must strive for themselves; so they that would have the benefit of the Son's intercession, must pray for themselves.

VII. We should come from this ordinance with a charitable disposition.—Anciently, the Christians had their love-feasts, or feasts of charity, annexed to their

Eucharist; but what needed that, while the Eucharist itself is a love-feast and a feast of charity? And surely that heart must be strangely hardened and soured, that can go from under the softening, sweetening powers of this ordinance in an uncharitable frame.

The fervent charity which we now should have among ourselves, must be a loving, giving, and forgiving charity. Thus it must have its perfect work.

We must come from this ordinance with a disposition to love our fellow Christians. Here we see how dear they were to Christ, for he purchased them with his own blood; and from thence we may infer how dear they ought to be, and how near they should lie, to our hearts. Shall I look strangely upon them that have acquaintance with Christ? or be indifferent towards them whom he has so much concern for? No; we that are many, being one bread and one body, and having been all made to drink into one Spirit, my heart shall be more closely knit than ever to all the members of that one body, who are quickened and acted by that one Spirit. I have here beheld the beauty of the Lord, and therefore must love his image wherever I see it on his sanctified ones. I have here joined myself to the Lord in an everlasting covenant, and thereby have joined myself in relation, and consequently in affection, to all those who are in the bond of the same covenant. I have here bound myself to keep Christ's commandments, and this is his commandment, "that we love one another," and that brotherly love continue.

Those from whom we differ in, the less weighty matters of the law, though we agree in the great things of God, we should now think of, with particular thoughts of love and kindness, because from them our minds are most in temptation to be alienated; and of those to whom we have given the right hand of fellowship in this and in other ordinances, we should likewise be mindful, with particular endearments, because of the particular relation we stand in to them, as our more intimate companions in the kingdom and patience of Jesus Christ. Yea, after such an ordinance as this, our catholic charity must be more warm and affectionate, more active, strong, and steadfast, and more victorious over the difficulties and oppositions it meets with; and, as the apostle speaks, we should " increase and abound in love one towards another, and towards all men;" and in all the fruits and instances of that love.

We must come from this ordinance with a disposition to give to the poor and necessitous, according as our ability and opportunity is. It is the laudable custom of the churches of Christ, to close the administration of this ordinance with a collection for the poor; to which we ought to contribute our share, not grudgingly or of necessity, but with a single eye and a willing mind, that our alms may be sanctified and accepted of God; and not only to this, but to all other acts of charity, we must be more forward and free after a sacrament. Though our Saviour lived upon alms himself, yet, out of the little he had, he gave alms to the poor, particularly at the feast of the passover, to set us an example. Days of rejoicing and thanksgiving (and such our sacrament days are) used to be thus solemnized; for when we " eat the fat, and drink the sweet ourselves, we must send portions unto them for whom nothing is prepared," that when our souls are blessing God, the loins of the poor may bless us. If our hearts have here been opened to Christ, we must evidence they are so by being open-handed to poor Christians; for, since our goodness cannot extend to him, it is his will that it should extend to them. If we have here in sincerity given ourselves to God, we have, with ourselves, devoted all we have to his service and honour, to be employed and laid out for him; and thus we must testify that we have heartily consented to that branch of the surrender. " As we have opportunity, we must do good to all men, especially to them that are of the household of faith: remembering that we are but stewards of the manifold grace of God." If our prayers have here come up for a memorial before God, as Cornelius', our alms, like his, must accompany them. We have seen here how much we owe to God's pity and bounty towards us: having therefore obtained mercy, we ought to show mercy; knowing the grace of the Lord Jesus, "that though he was rich, yet for our sakes he became poor, that we through his poverty might be rich."

We must come from this ordinance with a disposition to forgive those that have been provoking and injurious to us. Our approach to the sacrament made it necessary for us to forgive, but our attendance on it should make it even natural for us to forgive; and our experience there of God's mercy and grace to us, should conquer all the difficulty and reluctancy of which we are conscious to ourselves therein, and make it as easy to forgive our enemies as it is to forgive ourselves, when at any time we have had a quarrel with ourselves. That which makes it hard to forgive, and puts an edge upon our resentments, is the magnifying of the affronts we have received, and the losses we have sustained. Now, in this ordinance, we have had honours put upon us sufficient to balance all those affronts, and benefits bestowed on us, sufficient to countervail all those losses; so that we may well afford to forgive and forget both. With ourselves we have offered up to God our names, estates, and all our interests; in compliance therefore with the will of God, (that God who bid Shimei curse David, and who took away from Job that which the Sabeans and Chaldeans robbed him of,) we must not only bear with patience the damage we sustain in those concerns, but must be charitably affected towards those that have been the instruments of that damage, knowing that men are God's hand, and to his hand we must always submit.

But the great argument for the forgiving of injuries, when we come from the table of the Lord, is taken from the pardons God has in Christ there sealed to us. The jubilee trumpet which proclaimed releases, sounded at the close of the day of atonement. Is God reconciled to us? Let us then be more firmly than ever reconciled to our brethren.

Let the death of Christ, which we have here commemorated, not only slay all enmities, but take down all partition walls; not only forbid revenge, but remove strangeness; and let all our feuds and quarrels be buried in his grave. Has our Master forgiven us that great debt, and a very great debt it was, and ought we not then to have compassion "on our fellow-servants?" Let us, therefore, who have in this ordinance put on the Lord Jesus Christ, put on, "as becomes the elect of God, holy and beloved, bowels of mercies and kindness, inclining us to forgive; humbleness of mind and meekness," enabling us to conquer that pride and passion which object against our forgiving; that if any man have a quarrel against any, it may be passed by, as God for Christ's sake has forgiven us.

VIII. We should come from this ordinance longing for heaven.—Every good Christian lives in the belief of the life everlasting, which God, that cannot lie, has promised, looking for the blessed hope; and doubtless much of the power of godliness consists in the joyful expectation of the glory to be revealed. But though we should look upon ourselves as heathens if we did not believe it, and as desperate if we had not some hopes of it; yet we have all reason to lament it, as not only our infelicity, but our iniquity, that our desires towards it are so weak and feeble. We are too apt to take up our rest here, and wish we might live always on this earth; and we need something to make us hunger and thirst after that perfect righteousness, that crown of righteousness, with which only we shall be filled. For this good end the Lord's Supper is very improvable, to hasten us towards the land of promise, and carry out our souls in earnest breathings after the felicities of our future state.

The complaints we find cause to exhibit at this ordinance, should make us long for heaven; for whatever is defective and uneasy here, we shall be for ever freed from when we come to heaven. When here we set ourselves to contemplate the beauty of God and the love of Christ, we find ourselves in a cloud, we see but through a glass darkly; let us therefore long to be there where the veil shall be rent, the glasses we now make use of laid aside, and we shall not only see face to face, but, which will yield us more satisfaction, we shall see as we are seen, and know as we are known. When here we would soar upwards upon the wings of love, we find ourselves clogged and pinioned; this immortal spirit is caged in a house of clay, and does but flutter at the best. Let us therefore long to be there, where we shall be perfectly delivered from all the incumbrances of a body of flesh, and all the entanglements of a world of sense; and love, in its highest elevations, and utmost enlargements, shall survive both faith and hope. When here we would fix for God, and join ourselves closely to him, we find ourselves apt to wander, apt to waver, and should therefore long to be there, where our love to God will be no longer love in motion, constant motion, as it is here, but love at rest, an everlasting rest. Here we complain, that, through the infirmity of the flesh, we are soon weary of well-doing; and, if the spirit be willing, yet the flesh is weak, and cannot keep pace with it; but there we shall run and not be weary, we shall walk and not faint; and shall not rest, because we shall not need to rest day nor night from praising God. O when shall I come to that world where there is neither sin, nor sorrow, nor snare; and to the spirits of just men made perfect there, who are as the angels of God in heaven!

The comforts which through grace we experience in this ordinance, should make us long for heaven. The foretastes of those divine joys should whet our appetites after the full fruition of them. The bunch of grapes that meets us in this wilderness should make us long to be in Canaan, that land of overflowing plenty, where we shall wash our garments in this wine, and our clothes in the blood of the grape. If communion with God and grace here afford us such a satisfaction, as surpasses all the delights of the sons of men, what will the fulness of joy be in God's presence, and those pleasures for ever more? If the shadows of good things to come be so refreshing, what will the substance be, and the good things themselves? If God's tabernacles be so amiable, what will his temple be? If a day at his courts, an hour at his table, be so pleasant, what then will an eternity within the veil be? If I find myself so enriched with the earnest of the purchased possession, what then will the possession itself be? If the joy of my Lord, as I am here capable of receiving it, and as it is mixed with so much alloy in this imperfect state, be so comfortable, what will it be when I shall enter into that joy, and bathe myself eternally in the spring-head of these rivers of pleasure?

Pant then, my soul, pant after those fountains of living water, out of which all these sweet streams arise; that boundless, bottomless ocean of delight into which they are all run. Rest not content with any of the contentments here below; no, not with those in holy ordinances, (which are of all others the best we meet with in this wilderness,) but long for the enjoyments above in the vision of God. It is good to be here, but it is better to be there; far better to depart, and be with Christ. Whilst thou art groaning under the burdens of this present state, groan after the glorious liberties of the children of God in the future state. Thirst for God, for the living God: O when shall I come and appear before God? That the day may break, and the shadows flee away, "make haste, my beloved, and be thou like to a roe or to a young hart upon the mountains of spices."

CHAPTER XIII.

AN EXHORTATION TO ORDER THE CONVERSATION ARIGHT AFTER THIS ORDINANCE.

I. In general, we must live so as to adorn our profession. II. To fulfil our engagements. III. To make grateful returns for favours shown us. IV. To preserve the comforts we have tasted. V. To evidence our communion with God. 1. In particular, we must be sincerely devout and pious. 2. Conscientiously just and honest. 3. Religiously meek and peaceable. 4. Strictly sober and chaste. 5. Abundantly charitable and beneficent. 6. More weaned from this world, and more taken up with another.

We will now suppose the new moon to be gone, the Sabbath to be past, and the solemnities of the sacrament-day to be over; and is our work now done? No: now the most needful and difficult part of our work begins; which is, to maintain such a constant watch over ourselves, that we may, in the whole course of our conversation, exemplify the blessed fruits and effects of our communion with God in this ordinance. When we come down from this mount, we must, as Moses did, bring the tables of the testimony with us in our hands, that we may in all things have respect to God's commandments, and frame our lives according to them. Then we truly get good by this ordinance, when we are made better by it, and use it daily as a bridle of restraint to keep us in from all manner of sin, and a spur of constraint to put us on to all manner of duty.

I shall endeavour, first, to give some general rules for the right ordering of the conversation after we have been at the Lord's Supper; and then, secondly, I shall mention some particulars, wherein we must study to conform ourselves to the intentions of that ordinance, and abide under the influence of it.

For the first, the Lord's Supper was instituted not only for the solemnizing of the memorial of Christ's death at certain times, but for the preserving of the remembrance of it in our minds at all times, as a powerful argument against every thing that is evil, and a prevailing inducement to every thing that is good; in this sense we must "bear about with us continually the dying of the Lord Jesus, that the life also of Jesus may be manifested in our mortal bodies." It was instituted, not only for the sealing of the covenant, that it may be ratified, but for the imprinting of it upon our minds, that we may be ever mindful of the covenant, and live under the commanding power of it.

We must see to it, that there be an agreement between our performances at the Lord's table, and at other times; that we be uniform in our religion, and not guilty of a self-contradiction. What will it profit us, if we pull down with one hand what we build up with the other; and undo in our lives what we have done in our devotions? That we may not do so, let us be governed by these rules:—

I. Our conversation must be such, that we may adorn the profession which in the Lord's Supper we have made.—We have in that ordinance solemnly owned ourselves the disciples and followers of the Lord Jesus; we have done ourselves the honour to subscribe ourselves his humble servants, and he has done us the honour to admit us into his family; and now we are concerned to walk worthy of the vocation wherewith we are called; that, our relation to Christ being so much an honour to us, we may never be a dishonour to it. We are said to be taken into covenant with God for this very end, that we may be unto him for "a name, and for a praise, and for a glory," that we may be witnesses for him, and for the honour of his name among men.

We must therefore be very cautious, that we never say or do any thing to the reproach of the gospel, and Christ's holy religion, or which may give any occasion to the enemies of the Lord to blaspheme. If those who profess to be devout towards God, be unjust and dishonest towards men, this casts reproach upon devotion, as if that would consist with, and countenance immorality. If those who call themselves Christians walk as other Gentiles walk, and do Satan's drudgery in Christ's livery, Christianity suffers by it, and religion is wounded in the house of her friends. Injuries are done it which cannot be repaired; and those will have a great deal to answer for another day, for whose sakes the name of God and his doctrine are thus evil spoken of. By our coming to the Lord's Supper, we distinguish ourselves from those whose profession of Christianity, by their being baptized in infancy, seems to be more their chance than their choice; and, by a voluntary act of our own, we surname ourselves by the name of Israel: now, if, after we have thus distinguished ourselves, and so raised the expectations of our neighbours from us, we do that which is unbecoming the character we bear; if we be vain, and carnal, and intemperate; if we be false and unfair, cruel and unmerciful, what will the Egyptians say? They will say, Commend us to the children of this world, if these be the children of God; for what do they more than others? Men's prejudices against religion are hereby confirmed, advantage is given to Satan's devices, and the generation of the righteous is condemned for the sake of those who are spots in their feasts of charity. Let us therefore always be jealous for the reputation of our profession, and afraid of doing that which may in the least be a blemish to it; and the greater profession we make, the more tender let us be of it, because we have the more eyes upon us, that watch for our halting; when we do good, we must remember the apostle's caution, "Let not your good be evil spoken of."

We must also be very studious to do that which will redound to the credit of our profession. It is not enough that we be not a scandal to religion, but we must strive to be an ornament to it, by excelling in virtue, and being forward to every good work. Our light must shine as the face of Moses did, when he came down from the mount; that is, our good works must be such, that they who see them may give religion their good word, and thereby "glorify our Father which is in heaven." " Our conversation must be as becomes the gospel of Jesus Christ," that they who will not be won by the word, may be won by it to say, We will go with you, for we have heard that God is with you. If there be any virtue, if there be any praise, more amiable and lovely than another, let us think on these things. Are we children? Let us walk as obedient children, well taught, and well managed. Are we soldiers? Let us approve ourselves good soldiers, well trained and well disciplined; so shall we do honour to him that has called us. If God's Israel carefully keep and do his statutes, it will be said of them to their honour among the nations, " Surely they are a wise and understanding people." And this will redound to the honour of Christ; for thus wisdom is justified of her children.

II. Our conversation must be such, that we may fulfil the engagements which at the Lord's Supper we have laid ourselves under. — Having at God's altar sworn that we will keep his righteous judgments, we must conscientiously perform it in all the evidences of a holy, righteous, and sober conversation. The vows we have made, express or implicit, must be carefully made good by a constant watchfulness against all sin, and a constant diligence in all duty; because, " better it is not to vow, than to vow and not to pay."

When we are at any time tempted to sin, or in danger of being surprised into any ill thing, let this be our reply to the tempter, and with this let us quench his fiery darts, " Thy vows are upon me, O God." Did I not say, " I would take heed to my ways, that I sin not with my tongue?" I did say so, and therefore " I will keep my mouth as with a bridle." Did I not make " a covenant with mine eyes?" I did; that therefore shall be to me a covering of the eyes, that they may never be either the inlets or outlets of sin. Did I not say, " I will not transgress?" I did so; and therefore, by the grace of God, I will " abstain from all appearance of evil, and have no

fellowship with the unfruitful works of darkness."
An honest man is as good as his word.

When we begin to grow slothful and careless in our duty, backward to it, and slight in it, let this stir up the gift that is in us, and quicken us to every good word and work: "O my soul, thou hast said unto the Lord, Thou art my Lord;" thou hast said it with the blood of Christ in thy hand; "he is thy Lord then, and worship thou him." "When a lion in the way, a lion in the streets," deters us from any duty, and we "cannot plough by reason of cold, nor sow or reap for fear of winds and clouds," let this help us over the difficulty with a steady resolution—It is what I have promised, and I must perform it; I will not, I dare not, be false to my God and my covenant with him: "I have opened my mouth unto the Lord; and, without incurring the guilt of perjury, I cannot go back."

III. *Our conversation must be such, that we may make some grateful returns for the favours which we have here received.*—The law of gratitude is one of the laws of nature; for the ox knows his owner, and the ass his master's crib: and some have thought that all our gospel-duty may very fitly be comprised in that of gratitude to our Redeemer. In the Lord's Supper we see what Christ has done for us, and we receive what he bestows on us; and, in consideration of both, we must set ourselves, not only to love and praise him, but to walk before him in the land of the living; that though we cannot return him any equivalent for his kindness, yet, by complying with his will, and consulting his honour, we may show that we bear a grateful mind, and would render again according to the benefit done unto us.

By wilful sin after a sacrament, we load ourselves with the guilt, not only of treachery, but of base ingratitude. It was a great aggravation of Solomon's apostasy, that "he turned from the Lord God of Israel, which had appeared unto him twice." More than twice, yea, many a time has God appeared, not only for us in his providences, but to us in his ordinances, manifesting himself in a distinguishing way to us, and not unto the world. Now, if we carry ourselves strangely to him who has been such a friend to us, if we affront him who has so favoured us, and rebel against him who has not only spared but ransomed us, we deserve to be stigmatized with a mark of everlasting infamy, as the most ungrateful wretches that ever God's earth bore, or his sun shone upon. Foolish people and unwise are we, thus to requite the Lord. Let us therefore reason thus with ourselves, when at any time we are tempted to sin:—after he has given us such a deliverance as this, shall we again break his commandments? Shall we spit in the face, and spurn at the bowels of such loving kindness? After we have eaten bread with Christ, shall we go and lift up the heel against him? No, God forbid; we will not continue in sin after grace has thus abounded.

By an exact and exemplary conversation, we show ourselves sensible of the mighty obligations we lie under to love him, and live to him who loved us, and died for us; we should, therefore, from a principle of gratitude, always abound in the work of the Lord, and lay out ourselves with zeal and cheerfulness in his service; thinking nothing too much to do, too hard to suffer, or too dear to part with, for him that has done and suffered, and parted with so much for us. Let the love of Christ constrain us.

IV. Our conversation must be such that we may preserve the comforts which we have tasted in the Lord's Supper.—Have we been satisfied with the goodness of God's house? Let us not receive the grace of God therein in vain, by the forfeiture or neglect of those satisfactions. "Fear the Lord and his goodness;" that is, fear lest you sin against that goodness, and so sin it away. Have we received Christ Jesus the Lord? Let us hold fast what we have received, that no man take our crown, and the comfort of it. Has God here spoken peace to us? Let us then never return to folly, lest we break in upon the peace that God has spoken; it is a jewel too precious to be pawned, as it is by the covetous for the wealth of this world, and by the voluptuous for the pleasures of the flesh. Have we tasted that the Lord is gracious? Let us not put our mouths out of taste to those spiritual and divine pleasures, by any carnal delights and gratifications. Has God made us to hear joy and gladness? Let us not set ourselves out of the hearing of that joyful sound, by listening to the voice of Satan's charms, charm he ever so wisely.

If we walk loosely and carelessly after a sacrament, we provoke God to hide his face from us, to take from us the cup of consolation, and to put into our hands instead of it the cup of trembling; we cloud our evidences, shake our hopes, and wither our comforts, and undo what we have been doing at this ordinance. That caution, therefore, which the apostle gives to the elect lady and her children, should be ever sounding in our ears, "Look to ourselves, that we lose not the things which we have wrought;" or, as the margin reads it, "the things that we have gained." Let us not, by our own folly and neglect, lose the benefit of what we have done, and what we have got at the Lord's table.

Especially, we should take heed lest Satan get an advantage against us, and improve that to our prejudice, which we do not take due care to improve as we ought, to our benefit. After the sop, Satan entered into Judas. If the comforts which we think we have received in this ordinance do not make us more watchful, it is well if they do not make us more secure. If they be not a savour of life unto life, by deterring us from sin, there is danger lest they prove a savour of death unto death, by hardening us in sin. It was one of the most impudent words which that adulterous woman spoke, and she spoke a great many, when she allured the young man into her snares: "I have peace-offerings with me this day, I have paid my vows, therefore came I forth to meet thee." I have been confessed, and absolved, and therefore can the better afford to begin upon a new score; I know the worst of it; it is but being confessed and absolved again. But shall we continue in sin, because grace has abounded, and that grace may abound? God forbid; far be it, far be it from us ever to entertain such a thought. Shall we suck poison out of the balm of Gilead, and wreck our souls upon the rock of salvation? Is Christ the minister of sin? Shall the artifices of our spiritual enemies turn this table into a snare, and that on it, which should be for our welfare, into a trap? Those are but pretended comforts in Christ, that are thus made real supports in sin: "Be not deceived, God is not mocked." Hell will be hell indeed to those who thus "trample under foot the blood of the covenant as an unholy thing, and do despite to the Spirit of grace." Their case is desperate indeed, who are emboldened in sin by their approaches to God.

V. Our conversation must be such, that we may evidence the communion we have had with God in Christ at the Lord's table.—It is not enough to say that we have fellowship with him; the vilest hypocrites pretend to that honour; but, by walking in darkness, they disprove their pretensions, and give themselves the lie. We must therefore show that we have fellowship with him, by walking in the light, and as he also walked. By keeping up communion with God in providences, having our eyes ever towards him, and acknowledging him in all our ways; receiving all our comforts as the gifts of his bounty, and bearing all our afflictions as his fatherly chastisements,—we evidence that we have had communion with him in ordinances. They who converse much with scholars, evidence it by the tongue of the learned; as one may likewise discover by the politeness and refinement of a man's air and mien, that his conversation has been much with persons of quality: thus they that have communion with the holy God, should make it appear in all holy conversation, not suffering any corrupt communication to proceed out of their mouth, but abounding in that which is good, and to the use of edifying, that, by our speech and behaviour, it may appear to what country we belong.

When Peter and John acquitted themselves before the council with such a degree of conduct and assurance, as one could not have expected from unlearned and ignorant men, not acquainted with courts, or camps, or academies; it is said, that they who marvelled at it, "took knowledge of them that they had been with Jesus." And from those who had been with Jesus, who had followed him, sat at his feet, and eaten bread with him, very great things might be expected. In this ordinance we have been with Jesus, we have been seeing his beauty, and tasting his sweetness; and now we should live so, that all who converse with us may discern it, and by our holy, heavenly converse, may take knowledge of us that we have been with Jesus.

For the second thing proposed, let us mention some particulars, wherein we ought, in a special manner, to approve ourselves well after this solemnity, that, "as we have received Christ Jesus the Lord, we may so walk in him."

After we have been admitted into communion with God, and have renewed our covenants with him at his table, it behoves us to be careful, in these six things:—

1. We must see to it, that we be sincerely devout and pious. It is not enough that we live soberly and righteously, but we must live godly, in this present world, and our sacramental engagements should stir us up to abound therein more and more. After an interview with our friends, by which mutual acquaintance is improved, and mutual affections confirmed, we are more constant and endearing in our correspondence with each other; so we should be with God after this ordinance, more frequent in holy ejaculations, and breathings of soul towards God, intermixed even with common business and conversation; more abundant in reading, meditation, and solemn prayer; more diligent in our attendance on public ordinances, more fixed and enlarged in closet

devotions, and more lively and affectionate in our family worship. Those religious exercises wherein we have formerly been remiss and careless, easily persuaded to put them by, or put them off, we should now be more constant to, and more careful in, more close in our application to them, and more serious in our performance of them.

If we have indeed found that it is good for us to draw near to God, we will endeavour to keep near him, so near him, as upon every occasion to speak to him, and to hear from him. If this sacrament has been our delight, the word will be our delight, and we will daily converse with it; prayer will be our delight, and we will give ourselves to it, and continue instant in it. They that have been feasted upon the sacrifice of atonement, ought to abound in sacrifices of acknowledgment, the spiritual sacrifices of prayer and praise, and a broken heart, which are acceptable to God through Christ Jesus; and having in our flock a male, we must offer that, and not a corrupt thing.

It is the shame of many who are called Christians, and have a name and a place in God's family, that they are as backward and indifferent in holy duties, as if they were afraid of doing too much for God and their own souls, and as if their chief care were to know just how much will serve to bring them to heaven, that they may do no more. They can be content to go a mile, but they are not willing to go twain. And does it become those on whom God has sown so plentifully, to make their returns so sparingly? Ought we not rather to inquire what free-will offerings we may bring to God's altar; and how we may do more in religion than we have used to do? They that have found what a good table God keeps, and how welcome they have been to it, should desire to dwell in his house all the days of their life; and blessed are they that do so, " they will be still praising him."

2. We must see to it, that we be conscientiously just and honest. We not only contradict our profes-

sion, and give ourselves the lie, but we reproach the religion we profess, and give it the lie, if, after we have been at this sacrament, we deceive or defraud our brethren in any matter; for this is that which the Lord our God requires of us, that we do justly; that is, that we never do wrong to any, in their body, goods, or good name; and that we ever study to render to all their due, according to the relation we stand in, and the obligation we lie under to them. "That, therefore, which is altogether just ("justice, justice," as the word is,) thou shalt follow." There are many who make no great pretensions to religion, and yet natural conscience, sense of honour, and a regard to the common good, keep them strictly just in all their dealings, and they would scorn to do a base and dishonest thing; and shall not the bonds of this ordinance, added to those inducements, restrain us from every thing that has but the appearance of fraud and injustice? A Christian, a communicant, and yet a cheat, yet a man not to be trusted, not to be dealt with, but standing on one's guard! How can these be reconciled? Will that man be true to his God whom he has not seen, that is false to his brother whom he has seen? Shall he be intrusted with the true riches, that is "not faithful in the unrighteous mammon?"

Let the remembrance of our sacramental vows be always fresh in our minds, to give a check to those secret covetings, which are the springs of all fraudulent practices. I have disclaimed the world for a portion: shall I then, for the compassing of a little of its forbidden gain, wrong my brother, to whom I ought to do good; wrong my profession, which I ought to adorn; and wrong my own conscience, which I ought to keep void of offence? God forbid! I have likewise renounced the hidden things of dishonesty, and promised not to walk in craftiness; "by the grace of God, I will therefore ever have my conversation in the world, in simplicity and godly sincerity, not with fleshly wisdom." They that are so well skilled in the arts of deceit, as to save themselves from the scandal of it, and to be able to say with Ephraim, though he had the balances of deceit in his hands, " In all my labours, they shall find no iniquity in me that were sin;" yet cannot thereby save themselves from the guilt of it, and the ruin that attends it; for doubtless " the Lord is the avenger of all such." Those that cheat their neighbours, cannot cheat their God, but will prove in the end to have cheated themselves into everlasting misery; and " what is a man profited, if he gain the whole world, and lose his own soul?"

3. We must see to it, that we be religiously meek and peaceable. We must not only come from this ordinance in a calm and quiet frame, but we must always keep ourselves in such a frame. By the meekness and gentleness of Christ, (which the apostle mentions as a most powerful charm,) let us be wrought upon to be always meek and gentle, as those that have learned of him. The storms of passion that are here calmed, must never be suffered to make head again; nor must the enmities that are here slain, ever be revived. Having eaten of this gospel passover, we must all our life long keep the feast, without the " leaven of malice and wickedness." Having been feasted at wisdom's table, we must always abide under the conduct and influence of that wisdom, which is " first pure, and then peaceable, gentle, and easy to be entreated." God was greatly displeased with those that, after they released their bond-servants, according to the law, recalled their releases, and brought them into subjection again. And so will he be with those who seem to set aside their quarrels when they come to the sacrament, but, as soon as the pang of their devotion is over, the heat of their passion returns, and they resume their quarrels, and revive all their angry resentments; thereby making it to appear, that they did never truly forgive, and therefore were never forgiven of God.

Let those that have had communion with God in this ordinance, be able to appeal to their relations and domestics, and all they converse with concerning this; and to vouch them for witnesses, that they have mastered their passions, and are grown more mild and quiet in their families than sometimes they have been; and that even when they are most provoked, they know both how to hear reason, and how to speak it. Whatever others do, let us never give occasion to the enemies of the Lord to say, that the seriousness of religion makes men sour and morose, and that zeal in devotion disposes the mind to peevishness and passion; but let us evidence the contrary, that the grace of God does indeed make men good-natured, and that the pleasures of serious godliness make men truly cheerful and easy to all about them. Having been here sealed " to the day of redemption, let us not grieve the Holy Spirit of God," that blessed dove; and that we may not, "let all bitterness, and wrath, and anger, and clamour, and evil-speaking, be put away from us, with all malice."

4. We must see to it, that we be strictly sober and chaste. Gluttony, and drunkenness, and fleshly lusts, are as great a reproach as can be to those that profess relation to Christ, and the expectation of eternal life. It becomes those that have been feasted at the table of the Lord, and have there tasted the pleasures of the spiritual and divine life, to be dead to all the delights of sense, and to make it appear that they are so, by a holy indifference to them. Let not the flesh be indulged to the prejudice of the spirit, nor provision made for the fulfilling of the lusts thereof. Have we been entertained with the dainties of heaven? Let us not be desirous of the dainties of sense, nor solicitous to have the appetite gratified, and all our enjoyments to the highest degree pleasing. When our Lord had instituted his Supper, and gave this cup of blessing to his disciples, he added, " I will not drink henceforth of this fruit of the vine:" now welcome the bitter cup, the vinegar, and the gall; teaching us after a sacrament to sit more loose than before to bodily delights, and to be better reconciled to hardships and disappointments in them. It was the sin and shame of the Israelites in the wilderness,

that while they were fed with manna, angels' food, they lusted, saying, "Who will give us flesh to eat?" And they sin after the similitude of that transgression, who, when they have eaten of the bread of life, and drunk of the water of life, yet continue to be as curious and careful about their meat and drink, as if they knew no better things, and had their happiness bound up in them; as if the kingdom of God were in this sense meat and drink, and a Turkish paradise were their heaven. Surely they that are of this spirit serve not our Lord Christ, but their own bellies.

But if they thus shame themselves who indulge the flesh, though their reason remains with them; what shall we think of those who, by their intemperance, put themselves quite out of possession of their own souls, unfit themselves for the service of God, and level themselves with the beasts? A Christian, a communicant, and yet a tippler, a drunkard, and a companion with those that run to this excess of riot! This, this is the sin that has been the scandal and ruin of many, who, having begun in the spirit, have thus ended in the flesh; this is that which has quenched the Spirit, hardened the heart, besotted the head, debauched the conscience, withered the profession, and so has slain its thousands, and its ten thousands. Against this sin, therefore, the Lord's prophet must cry aloud, and not spare; of the danger of this, the watchmen are concerned to give warning; and dare those who partake " of the cup of the Lord, drink of the cup of devils?" Can there be so much concord between light and darkness, between Christ and Belial? No, there cannot; these are contrary, the one to the other. If men's communicating will not break them off from their drunkenness, their drunkenness must break them off from communicating; for these are spots in our feasts of charity; and, if God be true, "drunkards shall not inherit the kingdom of God." Let me, therefore, with all earnestness, as one that desires to obtain mercy of the Lord to be faithful, warn all that profess religion and relation to Christ, to stand upon their guard against this snare, which has been fatal to multitudes. As you tender the favour of God, the comforts of the Spirit, the credit of your profession, and the welfare of your own souls here and hereafter, take heed of being entangled in any temptations to this sin; shun the society of these evil-doers, abstain from all the appearances of this sin; watch and be sober; he "that loved us, and washed us from our sins in his own blood, has made us unto our God kings and priests." Are we priests? This was the law of the priesthood, and it was a law made upon occasion of the death of Nadab and Abihu, who probably had "erred through wine." "Do not drink wine or strong drink, when ye go into the tabernacle of the congregation." Are we kings? " It is not for kings, O Lemuel, it is not for kings to drink wine; lest they drink and forget the law." It is not for Christians to drink to excess, and to allow themselves in those riotings and revellings, which even the sober heathen condemned and abhorred.

Adultery, fornication, uncleanness, and lasciviousness, are likewise lusts of the flesh, and defiling to the soul, which, therefore, all those must carefully avoid that profess to be led by the Spirit: they are abominable things which the Lord hates, and which we also must hate. Are not our bodies temples of the Holy Ghost? Dare we then defile them? Are they not members of Christ? And shall we make them the members of a harlot? Let those that eat of the holy things, be holy both in body and spirit, and "possess their vessels in sanctification and honour, and not in the lusts of uncleanness." Let those eyes never be guilty of a wanton look, that have here seen Christ evidently set forth crucified among us; let not lewd, corrupt communication proceed out of that mouth into which God's covenant has been taken; let not unclean, lascivious thoughts be ever harboured in that heart in which the holy Jesus vouchsafes to dwell. Let those that have eaten of wisdom's bread, and drunk of the wine that she has mingled, never hearken to the invitations of the foolish woman, who courts the unwary to stolen waters, and bread eaten in secret, under pretence that they are sweet and pleasant; "for the dead are there, and her guests are in the depths of hell."

5. We must see to it, that we be abundantly charitable and beneficent. It is not enough that we do no hurt, but if we would order our conversation aright, we must, as we have opportunity, do good to all men, as becomes those to whom God in Christ is good, and does good, and who profess themselves the disciples and followers of him who went about doing good. Shall we be selfish, and seek our own things only, who have here seen how Christ humbled and emptied himself for us? Shall we be sparing of our pains for our brethren's good, who have here seen Christ among us, as one that serves, as one that suffers, and as one who came not to be ministered unto, "but to minister, and to give his life a ransom for many?" Shall we be shy of speaking to, or speaking for our poor brethren, who have here seen our Lord Jesus not ashamed to own us, and intercede for us, notwithstanding our poverty and meanness? Shall we be strait-handed in distributing to the necessities of the saints, who have here found Christ so liberal and open-handed in imparting to us, not only the gospel of God, but even his own soul? After we have been at this ordinance, we should show how much we are affected with our receiving there, by being ready and forward "to every good work;" because our goodness extends not to God, it ought to extend to the saints that are in the earth. Thus we must be "followers of God as dear children; we must walk in love, as here we see Christ hath loved us, and given himself for us."

6. We must see to it, that we be more taken off from this world, and more taken up with another world. A Christian then lives like himself, when he lives above the things that are seen, which are temporal, and looks upon them with a holy contempt, and keeps his eye fixed upon the things that are not seen, which are eternal, looking upon them with a

holy concern. We are not of this world, but we are called out of it; we belong to another world, and are designed for it: we must, therefore, "seek the things that are above, and not set our affections on things beneath."

The thoughts of Christ crucified should wean us from this world, and make us out of love with it. The world knew him not, but hated him; the princes of this world crucified him; but he overcame the world, and we also by faith in him may obtain a victory over it; such a victory over it, that we may not be entangled with its snares, encumbered with its cares, or disquieted by its sorrows. By frequent meditation on the cross of Christ, "the world will be crucified to us, and we to the world;" that is, the world and we shall grow very indifferent one to another, and no love shall be lost between us.

The thoughts of Christ glorified should raise our hearts to that blessed place where Christ "sitteth on the right hand of God, and from whence we look for the Saviour." When we commemorate Christ's entrance within the veil as our forerunner, and have good hopes of following him shortly; when we think of his being in paradise, and of our being with him; how should our affections be carried out towards that joy of our Lord! How studious should we be to do the work of heaven, conform to the laws of heaven, and converse as much as may be with the glorious society there! Having received the adoption of sons, we should improve our acquaintance with, and raise our expectations of, the inheritance of sons.

CHAPTER XIV.

SOME WORDS OF COMFORT WHICH THIS ORDINANCE SPEAKS TO SERIOUS CHRISTIANS.

Four things premised. This ordinance may comfort us, I. Against the remembrance of our former sins and provocations. II. Against the sense of our sins and daily infirmities. III. Against the sad remainders of indwelling corruption. IV. Against prevailing doubts and fears about the spiritual state. V. Against the troubles and calamities of this life. VI. Against the fears of death.

The Lord's Supper was intended for the comfort of good people, not only while they are actually attending on God in it, but ever after; not only that their joy may be full, but that this joy may remain in them. It is a feast which was made for laughter; not that of the fool, which terminates in a sigh, and the end of it is heaviness, but that of the truly wise man who has learned to rejoice evermore, yea, to rejoice in the Lord always; not that of the hypocrite, whose triumphing is short, and his joys but "for a moment," but that of the sincere Christian, whom God causeth always "to triumph in Christ." The water that Christ here gives, is designed to be a well of water, living water, sending forth "streams that make glad the city of our God." This feast, if it be not our own fault, will be to us a continual feast, a breast of consolation, from which we may daily suck and be satisfied.

It is the will of God that his people should be a comforted people. The most evangelical part of the prophecy of Isaiah begins with this, "Comfort ye, comfort ye my people, saith your God." He takes pleasure in their prosperity, he delights to see them cheerful, and to hear them sing at their work, and sing in his ways. Religion was never intended to make people melancholy; wisdom's adversaries do her wrong if they paint her in mourning, and wisdom's children do not do her right, if they give them occasion to do so; for though they are, like St. Paul, as sorrowful, yet they should be like him, always rejoicing; because, though they seem perhaps to have nothing, yet really "they possess all things." So good a Master do we serve, that he has been pleased to combine interests with us, and so compound his glory and our comfort, that, in seeking the one, we seek the other also. He has made that to be our duty, which is indeed our greatest privilege; and that is, to delight ourselves always in the Lord, and to live a life of complacency in him. And it is the New Testament character of a Christian indeed, that he rejoices in Christ Jesus.

Good Christians have, of all people, most reason to rejoice and be comforted. As for those that are at a distance from God, and out of covenant with him, they have reason to be afflicted, and mourn and weep. "Rejoice not, O Israel, for joy as other people; for thou hast gone a whoring from thy God." To them that eat of the forbidden tree of knowledge, this tree of life also is forbidden; but those that devote themselves to God, have all the reason in the world to delight themselves in God. They that "ask the way to Zion with their faces thitherward, though they go weeping to seek the Lord their God," yet they shall go on rejoicing, when they have found him; for they cannot but find the way pleasantness, and the paths of it peace. Have not they reason to smile, on whom God smiles? If God has put grace into the heart, has he not put gladness there, and a new song into the mouth? Is Christ proclaimed king in the soul? And ought it not to be done with acclamations of joy? Is the atonement received, and the true treasure found? And shall we not rejoice with joy unspeakable? Have we good hope through grace of entering shortly into the joy of our Lord? And have we not cause now to rejoice in the hope of it?

Yet those who have so much reason to rejoice are often cast down and in sorrow, and not altogether without cause. This state of probation and preparation is a mixed state, and it is proper enough it should be so, for the trial and exercise of various graces, and that God's power may have the praise of keeping the balance even. In those whose hearts are visited by the day-spring from on high, the light is neither clear nor dark, it is neither day nor night. They have their comforts, which they would not exchange for the peculiar treasure of kings and princes; but withal they have their crosses, under which they groan, being burdened. They have their hopes, which are an anchor to the soul, both sure and steadfast, entering into that within the veil; but withal they have their fears, for their warfare is not yet accomplished; they have not yet attained, neither are already perfect. They have their joys, such as the world can neither give nor take away, joys that a stranger doth not intermeddle with; but withal they have their griefs, their way to Canaan lies through a wilderness, and their way to Jerusalem through the valley of Baca. Their Master was himself a man of sorrows, and acquainted with griefs, and they are to be his followers. While we are here, we must not think it strange, if, for a season, when need is, we are in heaviness; we cannot expect to reap in joy hereafter, unless we now sow in tears. We must not therefore think, that either the present happiness of the saints, which in this world they are to expect, or their present holiness, which in this world they are to endeavour after, consists in such delights and joys, as leave no room for any mourning and sense of trouble: no, there is a sorrow, that is a godly sorrow; a jealousy of ourselves, that is a godly jealousy. It is only a perfect love that casts out all fear and all grief, which we are not to expect in this imperfect state. All tears shall not be wiped away from our eyes, nor shall sorrow and sighing quite flee away, till we come to heaven: while we are here, we are in a vale of tears, and must conform to the temper of the climate; we are at sea, and must expect to be tossed with tempests; we are in the camp, and must expect to be alarmed; while without are fightings, no wonder that within are fears.

Our Lord Jesus has therefore provided such comforts for the relief of his people, in their present sorrowful state, as may serve to balance their griefs, and keep them from being pressed above measure; and he has instituted holy ordinances, and especially this of the Lord's Supper, for the application of those comforts to them, that they may never fear, may never sorrow as those that have no hope nor joy. The covenant of grace, as it is ministered in the everlasting gospel, has in it a salve for every sore, a remedy for every malady; so that they who have an interest in that covenant, and know it, may triumph with blessed Paul: " Though we are troubled on every side, yet we are not distressed; perplexed sometimes, but, thanks be to God, not in despair; persecuted by men, but not forsaken of God; cast down and drooping, but not destroyed and lost." This is that which bears them up under all their burdens, comforts them in all their griefs, and enables them to rejoice in tribulation: God is theirs, and they are his, and he has " made with them an everlasting covenant, well ordered in all things, and sure; and this is all their salvation, and all their desire, however it be."

The word of God is written to them for this end, " that their joy may be full—and that through patience and comfort of the Scriptures they may have hope." Precious promises are there treasured up, to be the foundations of their faith and hope, and consequently the fountains of their joy. Songs of thanksgiving are there drawn up for them to refresh themselves with in their weary pilgrimage, and to have recourse to for the silencing of their complaints. Ministers are appointed to be the helpers of their joy, and to speak comfort to such as mourn in Zion. The Sabbath is the day which the Lord has made for this very end, that they may rejoice and be glad in it. Prayer is appointed for the ease of troubled spirits, that in it they may pour out their complaints before God, and fetch in comfort from him. " Ask and ye shall receive, that your joy may be full."

This sacrament was ordained for the comfort of good Christians, for the confirmation of their faith, in order to the preservation and increase of their joy; and they ought to improve it both for the strengthening of the habit of holy cheerfulness, and their actual encouragement against the several particular grievances of this present time. And there is no complaint which a good Christian has cause to make at any time, which he may not qualify, and keep from growing clamorous, by comforts drawn from what he has seen and tasted, what he has done and received, at the Lord's table. Let us therefore be daily drawing water out of these wells of salvation; and when our souls are cast down and disquieted within us, let us fetch arguments from our communion with God in this ordinance, both in chiding them for their despondency, and encouraging them to hope and rejoice in God. What is it that grieves and oppresses us? Why is our countenance sad, and why go we mourning all the day long? Whatever the occasion of the heaviness is, let it be weighed in the balance of the sanctuary, and I dare say there is that comfort to be fetched from this ordinance, which is sufficient to be set in the scale against it, and outweigh it. Let us mention some of the most common causes of our trouble, and try what relief we may from hence be furnished with:—

I. Are we disquieted and discouraged by the remembrance of our former sins and provocations? There is that here which will help to quiet and encourage us in reference to this. Conscience sometimes calls to mind the sins of the unconverted state, and charges them home upon the soul, especially if they were heinous and scandalous; it repeats the reproach of the youth; rips up the old quarrels, and aggravates them; probes the old wounds, and makes them bleed afresh; and from hence the disconsolate soul is ready to draw such hard conclusions as these: —Surely it is impossible that so great a sinner as I have been, should be pardoned and accepted; that such a prodigal should be welcomed home, and such a publican ever find mercy! Can I expect to share in that grace which I so long slighted and sinned against? Or to be taken into that covenant of which I have so often cast away the cords? Will the holy God take one into the embraces of his love, who has been so vile and sinful, and fitter to be made a monument of his wrath? Can there be any hope for me? Or, if there be some hope yet, can there be any joy? If I may, through a miracle of mercy, escape hell at last, which I have deserved a thousand times, yet ought I not to weep mine eyes out, and to "go softly all my years in the bitterness of my soul?" Ought not I to go down to the grave mourning? Should not my soul refuse now to be comforted, which so long refused to be convinced?

These are black and sad thoughts, and enough to sink the spirit, if we had not met with that at the Lord's table which gives a sufficient answer to all these challenges. We have been great sinners, but there we have seen the great Redeemer, able to save to the uttermost all that come to God by him; and have there called him by that name of his, which is as ointment poured forth, "The Lord our righteousness." Our sins have reached to the heavens, but there we have seen God's mercy in Christ reaching beyond the heavens. We have been wretchedly defiled in our own ways, but there we have seen, not only a laver, but a fountain opened for the house of David to wash in; and have been assured that the blood of Christ cleanses from all sin, even that which, for the heinousness of its nature, and the multitude of its aggravations, has been as scarlet and crimson. That article of the covenant, which is so expressive of a general pardon, has been sealed to me upon gospel terms: "For I will be merciful to their unrighteousness, and their sins and their iniquities I will remember no more;" and this I rely upon. Great sinners have obtained mercy, and why may not I?

And though an humble remembrance of sin will be of use to us all our days, yet such a disquieting remembrance of it as hinders our faith in Christ, and our joy in God, is by no means good; even sorrow for sin may exceed due bounds, and penitents may be swallowed up with over-much sorrow. The covenant of grace speaks not only pardon, but peace to all believers; and not only sets the broken bones, but makes them to rejoice. When it says, "Thy sins be forgiven thee," it says also, "Son, daughter, be of good cheer." It is the duty of those who have received the atonement, to take the comfort of it, and to "joy in God through our Lord Jesus Christ." Acts of self-denial and mortification are means and evidences of our sanctification, and such as we ought to abound in; but they are not the grounds of our justification: it is Christ's blood that makes the satisfaction, not our tears. Therefore we must not so remember former sins, as to put away present comforts; a life of repentance will very well consist with a life of holy cheerfulness.

II. Are we disquieted and discouraged by the sense of our sins of daily infirmity? There is that here which will be a relief against this grievance also:—I have not only former guilt to reflect upon, contracted in the days of my ignorance and unbelief, but alas! I am still sinning, sinning daily. God knows, and my own heart knows, that in many things I do offend. I come short of the rule, and short of the glory of God every day; vain thoughts lodge within me, idle words proceed from me. If I would count either the one or the other, they are more in number than the sand. When I think of the strictness and extent of the divine law, and compare my own heart and life with it, I find that innumerable evils compass me about. Neglects of duty are many, and negligences in duty are more. Who can tell how oft he offends? If the righteous God should enter into judgment with me, and be extreme to mark what I do amiss, I were not able to answer him for one of a thousand. It might have been expected, that when the God of mercy had, upon my repentance, forgiven the rebellions of my sinful state, taken me into his family, and made me as one of his hired servants, nay, as one of his adopted children, that I should have been a dutiful child, and a diligent servant; but, alas! I have been slothful and trifling, and in many instances undutiful; I am very defective in my duty, both to my Master, and to my fellow-servants, and in many things transgress daily. For these things I weep; mine eyes, mine eyes run down with tears.

But there is that in this ordinance which may keep us from sinking under this burden, though we have cause enough to complain of it. It is true, I am sinning daily, and it is my sorrow and shame that I am so; but the memorial of that great sacrifice which Jesus Christ offered once for all upon the cross, is therefore continually to be celebrated on earth, because the merit of it is continually pleaded in heaven, where Christ ever lives to make intercession in the virtue of his satisfaction. Having therefore celebrated the memorial of it at the table of the Lord here in the outer court, I ought to take the comfort of the continual efficacy of it within the veil, and its prevalency for the benefit of all believers. The water out of the rock, the rock smitten, follows God's Israel through this wilderness, in the precious streams of which, they that are washed are welcome to wash their feet from the pollutions they contract in their daily walk through this defiling world; and the best have need of this washing. That needful word of caution, "that we sin not," is immediately followed with this word of comfort, but "if any man sin, we have an advocate with the Father;" one to speak for us, and to plead our cause; and he has a good plea to put in, in our behalf, for "he is the propitiation for our sins."

Add to this, that the covenant of grace, which is sealed to us in this ordinance, is so well ordered in all things, and so sure, that every transgression in the covenant does not presently throw us out of covenant. We do not stand upon the same terms that Adam in innocency did, to whom the least failure was fatal. No; to us God has "proclaimed his name gracious and merciful, forgiving iniquity, transgression, and sin." If we mourn for our sins of daily infirmity, are ashamed of them, and humble ourselves for them; if we strive and watch, and pray against them, we may be sure they shall not be laid unto our charge, but in Christ Jesus they shall be forgiven to us, for we are under grace, and not under the law. The God we are in covenant with is a God of pardon; "with him there is forgiveness." We are instructed to pray for daily pardon as duly as we pray for daily bread, and are encouraged to come boldly to the throne of grace for mercy: so that, though there be a remembrance made of sin every day, yet thanks be to God there may be a remembrance made of the sacrifice for sin; by which an everlasting righteousness was brought in.

III. Are we disquieted and discouraged by sad remainders of indwelling corruption?—We may from hence derive support under this burden. All that are enlightened from on high, lament the original sin that dwells in them, as much as the actual transgressions that are committed by them; not only that they are defective in doing their duty, but that they labour under a natural weakness and inability for it; not only that they are often overtaken in a fault, but that they have a natural proneness and inclination to that which is evil. It was the bitter complaint of blessed Paul himself, "O wretched man that I am, who shall deliver me from the body of this death?" And it is the complaint of all that are spiritually alive, while they are here in this imperfect state.

The most intelligent find themselves in the dark and apt to mistake; the most contemplative find themselves unfixed, and apt to wander; the most active for God find themselves dull and apt to tire; when the spirit, through grace, is willing, yet the flesh is weak; and when we would do good, evil is present with us. Corrupt appetites and passions often get head, and betray us into many indecencies. This makes the heart sad, and the hands feeble;

and, by reason of these remaining corruptions, many a good Christian loses the comfort of his graces. These Canaanites in the land are as thorns in the eyes, and goads in the sides of many an Israelite.

But be not cast down, my soul! the covenant which was sealed to thee at the table of the Lord, was a covenant of grace, which accepts sincerity as gospel perfection, not a covenant of innocency, which accepts of nothing less than a sinless, spotless purity. Were not these complaints poured out before the Lord, and did he not say, "My grace is sufficient for thee?" And what canst thou desire more? Were not orders given at the banquet of wine, for the crucifying of the adversary and enemy, this wicked Haman; so that, though it be not yet dead, it is a body of death, and ere long it shall be put off for ever? Was it not there said to thee, was it not sealed, "that sin shall not have dominion over thee; but the God of peace shall bruise Satan under thy feet shortly;" so that, though he may for a while disturb thy peace, and his troops may foil thee, yet, like Gad, in Jacob's blessing, thou shalt "overcome at the last?" "The bruised reed shall not be broken, nor the smoking flax quenched, but judgment shall in due time be brought forth unto victory." Grace shall get the upper hand of corruption, and be a conqueror, yea, "more than a conqueror, through him that loved us.—Come then, come set thy feet upon the necks of these kings," and rejoice in the hope of a complete victory at last. These lusts which war against thee, make war with the Lamb too, and oppose his interests; but, for certain, "the Lamb shall overcome them; for he is the Lord of lords, and King of kings, and they that are with him are called, and chosen, and faithful." Thou hast seen on how firm a rock the kingdom of God within thee is built, and mayest be sure that the gates of hell shall not prevail against it. Christ has given thee a banner to be displayed because of the truth; "and through him thou shalt do valiantly, for he it is that shall tread down thine enemies."

Go on, my soul, go on to fight the Lord's battles, by a vigorous resistance of sin and Satan; maintain a constant guard upon all the motions of thy spiritual enemies, hold up the shield of faith, and draw the sword of the Spirit against their assaults. Suppress the first risings of corruption, make no provision for it, resolve not to yield to it, walk in the Spirit, that thou mayest not fulfil the lusts of the flesh; never make league with these Canaanites, but vex these Midianites, and smite them; mortify this body of death, and all its members; strengthen such principles, and dwell upon such considerations as are proper for the weakening of the power of sinful lusts; and then, be of good comfort, this house of Saul shall wax weaker and weaker, and the house of David stronger and stronger. Thou hast seen, my soul, thou hast tasted the bread and wine which the Lord Jesus, that blessed Melchizedek, has provided for the support and refreshment of all the followers of faithful Abraham, when they return weary (and wounded perhaps) from their spiritual conflicts. Make use of this provision then, feast upon it daily, and go on in the strength of it. Thank God (as St. Paul did in the midst of these complaints) for Jesus Christ, who not only has prayed for thee, that thy faith fail not, but is now, like Moses, interceding on the top of the hill, while thou art, like Joshua, fighting with these Amalekites in the valley. Be faithful therefore unto the death, and thou shalt shortly have a place in that New Jerusalem, into which no unclean thing can enter. Now thou groanest, being burdened, but in heaven there shall be none of these complaints, nor any cause for them.

IV. Does the trouble arise from prevailing doubts and fears about thy spiritual state?—We may draw that from this ordinance which will help us to silence those fears, and solve those doubts, and to clear it up to us that God in Christ is ours, and we are his, and that all shall be well shortly. Many good Christians, though they are so far willing to hope the best concerning themselves, as not to decline coming to the Lord's table, and there perhaps they may meet with some satisfaction; yet afterwards the tide of their comforts ebbs, a sadness seizes their spirits, the peace they have had they suspect to have been a delusion, and are ready to give up all for gone; unbelief makes hard conclusions, clouds the evidences, shakes the hopes, withers the joys—that it is as good to give up all pious pursuits, as thus keep them up in vain; as good make a captain, and return into Egypt, as perish in this wilderness, for this is not the way to Canaan. And thus many are kept by unbelief from entering into the present Sabbatism or rest, which is intended for the people of God in this life.

But, "O thou of little faith, wherefore dost thou doubt?" Come, call to remembrance the former days, the former sacrament days, and the sweet communion thou hadst with God in them; days never to be forgotten. Thou doubtest whether God loves thee, and thou art ready to say as they did, "Wherein hath he loved me?" But dost thou not remember the love tokens he gave thee at his table, when he embraced thee in the arms of his grace, kissed thee with the kisses of his mouth, and his banner over thee was love? Thou doubtest whether thou be a child of God, and a chosen vessel or not, and art sometimes tempted to say, "Surely the Lord hath utterly separated me from his people, and I am a dry tree." "How shall he set me among the children, and give me a pleasant land?" But dost thou not remember the children's bread thou hast been fed with at thy Father's table, and the Spirit of adoption there sent forth into thy heart, teaching thee to cry, Abba, Father? Thou calledst thyself a prodigal, and no more worthy to be accounted a son, because thou didst bear the reproach of thy youth, which made thee ashamed, yea, even confounded. But did not God, at the same time, call thee, as he did penitent Ephraim, a dear son, a pleasant child; were not his bowels troubled for thee? And did he not say, I will surely have mercy on thee? Did not thy Father meet thee with tender compassions? Did he not call for the best robe, and put it on thee? Did he not invite thee to the fatted calf? and, which was best of all, give thee a kiss which sealed thy pardon? And wilt thou now call that point in question which was then so well settled? "Is God a man, that he should lie, or the Son of man that he should repent?" No; "He is God, and not man." Thou doubtest whether Christ be thine or not; whether thou hast any interest in his mediation and intercession; whether he died for thee or not. But didst thou not, at his table, accept of him to be thine, and consent to him upon his own terms? Didst thou not say to him, with thy finger in the print of the nails, "My Lord, and my God?" And did he not answer thee with good and comfortable words, saying unto thee, I am thy salvation? Hast thou revoked the bargain? Or dost thou fear that he will revoke it? Was it not an everlasting covenant, never to be forgotten? Why art thou troubled? And why do thoughts arise in thy heart? Was not Christ present with thee, and did he not show himself well-affected to thee, when, at his table, he said unto thee, "Behold my hands and my feet, that it is I myself?" Thou doubtest whether thou hast any grace or not, any love to God, any faith, any repentance. But hast thou forgotten God's workings on thy heart, and the workings of thy heart towards God at his table? Did not thine heart burn within thee when thy dear Redeemer talked with thee there? Didst thou not sit down under his shadow with delight, and say, "It is good to be here?" Didst thou not desire a sign of the Lord, a token for good? Didst thou not say, "Do not deceive me?" And was there not a token for good shown thee? Was not thy heart melted for sin? Was it not drawn out towards God? Did it not appear that God was with thee of a truth? Wherefore, then, dost thou doubt of that, of which thou hadst then such comfortable evidences? "Why sayest thou, O Jacob, and speakest, O Israel, My way is hid from the Lord, and my judgment is passed over from my God?" Why dost thou entertain such hard thoughts of God and thy own state? "Hast thou not known, hast thou not heard, that the everlasting God, the Lord, the Creator of the ends of the earth, fainteth not, neither is weary?"

And why art thou fearful and faint-hearted? Why dost thou look forward with terror and trembling, while thou hast so much reason to look forward with hope and rejoicing? Alas, says the troubled spirit, God hath cast me out of his sight, and I fear will cast off for ever, and will be favourable no more: I shall no more see the Lord, even the Lord in the land of the living! My comforts are removed, and all my pleasant things are laid waste. "My bones are dried, my hope is lost, and I am cut off for my part." But hearken to this, thou who thus fearest continually every day, dost thou not remember the encouragements Christ gave thee at his table to hope in him, and to expect all good from him; did he not say, "I will never leave thee nor forsake thee?" And didst not thou promise, that thou wouldst never leave nor forsake him? Nay, did he not promise "to put his fear into thy heart, that thou mightest not depart from him?" He did, "and is not he faithful that hath called thee," faithful that hath promised, who also will do it? Thou art afraid that some time or other Satan will be too hard for thee, and thou shalt one day perish by his hand; but hast thou not had that precious promise sealed to thee, that "the faithful God will never suffer thee to be tempted above what thou art able, but will with the temptation make a way for thee to escape? His providence shall proportion the trial to the strength; or, which comes all to one, his grace shall proportion the strength to the trial. Thou art afraid, that, after all, thou shalt come short; that by reason of the violence of the storm, the treachery of the sea, and especially thine own weakness and unskilfulness, thou shalt never be able to weather the point, and get safe into the harbour at last. But shall I ask thee, thou that followest Christ trembling, "Dost thou not know in whom thou hast believed?" Is thy salvation intrusted with thyself, and lodged in thine own hands? No; it is not. If it were, thou wouldst have reason to fear the loss of it. But has not God committed it, and hast not thou committed it, to the Lord Jesus? And is not he "able to keep that which is committed to him against that day," that great day, when it shall be called for? Is not that a divine power that keeps thee; a divine promise that secures thee? Be not fearful then, "Be not faithless, but believing."

V. Are we disquieted and discouraged by the troubles and calamities of this life?—From our communion with God in the ordinance of the Lord's Supper, we may bring comfort and support under all the afflictions of this present time, whatever they be. Our Master instituted this sacrament on the night wherein he was betrayed;—and soon after he put off the body, and pleasantly said, "Now I am no more in the world;" but when we have received this sacrament, we find ourselves still in a world which is vexation of spirit; the soul still in a house of clay, liable to many shocks; and so close is the union between the soul and the body, that what touches the bone and the flesh cannot but affect the spirit at second hand. We are born and born again to trouble; besides, that we are exposed with others to the common calamities of human life, and the persecutions which all that will live godly in Christ Jesus must count upon; we are under the discipline of sons, and must look for chastisement. Afflictions are not only consistent with the love of God, but they flow from it: "As many as I love, I rebuke and chasten." They are not only reconcilable with the covenant, but a branch of it. I will chasten their transgressions with the rod, and their sins with stripes, is an article of the agreement with David and his seed, with this comfortable clause added, "Nevertheless, my loving-kindness will I not utterly take from him; my covenant will I not break."

There is no disputing against sense. Christianity was not designed to make men stocks and stones and Stoics under their calamities. " No affliction for the present is joyous, but grievous." Hence the best men, as they have their share of trouble, so cannot but have the sense of it; that is allowed them; they groan, being burdened; but this sense of trouble is apt to exceed due bounds: it is hard to grieve and not to over-grieve; to lay to heart an affliction, and not to lay it too near the heart. When grief for any outward trouble overwhelms our spirits, imbitters our comforts, and hinders our joy in God, stops the mouth of praise, takes off her chariot wheels, and makes us drive heavily on our way to heaven; then it is excessive and inordinate, and turns into sin to us. When sorrow fills the heart and plays the tyrant there, when it makes us fretful and impatient, breaks out in quarrels with God in his providence, and robs us of the enjoyment of ourselves, our friends, and our God; it is an enemy that we are concerned to take up arms against.

And from our sacramental covenants and comforts we may fetch plenty of arguments against the unreasonable insinuations of inordinate grief. Did I not see at the table of the Lord a lively representation of the sufferings of Christ, the variety and extremity of his sufferings? Did I not see his tears, his sweats, his agonies, his stripes, the pain and shame he underwent? And is the servant better than his master, and the disciple than his Lord? Did Christ go by the cross to the crown, and shall a Christian expect to go any other way? The Captain of our salvation was made perfect through sufferings; have not we much more need of them for the perfecting of what is lacking in us? Is not this one part of our conformity to the image of Christ, that, as he was a man of sorrows and acquainted with grief, so we should be, that he might be the firstborn among many brethren? A sight of Christ's afflictions should reconcile us to our own, especially if we consider not only what he suffered, but how he suffered; and with what an invincible patience and cheerful submission to his Father's will, leaving us example, (1 Pet. ii. 21.) Have we so often celebrated the memorial of Christ's sufferings? and have we not yet learned of him to say, "The cup that my Father hath given me, shall I not drink it?" Though it be a bitter cup, "Father, not my will, but thine be done." Have we not yet learned of him, who was led as a lamb to the slaughter, to be dumb, and not to open our mouths against any thing that God does: to forgive our enemies, and pray for our persecutors, and cheerfully commit ourselves to him that judges righteously? Let the same mind be in us which here we have seen to be in Jesus Christ.

Yet this is not all: in the Lord's Supper we give up ourselves, and all we have, unto the Lord, with a promise to acquiesce in all the disposals of his providence concerning us and ours; let us not therefore, by our discontent and uneasiness, revoke the surrender that we then made, or go counter to it. We there said it, and sealed it, that we would be the Lord's; and may he not do what he will with his own, especially when it is so by our own consent? God there said it, and sealed it to us, that he would be to us a Father; and can we take any thing amiss from a Father; such a Father, who never chastens us, but for our own profit, that we may be partakers of his holiness? Inviolable assurances were there given to us, that all things should work together for our present good, and for our future glory; that, as afflictions abound, consolations should so much the more abound; and some experience we there had of the sweetness and power of those consolations, which we ought to treasure up, that we may have them ready for our supports in the evil day. Can we forget how sweet God's smiles were, which there we saw? How reviving his comforts were, which we there tasted? And are not those sufficient to countervail the loss of the world's flattering smiles, and the comforts we have in the creature? It is generally supposed, that the comfortable sermon which Christ preached to his disciples on that text, "Let not your hearts be troubled," immediately followed the administration of the Lord's Supper; for it is the will of Christ, that those whom he has raised up to sit with him by faith in heavenly places, should not be cast down or disquieted for any cross or disappointment in earthly things.

Art thou sick, languishing perhaps under some wasting distemper, which consumes thy strength and beauty like a moth? Or chastened, it may be, with pain upon thy bed, and the multitude of thy bones with strong pain? Or labouring under the infirmities and decays of old age? Take comfort then, from thy communion with the Lord at his table. Didst thou not see there how Christ himself bore our sicknesses, and carried our sorrows then, when he bore our sins in his own body upon the tree, and so took away the sting of them; extracted out of them the wormwood and gall, which he himself drank in a bitter cup, and infused into them the comforts of his love, which he has given us to drink of? Didst thou not there receive a sealed pardon? Did not God, in love to thy soul, cast all thy sins behind his back, and tell thee so? Thou hast then no reason to complain of bodily distempers: "The inhabitants shall not say, I am sick." How so? Can one that is sick avoid saying, I am sick? Why, it follows, "The people that dwell therein shall be forgiven their iniquity." Sickness is next to nothing, to those who know that their sins are pardoned. When thou didst present thy body to God in that ordinance a living sacrifice, and didst engage that it should be for the Lord, was it not graciously added—"and the Lord for the body?" 1 Cor. vi. 13. And if the Lord be for the body, he will strengthen thee upon the bed of languishing; and though he may not presently help thee off it, yet he will sit by thee; and what speaks the wonderful condescension of Divine goodness, "he will make all thy bed in thy sickness." And that bed cannot but be easy which he makes.

Art thou poor, crossed in thine affairs, disappointed in lawful and hopeful designs, clogged with cares, and perhaps reduced to straits? Let the spiritual riches secured to thee in that sealing ordinance, be a balance to the affliction of outward poverty. The God of truth has said it, and thou mayest rely upon it, That those that fear him and seek him, shall not want any good thing, not any thing that infinite wisdom sees really good for them. " Trust in the Lord, therefore, and do good with the little thou hast; so shalt thou dwell in the land, and verily thou shalt be fed." It is not promised that thou shalt be feasted with varieties and dainties; those that are feasted at God's table, need not to complain, though they be not feasted at their own; but thou shalt be fed, fed with food convenient for thee. Some good Christians who have been in a very poor condition have said, that they have made many a meal upon the promises, when they wanted bread: " Verily thou shalt be fed," be fed with faith. The just shall live by his faith." " Though the fig-tree do not blossom, and there be no fruit in the vine; yet, while thou hast in the Lord's Supper seen the rose of Sharon blossoming, and tasted of the true vine, thou hast reason enough to " rejoice in the Lord, and joy in the God of thy salvation."

Are thy relations a grief to thee? Do those afflict thee of whom thou saidst, These same shall comfort me? Suppose thy yoke-fellow unsuitable, children undutiful, parents unkind, friends ungrateful, neighbours injurious, the comfort of our relation to God may suffice to make up the loss of any earthly comfort. If man be harsh, yet God is gracious. Though the waters of our rivers may be mudded or turned into blood, yet the fountain of life runs always clear, and its streams pure as crystal. On the supposition of family disappointments, David in his last words took comfort from the covenant of grace made with him.

Are those dear to thee removed by death? It is fit that that which is sown should be watered. But sacrament comforts will keep us from sorrowing as those that have no hope. We have lost the satisfaction we used to have in them; but is not God better to us than ten sons; far better than ten thousand such relations could have been? And yet they are not lost; they are only gone before, and death itself cannot wholly cut us off from communion with them; for we are come to the spirits of just men made perfect, and hope to be with them shortly.

Are the calamities of the church and of the nation our affliction? It is fit they should be so, for we have eaten and drunk into the great body, and, as living members, must feel its grievances; but in the Lord's Supper we have seen what provision the grace of God has made for his household, and from thence may infer the protection under which the providence of God will always keep it safe. The promises that are sealed to us, are sure to all the seed, and the covenant of grace is the rock on which the church is built, so firm that the gates of hell shall not prevail against it. The Lord we see, has founded Zion, and the poor of his people shall trust to that. Let us at this ordinance learn this new song, and sing it oft,—" Hallelujah, the Lord God omnipotent reigneth."

VI. Are the fears of death a trouble and terror to us?—We may fetch from the Lord's Supper that which will enable us through grace to triumph over these fears. This is a fear which is often found to have torment, and by reason of it, many weak Christians have been all " their life time subject to bondage." It is also a fear which often brings a snare, exposes us to many temptations, and gives Satan advantage against us. There are many who we hope, through grace, are saved from the second death, and yet are afraid of the first death, being more solicitous than they need be about a dying life, and more timorous than they need to be of a living death, a death that is their way to life. But the arrests of death, and its harbingers, would not be at all dreadful, if we did but know how to make a due improvement of the comforts we are made partakers of at the table of the Lord. We there saw Christ dying, dying so great a death, a death in pomp, armed and attended with all its terrors, dying in pain, in shame, in darkness, in agonies, and yet the Son of God, and the heir of all things. This takes off the reproach of death, so that now we need not be ashamed to die: if Christ humbled himself, and became obedient to death, why should not we? It likewise takes off the terror of death, so that now we need not be afraid to die. When we walk through that dark and dismal valley, we have no reason to fear any evil, while the great Shepherd of the sheep is not only gone before us, but goes along with us; "his rod and his staff they comfort us." He is our leader, and we do not approve ourselves his good soldiers, if we be not willing to follow him whithersoever he goes. He went through death to the joy set before him, and by that way only can we follow him. Through this Jordan must we enter Canaan.

Christ's death has broken the power of death, and taken from it all the armour wherein it trusted; so that now, let it do its worst, it cannot do a good Christian any real prejudice; for it cannot "separate him from the love of God. Surely the bitterness of death is now past," by Christ's tasting it. The sharpness of death, Christ has overcome, by submitting to it, and so hath opened the kingdom of heaven to all believers: "The sucking child may now play upon the hole of the asp, and the weaned child may put his hand on the cockatrice' den; for death itself shall not hurt or destroy in all God's holy mountain."

Nay, the death of Christ has quite altered the property of death. It not only ceases to be an enemy, but it is become a friend: the covenant of grace, sealed to us in the Lord's Supper, assures us of the unspeakable kindness that even death itself shall do us: "All things are yours," and death amongst the rest. As the death of Christ was the purchase of our happiness; so our own death is the passage to our happiness; it discharges us from our prison, and conveys us to our palace. The promise of eternal life sealed to us, and its earnests communicated to us in this ordinance, enable us to look with comfort on the other side death, and then we need not look with terror on this side of it.

Art thou afraid to give up thy soul? Thou hast already given it up to God in Christ to be sanctified, and therefore thou mayest, with holy cheerfulness, give it up to God in Christ to be saved. The dying Jesus, by committing his spirit into the hands of his Father, has emboldened all his followers in a dying hour to do the same. Why should that soul be afraid to go out of the body, and leave this world of sense, which is through grace allied to, and by faith acquainted with the blessed world of spirits, and is sure of a guard of angels ready to convey it to that world, and a faithful Friend ready to receive it?

Art thou afraid to put off thy body? The covenant sealed to thee at the Lord's table is a covenant with thy dust, and gives commandment concerning thy bones. Fear not the return of thine earth to its earth; it is in order to its being refined, and in due time restored to its soul, a glorious and incorruptible body. Spiritual blessings are perhaps for this reason, in the sacraments, represented and applied by outward and sensible signs, in the participation of which, the body is concerned, that we might thereby be confirmed in our believing hope of the glory prepared and reserved for these bodies of ours, these vile bodies, which even, while they lie in the grave, still remain united to Christ, and, when they shall be raised out of the grave, shall be made like unto his glorious body.

Let the sinners in Zion be afraid to die, let fearfulness surprise the hypocrites, when their souls shall be required of them; let their hearts meditate terror, and their face gather blackness, who, having lived a carnal, worldly, sensual life, have no interest in Christ and the promises; for they shall call in vain to rocks and mountains to shelter them from the wrath of the Lamb. But let them that have joined themselves to the Lord in an everlasting covenant, and have obtained mercy of the Lord to be faithful to that covenant, lift up their heads with joy, for their redemption draws nigh. Death will shortly rend the interposing veil of sense, and time will shortly scatter all the dark and threatening clouds which here hang over our heads, and open to us a bright and glorious scene in that blessed world of life, and love, where we shall enjoy the substance of those things, with the shadow of which we are refreshed at the Lord's table, and the full vintage of those joys of which here we have the first fruits.

Learn then, my soul, learn thou to triumph over death and the grave; "O death, where is thy sting? O grave, where is thy victory?" Having laid up thy treasure within the veil, and remitted thy best effects, and best affections thither; and having received the earnest of the purchased possession, be still looking, still longing for that blessed hope. Fear not death, for it cannot hurt thee; but desire it rather, for it will greatly befriend thee. When the "earthly house of this tabernacle shall be dissolved," thou shalt remove to the "house not made with hands, eternal in the heavens." Wish then, wish daily, for the coming of the Lord, for he shall appear to thy joy; "the vision is for an appointed time, and at the end it shall speak and shall not lie." Look through the windows of this house of clay, like the mother of Sisera, when she waited for her son's triumph, and cry through the lattice, "Why is his chariot so long in coming? Why tarry the wheels of his chariot? Come, Lord Jesus, come quickly."

THE END.

Other Solid Ground Titles

In addition to the book *The Communicant's Companion* which you hold in your hand, Solid Ground is honored to offer many other uncovered treasure, many for the first time in more than a century:

THE CHIEF END OF MAN by John Hall
THE CHILD AT HOME by John S.C. Abbott
THE LIFE OF JESUS CHRIST FOR THE YOUNG by Richard Newton
THE KING'S HIGHWAY: *The 10 Commandments for the Young* by Richard Newton
HEROES OF THE REFORMATION by Richard Newton
FEED MY LAMBS: *Lectures to Children on Vital Subjects* by John Todd
LET THE CANNON BLAZE AWAY by Joseph P. Thompson
THE STILL HOUR: *Communion with God in Prayer* by Austin Phelps
COLLECTED WORKS of James Henley Thornwell (4 vols.)
CALVINISM IN HISTORY *by Nathaniel S. McFetridge*
OPENING SCRIPTURE: *Hermeneutical Manual by Patrick Fairbairn*
THE ASSURANCE OF FAITH *by Louis Berkhof*
THE PASTOR IN THE SICK ROOM *by John D. Wells*
THE BUNYAN OF BROOKLYN: *Life & Sermons of I.S. Spencer*
THE NATIONAL PREACHER: *Sermons from 2nd Great Awakening*
FIRST THINGS: *First Lessons God Taught Mankind Gardiner Spring*
BIBLICAL & THEOLOGICAL STUDIES *by 1912 Faculty of Princeton*
THE POWER OF GOD UNTO SALVATION *by B.B. Warfield*
THE LORD OF GLORY *by B.B. Warfield*
A GENTLEMAN & A SCHOLAR: *Memoir of J.P. Boyce by J. Broadus*
SERMONS TO THE NATURAL MAN *by W.G.T. Shedd*
SERMONS TO THE SPIRITUAL MAN *by W.G.T. Shedd*
HOMILETICS AND PASTORAL THEOLOGY *by W.G.T. Shedd*
A PASTOR'S SKETCHES 1 & 2 *by Ichabod S. Spencer*
THE PREACHER AND HIS MODELS *by James Stalker*
IMAGO CHRISTI: *The Example of Jesus Christ by James Stalker*
LECTURES ON THE HISTORY OF PREACHING *by J. A. Broadus*
THE SHORTER CATECHISM ILLUSTRATED *by John Whitecross*
THE CHURCH MEMBER'S GUIDE *by John Angell James*
THE SUNDAY SCHOOL TEACHER'S GUIDE *by John A. James*
CHRIST IN SONG: *Hymns of Immanuel from All Ages by Philip Schaff*
COME YE APART: *Daily Words from the Four Gospels by J.R. Miller*
DEVOTIONAL LIFE OF THE S.S. TEACHER *by J.R. Miller*

Call us Toll Free at 1-877-666-9469
Send us an e-mail at sgcb@charter.net
Visit us on line at solid-ground-books.com
Uncovering Buried Treasure to the Glory of God

www.ingramcontent.com/pod-product-compliance
Lightning Source LLC
Chambersburg PA
CBHW031944080426
42735CB00007B/255